Masculinities in the US Hangout Sitcom

Masculinities in the US Hangout Sitcom examines how four sitcoms – *Friends, How I Met Your Mother, The Big Bang Theory*, and *New Girl* – mediate the tense relationship between neoliberalism and masculinities.

Why is Ross in *Friends* so worried about everything? This book argues that the men in *Friends* and similar shows that follow young, straight, mostly white twentysomethings in major US cities are beset by a range of social and economic concerns about their place in society. Using multiple methods of analysis to examine these shows – including conjunctural analysis, historiographical method, and critical discourse analysis – a range of topics in these shows are examined, from sexuality through to homosociality, from race through to nationality.

This book makes an insightful contribution to work on the television sitcom and on neoliberalism in culture and society. It will be an ideal resource for upper-level undergraduates, post-graduates, and researchers in a range of disciplines including television and screen studies, critical studies on men and masculinities and humor studies.

Greg Wolfman is an independent researcher who received his PhD from the University of Huddersfield, UK, in 2020. He is primarily interested in the confluence of and tension between neoliberalism and masculinity, and particularly how this is reflected in cultural forms. His work has been published in *NORMA: International Journal for Masculinity Studies*, and the *Journal of Bodies, Sexualities, and Masculinities*.

Masculinity, Sex and Popular Culture

Books in the Masculinity, Sex and Popular Culture series promote high quality research that is positioned at the nexus of masculinity, sex and popular culture. The series brings a media and cultural studies approach to the analysis of contemporary manifestations of masculinity in popular culture. It includes titles that focus on the connections between masculinities and popular culture that extend out from media cultures to examining practices – focusing on forms of participatory action in public spaces (such as bodybuilding and 'Lad' culture), and in more traditionally private arenas of sexual practice acknowledging that cultures of exhibitionism and display and the distinctions between the public and the private are increasingly important considerations in the digital age.
Series Editors: John Mercer and Clarissa Smith

Men, Masculinities, and Popular Romance
Jonathan A. Allan

Bareback Porn, Porous Masculinities, Queer Futures
The Ethics of Becoming-Pig
João Florêncio

Hipster Porn
Queer Masculinities and Affective Sexualities in the Fanzine *Butt*
Peter Rehberg

Men, Masculinities, and Infertilities
Jonathan A. Allan

Toxic Masculinity
Men, Meaning, and Digital Media
Edited by Mark McGlashan and John Mercer

Exploring the Cultural Phenomenon of the Dick Pic
Andrea Waling

Masculinities in the US Hangout Sitcom
Greg Wolfman

https://www.routledge.com/Masculinity-Sex-and-Popular-Culture/book-series/MASCSEXPOPCULT

Masculinities in the US Hangout Sitcom

Greg Wolfman

LONDON AND NEW YORK

First published 2023
by Routledge
4 Park Square, Milton Park, Abingdon, Oxon OX14 4RN

and by Routledge
605 Third Avenue, New York, NY 10158

Routledge is an imprint of the Taylor & Francis Group, an informa business

© 2023 Greg Wolfman

The right of Greg Wolfman to be identified as author of this work has been asserted in accordance with sections 77 and 78 of the Copyright, Designs and Patents Act 1988.

All rights reserved. No part of this book may be reprinted or reproduced or utilised in any form or by any electronic, mechanical, or other means, now known or hereafter invented, including photocopying and recording, or in any information storage or retrieval system, without permission in writing from the publishers.

Trademark notice: Product or corporate names may be trademarks or registered trademarks, and are used only for identification and explanation without intent to infringe.

British Library Cataloguing-in-Publication Data
A catalogue record for this book is available from the British Library

Library of Congress Cataloging-in-Publication Data
Names: Wolfman, Greg, author.
Title: Masculinities in the US hangout sitcom / Greg Wolfman.
Description: London ; New York : Routledge, 2023. |
Series: Masculinity, sex and popular culture | Includes bibliographical references and index.
Identifiers: LCCN 2023010836 (print) | LCCN 2023010837 (ebook) | ISBN 9781032426211 (hardback) | ISBN 9781032426228 (paperback) | ISBN 9781003363538 (ebook)
Subjects: LCSH: Situation comedies (Television programs)--United States. | Situation comedies (Television programs)--Great Britain. | Male friendship on television. | Masculinity on television.
Classification: LCC PN1992.8.C66 W66 2023 (print) | LCC PN1992.8.C66 (ebook) | DDC 791.45/617--dc23
LC record available at https://lccn.loc.gov/2023010836
LC ebook record available at https://lccn.loc.gov/2023010837

ISBN: 978-1-032-42621-1 (hbk)
ISBN: 978-1-032-42622-8 (pbk)
ISBN: 978-1-003-36353-8 (ebk)

DOI: 10.4324/9781003363538

Typeset in Sabon
by Deanta Global Publishing Services, Chennai, India

Contents

	Acknowledgements	*vi*
1	The hangout sitcom: Could it *be* more culturally relevant?	1
2	A brief historiography of US sitcom masculinities	40
3	A typology of straight white men in the hangout sitcom	62
4	Bromantic comedy: Male homosociality, heterosexuality, and relationships	89
5	Breaking the circle: Challenging whiteness in the hangout sitcom's surrogate families	115
6	First as farce, then as tragedy: Failing and flailing neoliberal men in the UK's hangout(-style) sitcoms	143
7	Masculinities after the hangout sitcom	170
	Index	*187*

Acknowledgements

While writing this book, I quite regularly wondered why there is not a sub-discipline of television studies called "*Friends* studies", so enormous has the show, and the hangout sitcom more generally, become to the cultural imaginaries on both sides of the Atlantic. Having written one chapter about it for my PhD thesis, extending it into a book has been, mostly, quite enjoyable. The "Masculinity, Sex and Popular Culture" series, which has produced some excellent and fun titles so far, felt ideal for doing so, so thanks to John Mercer and Clarissa Smith for editing the series, and for providing this opportunity. Thanks, too, to Routledge, and to the editing staff that have helped me through this process, including Charlotte Taylor and Eleanor Catchpole Simmons, who was a reliable point of contact.

There are people who have helped significantly. There are those who have provided feedback at the several conferences and symposiums where I presented some of these ideas, notably in Warwick and in Cardiff. Chris Moeller offered advice on the proposal, while the anonymous reviews on that proposal and sample chapters were gratefully received, as well as other anonymous reviewers for previously published parts of Chapter 3. Thanks to Archie Wolfman, too, for providing feedback and proofing. Tray Yeadon-Lee and Jeff Hearn both deserve many thanks for advice, general support, and assistance, both on this project and in general.

Thank you to my students over the past several years for giving me purpose during a pandemic. Also, I am grateful to the many café staff who have put up with my lengthy table occupations following a purchase of a single filter coffee.

Thanks to Phoebe, for everything, but particularly for an encyclopaedic knowledge of *Friends* that worked better than Google when I needed to know "which episode is this particular scene in". On the same note, I owe a debt of gratitude to whoever compiles the pages at the various wiki websites of the four shows, as well as the editors of the website TV Tropes, which both made cross referencing and trying to recall bits where my memory had failed significantly easier.

Thank you to Mum and Dad, of course, for everything else.

I acknowledge that large parts of Chapter 3 have been previously published in *Journal of Bodies, Sexualities, and Masculinities*, under the title

"Exfoliation, Cheese Courses, Emotional Honesty, and Paxil: Masculinity, Neoliberalism, and Postfeminism in the US Hangout Sitcom", in 2020, in volume 2, issue 2 (doi: 10.3167/jbsm.2021.020205), and am grateful for retaining the rights to republish them.

1 The hangout sitcom
Could it *be* more culturally relevant?

It is possible but not easy to overstate the intergenerational and transnational cultural importance of the sitcom *Friends* (1994–2004). Any readers whose teenage years, like mine, took place in any part of the noughties in the UK will likely be quite familiar with a variety of the show's actors, catchphrases, storylines, and guest stars. For example, from 1999 most weekends I would watch the UK kids' morning television show *SMTV Live*, which featured a regular five-minute skit called *Chums*. In it, the three presenters played fictional versions of themselves living in an urban flat garishly decorated with lilac walls and blue kitchen units, with a theme tune stating "no one's ever told you comedy could ever be this way", and that "we'll be chums forever", echoing the Rembrandts' song "I'll Be There for You" used by *Friends* as its theme, with its opening line "no one told you life could ever be this way". My friends and I used to re-enact *Chums* in the playground, blissfully unaware of our postmodern homage of a pastiche of a hit US sitcom.

The stories are not limited to childhood. In 2015, an annual months-long festival called Friendsfest was launched in Milton Keynes in the UK, with recreated sets of the iconic apartments, Central Perk café, and an imitative fountain complete with umbrellas to re-enact the show's iconic opening credits. In that summer of 2015, my social media feeds were inundated with photos of friends and acquaintances posing at these locations, reconstructing famous scenes and stills from the show. On the homepage of Friendsfest that lists the available activities, there is an image of a sofa being carried up some angled stairs, with the caption "pivot!", a fairly banal image nevertheless familiar to fans as a reference to a single episode in which Ross moves to a new apartment and, struggling to get his sofa up a flight of stairs, shouts repeatedly to Rachel and Chandler, "pivot!".

The cultural impact of *Friends* need not rely on anecdotes, either. Its global reach and import can be easily measured. Simone Knox and Kai Schwind (2019), in what is so far the only book-length study of the show, detail its cultural enormity:

> [It was] the most binge-watched television show of 2018, according to a study based on the behaviour of 12 million registered users worldwide. It is thus not surprising that it would be *Friends* for whose

DOI: 10.4324/9781003363538-1

2 *The hangout sitcom: Could it be* more *culturally relevant?*

streaming rights Netflix paid WarnerMedia roughly $100 million to retain for another year in late 2018, even though the programme is still readily available by linear television ... It would be *Friends* that would receive a global profile, shown in countries that include Australia, China, Egypt, France, Germany, Greece, India, Japan, Norway, the Philippines, Spain and the UK. It would be *Friends* whose ratings in the latter – despite having been available via constant reruns across different British channels for years and the popularity of its DVD box set – would see an actual year-on-year increase on Comedy Central UK in 2015. It would be *Friends* that would become a multi-billion dollar franchise, whose strong tie-in merchandise market would find its perhaps most vivid embodiment in the Mockolate bars on sale at the Friendsfest gift shop.

In short, it was and remains a show of huge intergenerational appeal even in the age of the hegemony of streaming – Hannah Hamad (2018, 692) suggests that *Friends* remains an "unacknowledged ur-text of millennial postfeminism". Its premises, character types, and storylines became the basis of a whole range of copycat shows, establishing *Friends* as the progenitor of a wider subgenre that this book calls the "hangout sitcom": in short, a group of largely white heterosexual twentysomethings in a major US city working their way through relationships and careers while relying on one another

Figure 1.1 Members of the public visiting the recreated set of *Friends*, at "Friendsfest" in Milton Keynes, UK. Copyright: Matthew King.

The hangout sitcom: Could it be *more culturally relevant*?

for moral and emotional support, "a makeshift clan that seemed familiar to Gen Xers who were forming their own similar connections" (Ihnat 2014). It was followed in 2005 by *How I Met Your Mother* (2005–2014), which deployed a very similar formula, following a group of white heterosexual twentysomethings in New York City, except they hung out in a bar rather than a café. Attracting large viewing figures for both *Friends* and *How I Met Your Mother*, the early 2000s saw the hangout sitcom's most dominant period. Over the next several decades, however, while these shows waned in and out, a series of societal challenges and changes took place.

In particular, the past decade or so has seen a variety of societal "privileges", from whiteness to heterosexuality to cis-genderedness, and particularly maleness, undergo what might be considered something of a popular introspective moment across culture and society more widely (Kanai and Gill 2020). As a result, popular culture's representations of race, gender, sexuality, and more have been the subject of significant debate. In 2020, for example, amid a groundswell of discussion about the injustice of the global politics of race, episodes of a wide range of television shows that had used blackface were removed from streaming platforms (Alter 2020).

In wider society, the social position of men has been questioned in moments such as #MeToo and #TimesUp, contributing to and culminating in a shift in the way the politics of masculinity, both as anti- and profeminist, are discussed (Maricourt and Burrell 2021). Within this debate over popular culture, *Friends* has been in the thick of it. An internet search for "friends sitcom toxic masculinity" returns over 500,000 results for articles titled "*Friends* superfans reveal worst and most problematic storylines" (Griffin 2020), and "*Friends* is the epitome of toxic masculinity" (Speich 2019), or, upon the momentous occasion of Netflix gaining the rights to stream *Friends* in the UK, "could *Friends* *be* any more problematic?" (Wright 2018).

Similarly, when I carried out my PhD research examining neoliberal masculinities, I used clips from three sitcoms, including *Friends*, to elicit responses about masculinity from the male participants. All of them knew *Friends*, and most of them remembered it fondly, pondering on their favorite characters and musing on how the show informed their formative years. Yet they were critical, particularly of the male characters, and most notably of Ross. The insecurity of his masculinity was derided several times as toxic and/or insecure, his controlling behavior of on-off girlfriend Rachel was criticized, and some incidences such as his discomfort with his son having a male nanny were recounted with disdain. Indeed, in terms of masculinity (as well as with race and sexuality), it is often difficult to defend *Friends*, such as the season three episode in which Ross repeatedly confiscates a Barbie doll that his son Ben wants to play with, trying to give him monster trucks instead, only to receive no narrative comeuppance. Ross's actions, it seems, are relatively fine. Yet, this does not seem to have alienated many millennial and Gen Z viewers, such that some generations of fans who did not even grow up with it are watching and loving the show *despite* their own reticence toward its gender politics.

Perhaps partially in response to this, culture industries have both actively worked to improve the diversity of representation of marginalized communities and identities on-screen, and even begun to interrogate social and political issues, particularly pertaining to gender, sexuality, and race (a visibility that Kanai and Gill (2020) argue is often purely cosmetic, not challenging the oppressive structures that contribute to the marginalization of such groups). As such, more recent offshoots of the hangout sitcom have attempted to construct a more profeminist gender politics, rejecting what is now often seen as the domineering and controlling masculinities of *Friends*, creating female characters with more agency, all while embracing the pseudo-family of the hangout sitcom. *New Girl* (2011–2018) was a hangout sitcom that centered a woman, with Jess Day as the eponymous new girl in the flat. Played by Zooey Deschanel, Jess sung the theme tune – "Who's that girl? It's Jess!" – with the opening credits placing her physically in the center of the shot, and her three new male flatmates acting out their metaphorical role as profeminist helpers, constructing a set around her that aesthetically reconstructs Jess's quaint feminine possessions, with decorative mirrors and smiling clouds. These opening credits set the scene for *New Girl*'s gender politics, with male characters that perform masculinities resembling Eric Anderson's (2009, 8–9) conception of "inclusive masculinities", men's gendered performances that rely on inclusivity and care rather than control and domination. The male characters' "guys' night" ends with them talking about love, sat under a homemade sleepover den, drinking sangria, and singing Foreigner's "I Wanna Know What Love Is" (*New Girl*, "Teachers"). Characters in the show deride "caveman ideas about masculinity" (*New Girl*, "Parents"), while the initially womanizing Schmidt finishes the show as a full-time stay-at-home dad while his wife Cece provides financially.

Meanwhile, sitcom phenomenon *The Big Bang Theory* (2007–2019) turned its attention toward an oft-maligned and subordinated masculine identity, the nerd, which turned out to be a presciently zeitgeist-aware narrative decision (Jahromi 2019). The show was a huge cultural and commercial success that foregrounded issues of gender and masculinities. In doing so, albeit in different ways to *New Girl*, it too sought to critique perceived outdated forms of masculinity. In the sixth episode of *The Big Bang Theory*, when jealous of another, bigger and more physical imposing, man flirting with their neighbor Penny, Leonard posits a theory about masculinity: "our society has undergone a paradigm shift. In the information age, Sheldon, you and I are the alpha males. We shouldn't have to back down. I'm going to assert my dominance face-to-face" (*The Big Bang Theory*, "The Middle Earth Paradigm"). Leonard's new theory of alpha (potentially hegemonic?) masculinity suggests that intelligence and technological ability are more important to contemporary masculinity than physical dominance, a theory popular within Western cultures (Roeder 2013). In fact, Leonard's "information age" masculinity – formulations of which have been found in what Winifred Poster (2013) calls "techno-masculinity" – is not unrecognizable in the geeky Ross in *Friends*, the nerdy Ted in *How I Met Your Mother*, or the neurotic Schmidt in *New Girl*. Is there a consistent theory of masculinity within the hangout sitcom, despite its internal diversity?

This is the main question this book aims to answer: what characterizes the masculinities of the hangout sitcom? Other tangential questions arise from the background in which the masculinities of the hangout sitcom become pertinent: why, for example, do *Friends* and its inheritors offer such apparent intergenerational appeal? And why and how do several generations seem to enjoy *Friends* amidst significant cognitive dissonance concerning the show's politics and their own, particularly considering that some of its most ardent fans were born after the show's initial run was over?

These questions provide the context in which the hangout sitcom's politics of masculinity are pertinent: if we are to understand why we are questioning how, why, and if we ever considered Ross, Chandler, and Joey to be male role models, we first must understand the context in which their fictional masculinities were produced. I argue, following a variety of television and genre studies scholars (Attallah 2003, Mills 2009, Mittell 2004, Marc 1997, Hamamoto 1989) that as the sitcom and its themes as a wider genre are profoundly socially, discursively, and ideologically contextual, the hangout sitcom's politics of masculinities should be understood from within the ideological conjuncture the subgenre emerged. Specifically, this was a moment in the early 1990s in which neoliberal ideology and postfeminism were achieving a hegemony that appeared to threaten masculinities and patriarchies more widely (Modleski 1991, Faludi 1991). The central argument of this book therefore is that masculinities in the hangout sitcom reflect a wider material-discursive tension between masculinities, patriarchies, men, and neoliberalism.

More specifically, I argue that the demands that neoliberalism makes of its arguably feminized subjects (Gill 2007, 2017) emerge in the hangout sitcom as a series of anxious hybridized masculinities that remain for the most part almost drearily familiar from the inception of the genre, if somewhat hybridized by neoliberalism. Such hybridization does not indicate a significant structural change or shift in discourses on masculinity or wider power structures. However, at the same time I argue that, read via specific lenses, and at specific moments, we can decode in the hangout sitcom some gender performances that offer more subversive/progressive masculinities, indicating occasional glimmers of hope around the edges of masculinity, particularly surrounding male homosocial relationships.

6 *The hangout sitcom: Could it be* more *culturally relevant?*

What's that genre? It's socially contextual comedy!

Television studies critically examines television via its industrial practices, social contexts, artistic endeavors, and audiences. Though studies of television existed prior to it, the University of Birmingham's famous Centre for Contemporary Cultural Studies (CCCS) produced many of the tools that contemporary scholars of television deploy today. Members of the CCCS rejected ideas that existed within the academy that only so-called "high culture" was worthy of value, arguing that popular culture was just as important a location of the construction of popular cultural meaning. Jonathan Gray and Amanda Lotz (2019, 14) write:

> Hence, rather than study cultural products ("texts") as works of art from which we should glean as much enlightenment as possible, the CCCS approach sought to explore texts' varying roles within society, especially as purveyors of power. Moreover, the CCCS refused to regard texts as mere "conveyor belts" that unproblematically transferred ideas from producer to consumer, nor did they regard audiences as mere dupes; thus a great deal of their efforts were expended studying exactly how power and ideology worked at the level of the text.

For the CCCS, as codified by Stuart Hall in his famous essay "Encoding, decoding" (Hall 1993), meaning is produced at both points of production and consumption, suggesting that scholars of television too need to acknowledge their own role in meaning production. As such, one of their insights, which seems somewhat banal today, was that the study of television requires actually watching television, and not just the study of its effects: what specific forms of power do these shows uphold or challenge? Television studies often therefore tends to focus on deeper readings of either individual shows or (sub)genres. Hence, this book examines the specific discursive context of masculinities in the moment that the hangout sitcom subgenre emerged. What, then, defines the hangout sitcom as a subgenre? Importantly, too, why the sitcom? In short, the sitcom as a wider genre offers a uniquely lucid insight into its contemporaneous sociocultural context.

Genre studies

Jason Mittell (2004, 28) argues that genre analysis entails five facets: "genre historiography, industrial practices of genre constitution, audience use of genres and structures of taste, generic textual analysis, and generic mixing". Analyzing and identifying genre therefore is not just a case of identifying its formal structures, but also its sociohistorical context. Jane Feuer (1992, 105), drawing from Todorov, thereby argues that television genres are *historical* rather than *theoretical*; that is, they are derived from observing an existing body of evidence. The labeling of the situation comedy is a case in point, such that the word sitcom was not widely applied to the now-established genre's originating shows until at least the 1960s, several years after their creation (Marc 2016).

To an extent, for those in the industry, this then becomes a theoretical pursuit to reproduce the norms of the subgenre with some small innovations – when Carter Bays and Craig Thomas pitched *How I Met Your Mother* to CBS, they would not have done so without the success of *Friends* before it, even though they were not aiming just to copy. Yet, as scholars of both television studies and genre studies have pointed out, television genres tend to be more dynamic than genres within other media (Dalton and Linder 2016, Mills 2009). The combined pressures of audience engagement and institutional interests are more intensely felt, following the quick turnaround of television episodes – it is not uncommon for later episodes in a season to not yet be filmed while early episodes are already being broadcast. Meanwhile, there is also a relative lack of a single authorial voice in comparison to both movies and literature, putting it further at the mercy of wider social influences (Marc 1997).

Feuer (1992, 108), for example, observes that less than two decades since its creation, "[t]he TV sitcom in the 1970s and after also moved away from the nuclear family as its basic setting and toward "families" of unrelated adults that formed in the workplace". This is not to say that the sitcom genre dramatically changed in this period, as there was a clear lineage between, for example, the workplace family of *The Mary Tyler Moore Show* (1970–1977) and the nuclear family of *I Love Lucy* (1951–1957). Rather, the change of setting reflected sociocultural shifts of the time, congealing into an emerging subgenre that remained within the strictures of the previous genre.

The sitcom genre

Although sitcom scholarship today is not difficult to come by, Paul Attallah (2010, 13) argued in the 1980s that

> [a]s a rule, one does not talk about situation comedy ... This is due to the way television is talked about in general, to the unworthiness that accrues to it and its products, to its institutional functioning, and to the various modes of availability of its products.

He suggests, in short, that "in the classic dichotomy between high art and low art, television definitely occupies the region of low art" (Attallah 2010, 14). Yet, particularly in US culture (and the US's predominance in global culture is important here), the sitcom occupies a hallowed position on television; since the advent of mass television ownership in the 1950s, it has been an extremely rare occurrence for a sitcom not to be somewhere near the top of the ratings. What does the sitcom do that has made it so enduringly popular?

In short, it is the sitcom's use of humor and narrative to mediate contemporaneous social and ideological clashes that ensures its continually high ratings and cultural position. Even for a TV genre, the sitcom is acutely sensitive to its context, not just discursively contextual (like all culture), but directly discursively involved in the social/ideological/conjunctural debates into which it regularly wades. Where Mittell (2004) talks of the importance of historiography in television genre studies, my historiography in Chapter 2 will demonstrate the sitcom's continuing mediation, and perhaps even regulation, of social clashes. Such a role means that the sitcom frequently reflects the everyday experiences of specific demographics of the US. More specifically, I argue, it mirrors everyday experiences of collective organization and affective belonging in the US. In the 1950s through the 1960s, this involved negotiating the contradictions and concerns of the nuclear family in an era of post-war reconstruction (Landay 2016, Pheasant-Kelly 2018); in the 1970s and 1980s, the suburban nuclear family also dealt with issues of race (Jhally and Lewis 1992), while collective organization moved into the workplace, formed between colleagues (Kutulas 2016); for the hangout sitcom, affective belonging is formed among like-minded young people in the city (Cobb et al. 2018, Sandell 1998, Roseneil and Budgeon 2004).

To achieve this, individual sitcom episodes follow paradigmatically basic narratives according to most understandings. Fiske (2010, 138–139), for example, draws again from Todorov:

> narrative begins with a state of equilibrium or social harmony. This is disrupted, usually by the action of a villain. The narrative charts the course of this disequilibrium and its final resolution in another, preferably enhanced or more stable, state of equilibrium,

while Neale (1980, 20) describes narrative as "the interruption of an initial equilibrium and the tracing of the dispersal and refiguration of its components".

If the situation of the sitcom is reflective of wider society, then comedy is the vehicle by which those societal values are normalized as shared ones. Humor theorists have shown how humor relies on some form of shared knowledge (Morreall 2009), and can act as a way of constructing a sense of solidarity or familiarity between individuals (McGraw and Warner 2014). For US and US-influenced cultures, the sitcom's use of humor allows ideological issues to be presented and solved in a familiar, comforting manner, allowing ideological axioms to become normalized. As Mills (2009, 9) suggests, in the sitcom "group laughter at a joke serves to signal an agreement about the way things are, should be or are understood to be".

The sitcom's more formal conventions thereby reflect this culturally mediative position. The live studio audience, for example, mimic the home audience, emphasizing the intimacy of the television in the home, with the laugh track continuing this prosthesis (Keyes 1999).[1] The traditional multi-camera setup allows for quick and easy production, producing a conventionally large 20 + episodes per season, breeding familiarity. Sitcom characters thereby become household names, as recognizable to viewers as their own families.

Sitcoms in the postmodern era

Genre studies has faced some significant challenges in the postmodern era. Jim Collins (1992) argues that postmodern television virtually abandons firm genre boundaries, instead drawing from a range of genres. *Twin Peaks* (1990–1991) is often thought to be a turning point for postmodern television, a show that contains and deploys a vast range of genre conventions to a differing set of purposes, such that Collins describes it as "aggressively eclectic" (Collins 1992, 260). While some genre studies scholars argue this represents a problem for the discipline, Mittell (2004, xvii–xviii) argues "that genre mixing and parody point to the continued importance of genre as an organizing principle, bringing the conventions, codes, and assumptions of genres to the surface of texts and surrounding industry and audience discourses". Genre parody and pastiche contribute to the solidification and codification of different genres, confirming their continued cultural relevance.

Many contemporary, and indeed hangout, sitcoms follow similar postmodern conventions, aping and parodying a range of other genres beyond the sitcom, as well as showing self-awareness, and intertextually referencing other sitcoms of both the subgenre and wider genre; in *New Girl*, the character Coach's real first name is Ernie Tagliaboo, an obvious reference to the character Coach in *Cheers* (1982–1993), whose real name is Ernie Pantusso. In *New Girl*, an early love interest of Jess's named Sam leaves her for a character called Diane, referencing the romance of Sam and Diane in *Cheers*. In an episode of *How I Met Your Mother*, the characters are sitting at a coffee shop not talking to one another, when Ted pipes up "So I guess that decides it", to which Marshall responds, "Yep, hanging out at a coffee place isn't nearly as fun as hanging out at a bar", a parodic reference to the hangout location of *Friends*. In addition, crossover of actors is extremely frequent between sitcoms – in *The Big Bang Theory*, comedian Bob Newhart plays Professor Proton, a fictional TV personality who had his own eponymous science show that several of the characters watched as children, echoing Newhart's own eponymous sitcom in the 1980s, *The Bob Newhart Show* (1972–1978), while in *New Girl* Rob Reiner plays Jess's dad, a lazy bachelor who could feasibly represent the path taken by his character Mike Stivic in *All in the Family* (1971–1979).

The dominance of streaming as the method of content consumption has radically transformed television over the past decade, too. The industry no longer belongs exclusively to broadcast networks, but also to a group of companies whose presence in the market relies solely on their streaming platforms – notably, Netflix (who are the predominant force in the market and have at some point owned the rights to stream all four sitcoms in this book in both the USA and the UK), Amazon Prime, Disney+, and in the US, Hulu. The effects of this are multiple: first, these platforms allow audiences to watch what they want, when they want, resulting in a method of viewing called "binge-watching", where hours of the same show are watched in a single sitting (Jenner 2014). New programming is now regularly attuned to this way of watching, plotted and written to be watched in multiple blocks. Standalone "filler" episodes with discrete individual narratives are less common, and instead series are more focused on one or two plots that thread through the entire season. This is an environment that does not necessarily suit the sitcom format's discrete standalone narratives. And second, perhaps in a bigger challenge to the sitcom, "the liberation of viewership from its spatial and temporal constraints also brings the erosion of its collective dimension since such spatial and temporal limits provided the social contexts that once made the audience activity a shared one" (Özgün and Treske 2021, 305). For a genre that relies on the exposition of humor to construct shared values and norms, a platform defined by an individualization and fragmentation of audiences potentially poses a major problem. Yet, as I explore in the final two chapters of this book, the globalized nature of streaming and the shift in the forms of power it gives to audiences might just mean that the way sitcoms are made and become successes is changing.

From Cheers *to* Seinfeld *to* Friends

Though *Friends* popularized and codified the hangout sitcom, it did not originate all its premises. Two shows in the 1980s had set the precedent: *Cheers* and *Seinfeld* (1989–1998). These will be explored in a little more detail in the next chapter, but they both followed groups of relatively young people in major US cities as they hung around together in a variety of places. In *Cheers*, this was in a bar after which the show was named (indeed, as a portion of the characters work for the bar, *Cheers* has also been dubbed a version of the workplace sitcom (Brown 2016), showing the porousness of subgenre categorization), while in *Seinfeld*, apartments and a diner were the most common locations. Both shows were enormously popular in the USA, both in terms of raw viewing figures reaching around 30 million, and in terms of the huge cultural phenomena they became – the two hangout shows were even bedfellows shown one after the other on NBC for the four years that their broadcast crossed over, which was characterized in an ad campaign by the network as "Must See TV".

Cheers's contribution mainly consisted in extending the friendship group beyond the workplace, from the bar's workers to its clientele – however, its focus was slightly different, more on the democratization and pluralism of the public sphere than on the private relationships of both older family sitcoms and the subsequent hangout sitcoms (Hilmes 1990). *Seinfeld* took this

The hangout sitcom: Could it be *more culturally relevant?*

premise in more radical directions, following a friendship group of four – three men and one woman – living in New York City, primarily doing nothing, a fact that the show, with its postmodern sensibility, shows an awareness off in an episode where the character George pitches a "sitcom about nothing" to TV executives (*Seinfeld*, "The Pitch"). Most of the episodes focus on mundane conversations, nights out, or other hijinks, and the characters barely change, instead remaining the same for the show's run. Co-creator Larry David famously publicly declared his policy on character development via the axiom "no hugging, no learning". In many ways, *Seinfeld* is thereby a critical work; it is first a critique of the sitcom itself, whose characters, despite often learning lessons, do not often substantively change. Their jobs might change, their houses might change, their friendships might change, but the fundamental essence of the character does not. In *I Love Lucy*, Lucy never stops her schemes, while Sam Malone in *Cheers* never manages to deal with his sex addiction or settle down.

It is also, however, a critique of the ways in which neoliberalism rejects and makes difficult the sustenance of human bonds (Illouz 2007) (this is unpacked in depth later in the chapter), with solipsistic characters who most of the time are more interested in their own pleasure and wellbeing than that of others. *Friends*, rather than critiquing neoliberalism per se, offers a solution to collective organization in a neoliberal era other than the family, where the friendship group is instead communal sanctuary from the precarity of neoliberal labor (Harris 2017). In short, where *Seinfeld* is cold and occasionally warm and fuzzy, *Friends* is mostly just warm and fuzzy.

So, while creator Jerry Seinfeld opined that *Friends* was the same formula as his show but "with better looking people", the differences, Kutulas (2018) notes, are deeper than just the characters' appearances, instead built on the appeal of idiosyncratic characters themselves; as early reviewers noted of *Friends*, in relation to its obvious resemblance to *Seinfeld*, in *Friends*, the characters *do* hug and *do* learn. *Friends* is thereby a postmodern sitcom, too, for the way it genre-mixes, introducing to the sitcom notions of character development previously the reserves of dramatic television. Kutulas (2018, 1177) sums up the difference thus:

> Viewers returned to *Seinfeld* to see what crazy schemes the writers had cooked up that week. They returned to *Friends* as they might a drama, to see what happened next to people they cared about. *Friends* was the first sitcom to take advantage of the scripted drama's opportunity to really develop characters over time.

The formal structures of the hangout sitcom

From here, *Friends* cemented the hangout sitcom's position in the canon, and many of its tropes, storylines, and more, became reference points for the

12 *The hangout sitcom: Could it be more culturally relevant?*

subsequent shows, despite considerable variability. It is worth outlining the hangout sitcom's most basic formal structures.

Its characters find solace from the pressures of not just work and the outside world, but also from their own nuclear families, in an insular pseudo-family of friends. The family in the hangout sitcom is important in three ways. First, the characters' nuclear families act as a source of imbalance in their personalities – in *Friends*, Ross's insecurity and Monica's competitiveness are a result of their parents' game of favorites, while Schmidt's fear of commitment in *New Girl* is because of his absent father. Second, it acts as a narrative endgame for the characters to move toward – a simple head count of the four shows studied here finds that 21 of the 23 characters are either married or engaged by the end, with just one couple engaged at the beginning. Third, as Mills (2009, 44) has observed, the hangout sitcom "has repeatedly centred on surrogate families, symbolising the fragmentary nature of the family in contemporary society". These surrogate families offer unconditional support and love in place of the nuclear family. In short, as *Friends* co-creator Marta Kauffman put it, "if the show was about that time in your life when your friends are your family, once you have family on your own, it's no longer that time" (*Friends: The Reunion* 2021).

Within these pseudo-families, there is almost remarkably little action despite the huge numbers of episodes. In family sitcoms, action revolved around conjugal roles and gendered divisions in domestic labor, as well as the lessons learned by children. In the workplace sitcom, labor was again the subject, but in the public sphere. In the hangout sitcom, the action is more difficult to pin down precisely because they, most of the time, do nothing. In *Friends*, the majority of the show's plotlines take place in the characters' New York homes or in their local café, Central Perk, and revolve around their private lives and extremely everyday concerns. This is not to say the workplace does not feature for all the characters, but that the tribulations of labor in a late capitalist setting are not the narrative topic, as opposed to the sense of communal belonging achieved in friendship groups.

The hangout sitcom is always in a city. In the early family sitcoms of the 1950s, suburbia was a familial aspiration that spoke to the elevation of a particular form of the privatized nuclear family, and so the cluster of family sitcoms set in the suburbs mediated the contradictions and tribulations of suburban family life. With the uneven development between urban, suburban, and rural areas throughout the 1980s and 1990s (Harvey 2007, İçli and Özçelik 2012), the sitcom instead began to explore urban life, and the contradictions and hardships that come from living in a city (Rossi 2017).

The main characters in the hangout sitcom are heterosexual, mostly middle-class, mostly single, and mostly white (Chidester 2008), though the latter changes in later shows, which is explored in Chapter 5. In all four sitcoms explored here, there are long-term heterosexual couples within the main cast who frequently serve as aspirational examples to the rest of the cast. Yet, even then, the relationships are not plain-sailing. Whereas the family sitcom features stable families, the hangout sitcom explores single heterosexual life, with romance and sex being probably the most common storyline.

Last, while the hangout sitcom's characters aspire to career progression, this is only a function of a wider aspiration toward happiness and self-fulfillment. Characters' redemption arcs move not just toward career and marriage, but to a sense of becoming a well-adjusted individual. For the "douchebag" character type explored in Chapter 3, the redemption arc is particularly stark – Schmidt's sexist womanizing gives way to a stay-at-home dad, while Barney's sexist womanizing in *How I Met Your Mother* gives way to single fatherhood.

In line with our understanding of genre as socially contextual, and this being felt more acutely within the sitcom and its subgenres, what is the social context in which these specific genre structures become possible? I argue that the ambivalent relation to the nuclear family, the bustling city, heterosexual romance, and the individual redemption arc are linked by neoliberalism.

How neoliberalism met men

This book is primarily interested in structures and their material contexts, effects, and importantly, affects (Clough 2007, Reeser and Gottzén 2018). The hangout sitcom is a means by which to access and unpack such structures – in particular, the relations between masculinities, patriarchies, and capitalisms: all deliberately pluralized, all considered multiple, dynamic, and flexible, and all in a continually negotiated dialectic with one another. To examine these material-discursive relations, this book deploys the notion of the conjuncture (Hall 2017), which refers to the processes by which norms and common sense emerge, become hegemonic, and wither away; it highlights the imperfections in these transient moments, and the challenges they face to their legitimacy; it makes room for the fact that hegemony is not an achieved moment but must be continually justified. Thereby, the methods of conjunctural analysis aim to characterize such a conjuncture via discursive readings of culture.

Masculinities and transpatriarchies

Masculinities in this book are understood as discourses that are legible as gendered actions, rather than character traits (Connell 2005). This follows from a general consensus over the last few decades that gender is performed in relation to existing material and social contexts such that it reiterates and reproduces existing gendered power relations (Butler 1990, West and Zimmerman 1987). Conjuncturally shifting patriarchies and capitalisms are the contexts in which such discursive practices are legible, and the circumstances also in which masculinities' dynamism and flexibility are instantiated. The ongoing literature on "hybrid masculinities", for example, addresses how masculinities respond to structural challenges (Arxer 2011, Bridges and

Pascoe 2014). Demetrakis Demetriou (2001, 349) argues that "masculinity that occupies the hegemonic position at a given historical moment is a hybrid bloc that incorporates diverse and apparently oppositional elements". At threatening moments, the strength of masculinity is its porousness, its ability to re-adapt to existing circumstances. Tristan Bridges and C.J. Pascoe (2014, 58) take the concept of hybridization further, using it to refer to a variety of "men's selective incorporation of performances and identity elements associated with marginalized and subordinated masculinities and femininities". Masculinities at any given moment are contextually defined, and have perhaps always been hybrid; they are, in short, conjunctural, sensitive to conjunctural shifts of capitalism and patriarchies.

These conjunctural shifts are determinant of one another, too. Over the course of the 20th century, global capitalism in the West progressed from a post-industrial laissez-faire form. through to a Keynesian influenced post-war consensus, to the hegemony of a global neoliberal political economy with complex and confusing impacts transnationally (Mirowski and Plehwe 2009) that is currently in its fairly violent death throes (see Davies and Gane 2021). Similarly, patriarchy continues to morph and take different shapes across time and space; Carol Brown (1981) for example shows how the advent of industrial capitalism marked a shift from private patriarchy, in which the home was primary arena of patriarchal relations, to public patriarchy, where women's subjugation became legitimized by the separation of the domestic and workplace. Ortner (2014) similarly demonstrates patriarchy's ongoing links with 21st-century institutions of industrial production, the military, and corporations. It is this process of the legitimization of patriarchies, a process that I argue is a constant one rather than a single moment, that characterizes a lot of what masculinities do.

This process is directly at play in the concept of "hegemonic masculinity", a concept for which Raewyn Connell, among others, is best known. Initially defined as "the currently most honored way of being a man, it required all other men to position themselves in relation to it, and it ideologically legitimated the global subordination of women to men" (Connell and Messerschmidt 2005, 832), it is dialectically constructed against subordinated and marginalized masculinities. Most of the time, it is not used as a static or reified form, but instead temporally and geographically contextual, at least partially constructed by and within a particular moment. Legitimization is and has been from the beginning key to hegemonic masculinity, such as in the now heavily cited formulation from Connell (2005, 76) of hegemonic masculinity as "the currently accepted answer the problem of the legitimacy of patriarchy". I am less interested in decoding a theory of hegemonic masculinity proposed by the hangout sitcom, and more in the subgenre's general politics of gender and of masculinities and men. Within this context, it makes sense to conceive not of a global unified and static patriarchy, but, as Jeff Hearn has done, of competing and overlapping trans(national)patriarchies that vary not just temporally and geographically, but also in and between states, supranational organizations, cultures, and subcultures (Hearn 2015, 2009). Perhaps it would even make sense to talk of hybrid patriarchies as well as hybrid masculinities. The sitcom, I argue, among other things, mediates the process by which US patriarchies are legitimized.

The neoliberal conjuncture

Neoliberalism is, as is customary to note, a conceptually slippery, often misused, geographically variable, internally complex concept (Venugopal 2015). It most often refers to neoliberal capitalism as a mode of political economy that aims to deregulate markets and stems from a belief in individual political liberties (Mirowski and Plehwe 2009). In the US, these policies are usually associated with the presidency of Ronald Reagan, whose advisers and policy platform were built on the founding principles of what is known as the Chicago School of economics led by economists Milton Friedman and George Stigler. Yet, as a variety of authors have argued, neoliberal economics is often taken to be merely a function of a political aim to extend free market economic logic beyond markets. Philip Mirowski and Rob Van Horn (2009, 161) write that the "American" brand of "neoliberalism transcends the classical liberal tension between the self-interested agent and the patriotic duty of the citizen by reducing both state and market to the identical flat ontology of the neoclassical model of the economy". It was and is as much an economic doctrine as an ideology of the state, with the latter's role in public life diminished at the expense of the virtues of private business and corporate interests (Duggan 2004). Economics was not just policy, but its endgame was political and cultural – or, as UK Prime Minister Margaret Thatcher put it, "economics is the method – the aim is to change the soul", not just of the nation, but of its subjects, too.

Capitalism has always interpellated a form of subjectivity amenable to its demands; in the 1950s, throughout the post-war consensus, consumption was incorporated into capitalist subjectivity as Western economies shifted from industrial to consumer-based economies (Nickles 2002, Spigel 1992). Under neoliberal capitalism, subjectivity incorporates a radical individualism, manifesting a cultural realm also defined by a pervasive individualism. Neoliberalism thereby extends rational individualism into the social, cultural, and political domains (Brown 2015, Duggan 2004). Neoliberal ontology takes the primary unit of society to be the individual on their own, who is not beholden to any societal structure or condition, instead entirely self-responsible (Brown 2006).

The neoliberal subject adapts to new demands that surface in response to a shift in the types of labor brought about by late 20th-century capitalism, and specifically a shift away from manual labor toward forms of both immaterial (Lazzaroto 2006) and affective (Hardt 1999) labor. The ideal neoliberal subject works in an office or for themselves, not a factory or production line

(Boutang 2011); they are expected to be able to emotionally or at least affectively invest in their labor (Abstract 1989, Illouz 2007); they are expected to perform aesthetic labor (Witz et al. 2003), and have strict bodily discipline; they have capacities for intellectual teamwork, cooperation, and even care (Enderstein 2018). In short, this subject is one whose qualitative characteristics include a variety of modalities and expectations that are coded feminine. As Rosalind Gill (2007, 156) suggests, "it appears that the ideal disciplinary subject of neoliberalism is feminine".

Neoliberalism's feminized subject is further indicated by a compulsory individualization that adopts othered or countercultural aesthetics and modalities. Jim McGuigan (2014, 2009) argues that neoliberal culture and subjectivity exhibit individualism through the incorporation and adoption of formerly othered or at least non-hegemonic cultures into the mainstream – hence, he says, neoliberalism constructs a "cool-capitalist way of life that does not appear to insist upon conformity and even permits a limited measure of bohemian posturing, personal experimentation and geographical exploration" (McGuigan 2014, 234). Elsewhere, I have argued that this leads men to adopt feminine modalities (Wolfman et al. 2021), such that even when femininity is not explicitly on the agenda, notions of compulsory individualization make it a constant potentiality. This does not just go for individuals, either, but for hegemonic ideology, too. Thomas Frank (1998), for example, shows how the counter-cultures that fomented throughout the 1960s were eventually incorporated into dominant consumerist culture. Furthermore, Eagleton-Pierce (2016) demonstrates how neoliberal politics rearticulates the radical collective politics of the 1960s and 1970s, such as the women's and civil rights movements, through an individualized language, which goes on to characterize neoliberalism's gender politics, and the ways it hybridizes patriarchies.

Neoliberal gender

By now, the contradictions inherent in the gender politics of neoliberalism should be apparent. Neoliberal capitalism cannot shed the legacy of domestic and public labor that comes with 20th-century capitalism's imbrication with the nuclear family, and therefore its heteronormative and binary gender regimes too. Yet, with an individualist ontology and normativity, as well as its absorption of oppositional politics and aesthetics into the mainstream, neoliberal gender is tensely poised.

Neoliberalism reformulates a version of feminist politics that often gets labeled *postfeminism* (Banet-Weiser et al. 2020, Gill and Scharff 2011). Like neoliberalism, the literature on postfeminism is interdisciplinary, complex, and often contradictory; "post"-ing feminism has several possible implications, ranging from rejection to replacement, from evolution to the achievement of a feminist hegemony (Gill 2017, McRobbie 2009). Rosalind Gill (2007) calls it a "media sensibility", and indeed much literature on postfeminism explores media and culture. She cites several elements of this sensibility that she relates to neoliberal politics. It defines femininity as a bodily property, thereby re-encoding a gaze on the body as a potential source of empowerment, reflecting a neoliberal biopolitics that emphasizes outward appearance and aesthetic labor (Hakim 2016, Phipps 2014). Like neoliberal subjectivity, postfeminist sensibility relies on an individualist paradigm that rejects the collective identity on which earlier forms of feminism were based – as such, it incorporates certain feminist paradigms and regurgitates them as individualist ones (Gill and Scharff 2011). Postfeminist sensibility also emphasizes self-surveillance and self-discipline, and resultantly encourages self-improvement and the notion of the makeover, making individuals responsible for improving themselves and their bodies (Sender 2006).

At the very least, we can observe a coopting of feminist language in service of the sustenance of a normative individualism, both in cultural and corporate realms – Gill and Kanai (2020) show how corporate visibility of historically marginalized identities, particularly those who are not cisgendered men, not only ignores, but actively strengthens the structural background that causes marginalization, which they call "woke capitalism". Whatever we might call this (postfeminist patriarchies, neoliberal patriarchies, "woke" patriarchies), contemporary patriarchies appear to have a real penchant for adaptation.

However, the individualism of postfeminism and neoliberalism are in a more difficult relationship with that most patriarchal of institutions, the family. The traditional feminist critique of capitalism as a form of exchange that rests on the foundations of hours of unpaid labor by women remains true of neoliberal capitalism, too. Yet, as Wendy Brown (2015, 100–107) observes, how does the emotional, affective, and often sacrificial collectivism of the family fare when neoliberalism's homo economicus is so radically individualized? To quote Margaret Thatcher again, but to add the elliptically separated secondary clause that is often omitted, "there is no society, only individual men and women ... and their families". It is an ambivalence that is often to be filled ideologically by neoconservatism's nuclear family values (Brown 2006, Cooper 2016) – but, for the hangout sitcom, the family does not preclude a surrogate group of friends.

Neoliberal men ...

This book has "neoliberal men" in the title, by which is meant not men that are neoliberal (whatever that might mean), but the many transnational and multifaceted masculinities that are negotiated and constructed by, within, and in response to the neoliberal conjuncture – here, in a subgenre of US television. The relationship between neoliberalism and masculinities has received some attention (Cornwall et al. 2016, Walker and Roberts 2018, Garlick 2020), though more often, the attention has been on postfeminist masculinities, research that explores themes of emasculation, socioeconomic demotion, and anxiety. Ben Brabon and Stephanie Genz (2009, 143) argue this demotion is doubly encoded: "on the one hand, the 'postfeminist man' accommodates backlash scripts – drawing upon characteristics of the 'new lad'. On the other hand, he is more self-aware, displaying anxiety and concern for his identity while re-embracing patriarchal responsibilities". These two sides of the same postfeminist coin are visible in the range of literature on postfeminism and men. Dow (2006), for example, emphasizes the latter, demonstrating how postfeminist men on-screen support and respect their female friends and partners, embracing nurturing and caring responsibilities. Gill (2014, 200) emphasizes so-called backlash scripts more, citing media that portrays men as bumbling and inept in order to stake the claim "that men are the disadvantaged losers in the "new" gender stakes".

Postfeminist masculinities have too received attention in relation to some of the sitcoms explored here – notably in *Friends* (as might be expected of its cultural enormity) and in *How I Met Your Mother*. In an invaluable special edition of the journal *Television & New Media*, a variety of contributors explore the foundational postfeminism of *Friends*, from Neil Ewen's (2018) suggestion that Chandler's personal crisis of masculinity is indicative of his dead-end unfulfilling career, to Lauren Jade Thompson's (2018) acute analysis of gendered domestic spaces in the show that, while hinting at deconstruction, maintain conservative gendered assumptions. In a different paper, Thompson (2015) analyzes *How I Met Your Mother*, suggesting that the three male characters offer differing insights into contemporary postfeminist masculinities, representing residual, dominant, and emergent forms of masculinity in a postfeminist moment.

A series of anxieties frame this entire literature, anxieties that emerge in the hangout sitcom, too. These anxieties are about men struggling to adapt to a series of societal changes in the Global North – shifts in labor patterns, in patriarchy, in familial structures, and capitalism. In short, these are men on-screen struggling to come to terms with not just postfeminism, but with both neoliberal capitalism and subjectivity and its attendant patriarchal shifts.

… in the US hangout sitcom

To reiterate, the question this book asks is this: is there a unified theory of masculinities in the hangout sitcom? I am as such concerned specifically with how forms of masculinity serve to legitimize patriarchy, and additionally what those legitimacy problems might be. I argue that such problems are contextually defined – what challenges to patriarchies exist at a given time and place, and how does masculinity overcome them? In short, it hybridizes, taking on and absorbing what might previously have been seen as threats to patriarchies and to masculinities. Other intersections are very important here, and explored in

The hangout sitcom: Could it be *more culturally relevant?* 19

this book: those of racialization, of sexuality, and more. These contexts are all at play in the sitcom, a television genre that is deeply contextually constructed.

Masculinities and men in the hangout sitcom are neoliberal insofar as the hangout sitcom is a neoliberal subgenre – neoliberal in the sense that its discourses are organized around the conjunctural concerns and contradictions of neoliberalism, rather than for expressing any sort of neoliberal realpolitik. When Ugo Rossi (2017, 86) talks of a "neoliberalism-city nexus" in which "newly built urban districts are intended to trigger a process of economic growth, spurred by the formation of a class of urbanites consuming domestic products and demanding public services", he could very well be describing the main characters in *Friends*, belonging to a "class of urbanites" who seem to spend most of their time consuming coffee. Similarly, the hangout sitcom's pseudo-family seems to be a response to a question asked by Wendy Brown (2015, 102):

> when neoliberal reason costs each human, positively and normatively, across every domain of existence, as self-investing entrepreneurial capital, responsible for itself and striving to appreciate its value vis a vis other capital entities, how does this comport with the need-based, explicitly interdependent, effective, and frequently sacrificial domain of family relations?

I suggest that Shelley Budgeon and Sasha Roseneil (2004, 135, emphasis added) had a robust answer a decade earlier: "much that matters to people in terms of intimacy and care increasingly takes place beyond the 'family', between partners who are not living together 'as family', and within *networks of friends*". In the hangout sitcom, that domain belongs not within the normal nuclear family, but in the friendship group.

The neoliberal conjunctural dilemma in which I am interested, though, and which I argue characterizes the so-called problematic politics of masculinity of the hangout sitcom, is, to paraphrase Brown: when the neoliberal subject is interpellated as bodily disciplined, compulsorily individualized, reflexive, adaptable, and skeptical of the patriarchal structures of the nuclear family, what happens to a masculine subjectivity whose only flirtations with bodily discipline have been countercultural, whose fear of femininity has made it anxious of individualizing via otherness, whose labor has often been staunchly manual, and whose powers have historically resided within the private family unit? The hangout sitcom does not provide a unified answer but does give some insight into some forms of resolution.

The one with the four sitcoms

The four hangout sitcoms examined in this book are *Friends*, *How I Met Your Mother*, *The Big Bang Theory*, and *New Girl*. A good number more could have been selected, and were considered – *Seinfeld*'s (1989–1998) setting the scene for *Friends* made it a candidate, but it does not quite fit the bill

20 *The hangout sitcom: Could it be more culturally relevant?*

like the others and remains less popular globally than its successors; *Scrubs* (2001–2010) was another candidate, as it contains many similar characters and tropes to the hangout sitcom, but the characters are linked by their workplace; *Happy Endings* (2011–2013) was considered too, but was not included for its short run of only two seasons before cancellation. With a corpus of 869 episodes totaling over 300 hours or nearly 13 solid days of television, the four shows selected cover every year from 1994 until 2019.

All four shows adhere to the formal structures of the hangout sitcom identified in the previous chapter: groups of slightly emotionally damaged gen X-ers and millennials finding a sense of belonging among a pseudo-family of peers in similar situations, hanging out in a major US city, aspiring both to self-fulfillment, and to start their own heterosexual families. They include thirteen male main characters who remain in place for each show's full run, plus one *New Girl* character, Coach, who was a regular for two seasons and appeared as a guest in several more.

Table 1.1 Male characters from the four selected sitcoms.

Show	Character	Actor	Ethnicity	Class
Friends	Chandler Bing	Matthew Perry	White	Middle-class
	Ross Geller	David Schwimmer	White, Jewish	Middle-class
	Joey Tribbiani	Matt LeBlanc	White, Italian	Working-class background
How I Met Your Mother	Marshall Eriksen	Jason Segel	White	Working-class background
	Ted Mosby	Josh Radnor	White (implied Jewish)	Middle-class
	Barney Stinson	Neil Patrick Harris	White	Working-class background
The Big Bang Theory	Sheldon Cooper	Jim Parsons	White	Working-class background
	Leonard Hofstadter	Johnny Galecki	White (implied Jewish)	Middle-class
	Raj Koothrapali	Kunal Nayyar	Indian-American immigrant	Middle-class
	Howard Wolowitz	Simon Helberg	White, Jewish	Middle-class
New Girl	Winston Bishop	Lamorne Morris	Black	Working-class background
	Nick Miller	Jake Johnson	White	Working-class background
	Winston "Schmidt" Schmidt	Max Greenfield	White, Jewish	Middle-class
	Ernie "Coach" Tagliaboo	Damon Wayans Jr.	Black	Unclear

The hangout sitcom: Could it be more culturally relevant? 21

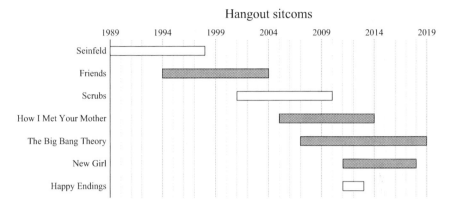

Figure 1.2 Timeline of US hangout sitcoms.

Here, I outline each of the four shows, with their basic institutional information (the period in which it was initially broadcast, creator, network, viewing figures, and current accessibility), their contemporary cultural status and position, and a description of the show's characters, their narrative arcs, relationships with one another, and any pertinent information about the actors. It is probably my duty to say that the remainder of this chapter is abundant with spoilers – so for those of you interested in the book who have not yet watched the shows, you may wish to skip at least this chapter.

Friends

Friends (1994–2004) was developed by David Crane and Marta Kauffman (who at the time were also running the family sitcom *Dream On* (1990–1996)) and began broadcasting in 1994. It is a multi-camera sitcom with a laugh track, filmed mostly in front of a live audience, which ran for ten years and ten seasons on NBC. Its episode titles, bar the first episode "Pilot", and "The Last One" all begin "The One Where/With/Without/In/After/At/That … ", on the basis that the show's writers thought that is how fans would identify and talk about the episodes – for example, "The One with the Male Nanny". At its height, and particularly at the finale, it was the most-watched show on television in the US and the Global North generally, at times reaching over 50 million viewers in the USA alone. It is still in syndication on NBC today, which is estimated to earn the network around $1 billion every year (Knox and Schwind 2019), while it has been picked up by streaming services and networks in over 50 countries, managing to reach newer and younger audiences every year.

I do not wish to belabor the point, but *Friends* was the frontpage of a number of magazines and newspapers for several years, and fashions and catchphrases from the show became ubiquitous – "the Rachel", the at-the-time

22   *The hangout sitcom: Could it be more culturally relevant?*

Figure 1.3 The cast of *Friends* from season two's opening credits. From left to right: David Schwimmer as Ross, Courtney Cox as Monica, Matthew Perry as Chandler (seated), Matt LeBlanc as Joey, Lisa Kudrow as Phoebe, Jennifer Aniston as Rachel.

unusual haircut given to Aniston in the show's early seasons, became hugely popular, while Joey's catchphrase chat-up line, "how you doin'?", and Chandler's sarcastic catchphrase "could [insert noun] *be* anymore [insert adjective]?" are all extremely familiar – as well as codifying many tropes that would be used in the other shows. Muzellec et al. (2013) even argue that parts of the show are hugely successful "fictional brands", breaking down the distinction between the physical and televisual realms. It was and remains a huge phenomenon (see Cobb et al. 2018, Hamad 2018).

Friends has six main characters. All six are, broadly, white (though Monica and Ross are Jewish, and Joey is from a family of New York Italian immigrants) and lead middle-class lifestyles. Ross and Monica Geller are a brother and sister living in New York City, where she works as a chef and lives in a rent-controlled apartment bequeathed to her by family, and he works as a palaeontologist living in his own apartment. They are both Jewish, which is largely a cultural rather than a religious identity for them (Brook 2010). Monica is played by Courteney Cox (later Cox Arquette), who was the most established of the six main actors prior to the show but is not of Jewish background herself. Monica, we learn from flashbacks, used to be overweight as a child, and is now a chef. She most embodies post-feminist femininity in *Friends* (Hamad 2018), with much of her storyline being about the choices she has to make between her career and starting a family – choices her partner Chandler does not consider in the same depth, a notable difference from later hangout sitcoms where male characters are more involved with domestic work. Conversely, Ross, played by David Schwimmer, who is of Jewish background, is a typical postfeminist male singleton (Brabon 2013), extremely nervous to find his female soulmate. Monica lives with her best friend from school, Rachel Green, who triggers the beginning of the show when she leaves her fiancé at the altar and appears on-screen as a runaway bride. She is played by Jennifer Aniston, who certainly had the most successful post-*Friends* career in Hollywood. Rachel is from an affluent background, somewhat protected from precarity, working as a waitress at the Central Perk café where the group spend most of their time after realizing she does not have the experience or skills to succeed in her dream of working in the fashion industry. Ross and Rachel's relationship has become a reference point for subsequent shows for their on-off romance.

Opposite Monica and Rachel's flat live Chandler Bing and Joey Tribbiani. Chandler, played by Matthew Perry, works a data-entry job in a company whose role and purpose is extremely unclear to the other characters as well as to the audience. Chandler is continually embarrassed by the gender of his father, Charles/Helena, who appears to live as a transgender woman (played, interestingly, by a cis woman), even while they are labeled frequently as a transvestite. Chandler marries Monica in season five, and the two remain stable through the rest of the show's run. Joey is a moderately successful Italian American actor best known for appearing on a fictional version of the real daytime soap opera, *Days of Our Lives* (1965–present) as Dr Drake Ramoray. He is played by Matt LeBlanc, and is something of a descendant of the jock character, successful with women if a little slow-witted, though is perhaps more well-intentioned than the jock character that preceded him. Joey, from a sprawling New York Italian family, as the only one of the main six characters not in a relationship at the finale, was the subject of his own short-lived spin-off, *Joey* (2004–2006), following him moving to Los Angeles to further his acting career. Finally, Phoebe Buffay is friend number six, a full-time masseuse initially befriended by Rachel. Portrayed by Lisa Kudrow, Phoebe's slightly off-kilter taste in fashion and sense of humor bely a tragic back story in which her mother committed suicide shortly before the show's beginning, and a not-evil-but-certainly-antagonist twin sister Ursula – Kudrow had previously played Ursula on the sitcom *Mad About You* (1992–1999), also set in New York, such that the writers decided to write both characters into the show. Phoebe marries a character named Mike Hannigan, played by the well-known comedy actor Paul Rudd, in the final season.

How I Met Your Mother

How I Met Your Mother (2005–2014) began in 2005, ran for nine years and nine seasons, and was created and run by duo Craig Thomas and Carter Bays. It is probably the most obvious simulacrum of the hangout subgenre

24 *The hangout sitcom: Could it be more culturally relevant?*

Figure 1.4 The cast of *How I Met Your Mother* from the show's opening credit. From left to right, Jason Segel as Marshall, Alyson Hannigan as Lily, Josh Radnor as Ted, Neil Patrick Harris as Barney, Cobie Smulders as Robin.

and of *Friends* in the USA; it is multi-camera, is set in New York, and while it was not filmed in front of a live studio audience, has a laugh track produced by recording audience reactions to episodes prior to broadcast. Their hangout location is the public space of MacLarens, mirroring Central Perk café, where the characters are always sitting on the same table, while the rest of the action takes place in several flats. Where it differs is that it has a central character, Ted, who acts as an unreliable narrator, via voice-over.

Though *How I Met Your Mother* never approached the same sort of ratings, nor cultural impact, as *Friends*, it was still an extremely popular show, at its peak hitting 15 million viewers. Broadcast on CBS, it remains syndicated, picking up not-insignificant viewing figures, and has been picked up internationally by over 20 different countries. It is on a variety of streaming platforms, where it consistently rates as one of the most-streamed shows. Whatever cultural longevity it has had can probably be attributed to Barney, whose catchphrases such as "legendary" and "wait for it!" have entered the popular lexicon, and the popularity of Neil Patrick Harris, whose fame led to him presenting the 2015 Academy Awards ceremony.

How I Met Your Mother tells the story of Ted Mosby, an architect and later architecture lecturer in New York City, who acts the titular "I" in the show's title. Ted narrates the story of how he met his wife, but as indicated by the title, addresses his two future children Penny and Luke Mosby who act as the television audience's proxy. The resultant overarching narrative then follows him, like Ross, searching for the "the one", his romantic soulmate. Ted is from a fairly ambiguous white middle-class background, and describes himself as "half-Jewish" at one point, suggesting one Jewish parent, though this is not addressed in any depth. Interestingly, Ted is played by two actors – the of-screen narrator version by comedian Bob Saget, and on-screen by the "wholly Jewish" Josh Radnor, who has focused his post-show career on direction rather than acting. He lives with his best friend Marshall Eriksen, who is initially a law student, later a lawyer, and eventually Supreme Court Justice in a flashforward episode. Marshall, who grew up in a rural working-class household in Minnesota, dreams of being an environmental lawyer, but accepts that the short-term makes that financially difficult, so works in corporate law for a portion of the show. He is portrayed by Jason Segel, who for several years made a career out of playing a certain type of emasculated male lead in romantic comedies such as *Forgetting Sarah Marshall* (2008), before more recently pivoting to a string of dramatic roles. Marshall is besotted with his fiancée, and later wife, Lily Aldrin, and the two are together for the whole show apart from one season. Lily is an aspiring artist and teacher who attended college with both Ted and Marshall. She is played by Alyson Hannigan, who was well-known for her six-year role as a main cast member of *Buffy the Vampire Slayer* (1997–2003).

Much of Ted's story focuses on his on-off love interest, Robin Scherbatsky, an aspiring journalist who eventually works her way into success, played by Cobie Smulders. Robin is portrayed as somewhat masculine, emotionally unavailable and skeptical of women who are overly feminine (Desjarlais 2018). Ted and Robin date for the entirety of season two, but do not rekindle a full relationship on-screen at any point, though are often depicted as having regular casual sex. In the final season, we are introduced to regular cast member Tracey McConnell, the titular "the mother", played by Cristin Milioti. We find out very little about her, other than that she performs a stellar version of the song "La Vie en Rose" on her ukulele. The group is finished by Barney Stinson, who is both comedy relief throughout most of the show, as well as a tragic masculine character. Barney, a "high-rise playboy" (Colwell 2014) who has a "playbook" in which he keeps detailed schemes to lure women into sleeping with him, works a shady and vaguely defined corporate job. He grew up in a working-class household, with a single mom and an absent father who he never knew. Barney's character is in an interesting dialectic with his actor, Neil Patrick Harris, a gay man known for not only his LGBTQ+ activism, but also for his proficiency in musical theatre, a similar theatricality that is applied to the artifice and extravagance of Barney's heterosexuality (Thompson 2015). The three male characters strongly mirror the male characters from *Friends* – Ted as Ross, the anxious Jewish male singleton; Marshall as Chandler, the office-worker in a long-term relationship; and Barney as Joey, the womanizer.

The Big Bang Theory

Set in Pasadena, California, *The Big Bang Theory* ran for 12 years and 12 seasons on the channel CBS, from 2007 to 2019, the longest of any show here, winning multiple Emmys and other awards. It is multi-camera, with a laugh track produced by a live studio audience. Its viewing figures made it, at times, the most popular show on US television, occasionally hitting over 20 million viewers, while it has been re-broadcast in over 30 other countries and is now in syndication, as well as available on multiple streaming platforms. *The Big Bang Theory* was filmed in front of a live studio audience, with a recorded laugh track, and was created by seasoned television writers Chuck Lorre and Bill Prady, whose joint writing credits span from *Roseanne* (1988–1997) to *Dharma & Greg* (1997–2002) to *Gilmore Girls* (2000–2007). Its episode titles are all written as tongue-in-cheek scientific theories, such as "The Big Bran Hypothesis", or "The Bow Tie Asymmetry".

The Big Bang Theory initially followed the lives of four nerdy men in Pasadena, California, and their hot female neighbor. Perhaps the central pairing, or at least the most publicly visible, are flatmates Leonard Hofstadter, an experimental physicist, and Sheldon Cooper, a theoretical physicist, both working at the California Institute of Technology. Leonard follows Ross and Ted as the male singleton of the series, an insecure nerdy guy who thinks he will never find love. He is portrayed by Johnny Galecki. Like those two, the character has a standard middle-class family background, while his surname "Hofstadter" hints at Ashkenazi Jewishness despite that not being explicitly

Figure 1.5 The cast of *The Big Bang Theory* from season five's opening credits. From left to right, Melissa Rauch as Bernadette, Simon Helberg as Howard, Johnny Galecki as Leonard, Kaley Cuoco as Penny, Jim Parsons as Sheldon, Mayim Bialik as Amy, Kunal Nayyar as Raj.

The hangout sitcom: Could it be more culturally relevant? 27

acknowledged. Sheldon is one of the most interesting characters of the entire subgenre, a mostly asexual former child prodigy who is almost certainly on the autistic spectrum (Walters 2013, Stratton 2016), and whose redemption arc is completed by happy heterosexual coupledom in the final few seasons (Stratton 2015) – he is currently the subject of an ongoing prequel show, *Young Sheldon* (2017–present), which narrates his childhood. Sheldon's asexuality being key to his character, it is interesting that, like Barney, he is portrayed by an openly gay man in Jim Parsons, again known for LGBTQ+ activism. At the beginning of the show, Penny, an attractive blonde aspiring actress whose surname is unknown, moves in opposite them, triggering an on-off romance between her and Leonard – they eventually marry. Penny works mostly as a waitress, until she gets a job as a sales representative, and comes from a white middle-class family. She is portrayed by Kaley Cuoco, who had previously had a starring role in the sitcom *8 Simple Rules* (2002–2005).

The initial cast of four is rounded off by Raj Koothrappali and Howard Wolowitz. Raj is an Indian-American particle astrophysicist who is literally unable to talk to women, losing the ability to speak in their presence. Portrayed by Kunal Nayyar, he was born in India and emigrated to the US for work, and gains the ability to speak to women later on in the series. Howard is a hypersexual Jewish aerospace engineer who is initially infatuated with Penny, though that dies down. Following the Jewish stereotype, he has an overbearing mother who is rarely seen on-screen and only usually heard off-screen. Interestingly, Simon Helberg, who is Jewish himself, was a recurring actor in the short-lived *Friends* spin-off *Joey* (2004–2006), playing Seth Tobin, a nerdy Jewish engineer. Howard marries first, completing his narrative arc relatively early on, meeting Bernadette Rostenkowski in season three, a graduate student also has an overbearing mother. Bernadette is played by Melissa Rauch. Finally, Sheldon surrenders his asexuality after a scientifically perfect match on an online dating site with Amy Fowler, a neurobiologist who struggles to get on with feminine women as well as with conversation and social interaction in general, but like many of the other characters, becomes more socially able as the series develops (McIntosh 2014). Amy shares some similarities with her actor Mayim Bialik, who has a PhD in neuroscience.

New Girl

Created and run by Elizabeth Meriwether, *New Girl* appeared toward the end of the hangout sitcom era in 2012, running for seven years and seven seasons, arguably riding a wave of popular feminism that began to take off the in the early 2010s (Kanai and Gill 2020) in installing a woman as not only its lead, but its eponymous character. In terms of ratings, it is the least popular show here, rarely achieving more than four million viewers per episode. These viewing figures will have been impacted by the emerging hegemony of streaming platforms over live television at the beginning of its broadcast, to

28 *The hangout sitcom: Could it be more culturally relevant?*

Figure 1.6 The cast of *New Girl* from season four's opening credits. From left to right, Lamorne Morris as Winston, Hannah Simone as Cece, Jake Johnson as Nick, Zooey Deschanel as Jess, Damon Wayans Jr. as Coach (above), Max Greenfield as Schmidt.

their established hegemony by the end. Despite this, *New Girl*'s network Fox discussed cancelling it before the writers wished to end it; in a Hail Mary, they successfully pitched and filmed a shortened seventh and final season of eight episodes set three years after the previous season to wrap up its ongoing narrative arcs. It is syndicated, and it has been broadcast in several countries internationally, but arguably had the least cultural impact of the four shows here, though such things are difficult to measure. It remains interesting, however, for a few hangout sitcom tropes from which it departed, from its female lead to more formal aspects such as its single-camera filming and its abandonment of the laugh track.

Set in Los Angeles, California, *New Girl*'s central character is Jess Day, an "adorkable" (a portmanteau of adorable and dorky that was used in advertising the show at its start, one from which Elizabeth Meriwether has since distanced herself (Radloff 2018)) primary school teacher who moves into a house with three single men after her boyfriend cheats on her. Jess is a white middle-class woman who enjoys a lot of typically feminine domestic activities, such as baking and arts and crafts. Jess is played by Zooey Deschanel, who was perhaps the best-known actor prior to her sitcom role of any of the main casts in this book, having starred in several major Hollywood movies beforehand (see McIntyre 2015). As the latest starting sitcom here, the move from Hollywood to primetime television perhaps indicates the increasing critical adulation for TV programs in the 21st century, and an increasing sense that television was and is no longer considered a "lower" art form (Albrecht 2015). Jess's love interest is flatmate Nick Miller, an underachieving bartender who studied law at university but decided it was not for him. Nick is from what might be fairly described as a working-class background, his dad a door-to-door salesman, and is regularly shown to be unfit for modern living, owning just one pair of jeans and refusing to open a bank account. He is played by Jake Johnson.

Winston "Schmidt" Schmidt is an insecure Jewish man known through most of the show only as Schmidt. Schmidt grew up with an absent father and a typically overbearing Jewish mother, and was overweight through his childhood and teenage years, and now quite preoccupied with his appearance, both body and fashion. Played by the actually Jewish Max Greenfield, Schmidt achieves redemption from his insecurities via his relationship with Cece Parekh, Jess's childhood friend and half-Indian model with, again, a stereotypically stern Indian mother (rather similar to Raj's parents). Cece's arc involves her career change from modeling into management, echoing career-focused forms of postfeminist femininity (Adamson 2016, Genz 2009). She is portrayed by Hannah Simone. The final flatmate is Winston Bishop, played by comedian Lamorne Morris, a black former basketball player who quits his career in Latvia and later becomes a police officer. Winston was a replacement character for the cocksure Ernie "Coach" Tagliaboo, who works as a personal trainer, played by Damon Wayans Jr. another black cast member, and who left to star in *Happy Endings*, and comes back as a main cast member for season four before leaving again when his character marries and moves to New York. As a result, at the beginning of the show, Winston's character is unrecognizable from a season later; it is initially implied he is quite hot-headed and competitive, but later becomes more caring, growing very attached to his cat Furguson, besotted with his girlfriend and later wife Aly, and enjoys light-hearted pranks.

Textual, subtextual, and paranoid masculinities

As the hangout sitcom subgenre morphs over time, alongside neoliberalism's ongoing sustaining and waning of its hegemony, it is notable how consciously salient gender generally and masculinity specifically become to an array of narratives and plot points. Some elements of this are present in *Friends*, such as in "The One with the Male Nanny", where Ross openly confesses his masculine insecurities to the male nanny after attempting to fire him. However, it becomes more obvious with Barney in *How I Met Your Mother*, whose entire narrative is essentially a study in white American heterosexual masculinity (Thompson 2015). His origin story, to be examined in more detail in the next chapter, involves heterosexual rejection, while his womanizing is shown to come from masculine insecurities. This lineage follows directly into Sheldon in *The Big Bang Theory*, and Schmidt in *New Girl*, characters with "tragic" origins whose masculinity is damaged goods. Masculinity is explicit in these characters' stories, rather than an implicit ideology or theory about gender – and not just explicit, but critiqued. How are we to deal with these textual societal critiques?

There is a risk here of what Eve Kosofsky Sedgwick (2003) famously called "paranoid" reading, defined by a "hermeneutics of suspicion" – in short, that the commitment to reading ideology from cultural texts gives way to *always* finding and anticipating all-encompassing ideological axioms. Even in moments when these sitcoms attempt to critique masculinity, it can be tempting to approach such critiques with suspicion. These are, after all, multi-billion-dollar networks, producing content with all the vested material interests that come with that. Surely there must be a profit motive behind these attempts to diversify and critique? So, if this book is about neoliberal masculinities, will I always find ideologies of neoliberalism and patriarchy lurking underneath the surface, or are other readings plausible too?

Sedgwick offers queer readings as an example of the type of "reparative" reading that has room for contingency, surprise, and intertextuality; reparative reading seems to indicate a position from which to consume texts, where suspicion gives way to an openness, or at least a willingness to find happy surprises and moments of disruption within texts. This, of course, does not mean to abandon the notion that texts arise from material conditions with material interests, but rather to not search for the ideology – to start with the question "what is here?" rather than with the question, "where is the ideology?". The text here is therefore primary, not assumed to encode ideology, and polysemic, readable in countless different ways. Reparative readings also need not take the social sciences' "linguistic turn" to be too literal, or rather to ensure that discourse is not analyzed at the expense of materiality – ideology is present within these sitcoms, but it is not funneled through them.

In other words, to say the hangout sitcom is neoliberal is not to say that it is dogma; to say that the hangout sitcom's masculinities are neoliberal is not to say that they are held up as some neoliberal ideal for men. Rather, to say the hangout sitcom is neoliberal is to say that the genre, as I have shown, mediates neoliberal ideology, with all its contradictions and structural complications. In particular, this book will show how the hangout sitcoms outlined in this chapter work to both undermine and legitimize US patriarchies.

The bibliophilic permutation

As conjunctural analysis is not as such a methodology as opposed to a theoretical starting point, most of this book is taken up with forms of critical discourse analysis, which are close textual readings of certain elements of the four sitcoms explored. Critical discourse analysis examines "the role of discourse in the (re)production and challenge of dominance" (van Dijk

The hangout sitcom: Could it be *more culturally relevant?* 31

1993), paralleling the discursive focus of the notion of the conjuncture. It is a method that addresses how discourses uphold, reflect and challenge power, a dialectic whose function is legible in the sitcom's clear and obvious narratives (Fiske 2010, Mills 2009). However, the methods of this book are somewhat more diverse.

In Chapter 2 I develop a historiography of masculinities in the US sitcom, arguing that the sitcom's narrative focus addresses how forms of collective organization and affective belonging are ideologically contextual, moving from the nuclear family to the workplace to friendship groups. I examine the gendered, and specifically masculinized, dimensions of these forms of organization, demonstrating the ways in which other subgenres and specific shows encode masculinities for their specific era. I show that masculinities remain remarkably similar throughout, despite some cosmetic changes.

In Chapter 3, I develop a typology of straight white masculinities in the hangout sitcom. I suggest that male heterosexuality in the hangout sitcom remains is not just resolutely heteronormative, but chrononormative, too, such that straight masculinity is organized around "straight time" (Freeman 2010). This, however, is not to say that all straight masculinities in the hangout sitcom are equally successful – instead, in response to perceived threats to chrononormativity, the family, and masculinity, male characters react rather differently. What results are three mostly distinct male character roles, variable subject positions who perform specific narrative and discursive functions rather than being defined by personality or biography (Fiske 2010). First, the postfeminist male singleton (Brabon 2013), concerned about how a perceived loss of power prevents heteronormative goals of marriage and family, anxiously spends 7 + seasons of a show searching for "the one". The douchebag instead resolves his anxiety via overcompensation, with a focus on creating a hyper-masculinized body, and a lack of commitment that culminates in womanizing behavior. Finally, the househusband, who finds himself happily married for most of the show's run, is allowed to demonstrate more comfort with neoliberal's feminized subjectivity, with his masculinity affirmed by heterosexual success.

Drawing on the pop culture trope of the "bromance", an extremely close homosocial, yet homoerotically coded, friendship between two men, Chapter 4 examines men's homosocial relationships in the hangout sitcom via one narrative from each sitcom that exemplifies a (or arguably, *the*) key "bromance" in each show – Chandler and Joey in *Friends*, Ted and Marshall in *How I Met Your Mother*, Leonard and Sheldon in *The Big Bang Theory*, and Nick and Schmidt in *New Girl*. I argue that over the period during which the hangout sitcom was hegemonic there was a significant shift away from the perpetual undermining of expressive and openly affective male friendship in *Friends*, to the textualization of something approaching, if not quite reaching, explicit homoeroticism in male friendship in *New Girl*. I show how homosocial male friendships in the hangout sitcom offer an important, if not revolutionary, departure from past US sitcom masculinities.

Chapter 5 unpacks the whiteness of the hangout sitcom's masculinities. The subgenre's approach to race and racialization over the period studied, at least consciously, shifts significantly, as it becomes more diverse as well as dealing with a range of social and political issues that pertain to race. I place this shift in the context of a neoliberal approach to race that gradually shifts from a post-race consensus (Jhally and Lewis 1992), in which racism is cast as a historical moment, to a post-white consensus (Hill 2004), in which white dominance is considered to be over. This post-white consensus, however, encodes a range of contradictory and often troublesome practices of fetishization that are not, perhaps, always positive. Non-white men continue to be marked by an othered masculinity throughout. I further explore how the post-white consensus has impacted the Jewishness of the hangout sitcom.

Drawing on ideological and institutional differences between the UK and the US concerning neoliberalism, the sitcom, and the masculinities within it, the next chapter compares the four US hangout sitcoms with three British sitcoms that riff on the same ideas – young people making their way in the city. After outlining some of these international differences, I show how *Spaced* (1999–2001), *Coupling* (2000–2004), and *Peep Show* (2003–2015) mediate the contradictions between masculinity and neoliberalism in more diverse ways, and with rather less optimism, with male characters whose anxieties are much more pronounced and who rarely have happy, resolved, endings.

In the final chapter of the book, I reflect on the recent relative demise of the hangout sitcom, and what that has to say about neoliberal masculinities, and masculinities on-screen moving forward. In recent years, the more popular sitcoms have included a breed of diversified workplace sitcom, such as *Parks and Recreation* (2009–2015) and *Brooklyn Nine-Nine* (2013–2021) and nostalgic re-emergences of a slightly queered but still mostly white family sitcom, notably *Modern Family* (2009–2020). We can read from these shows something of a legacy of masculinities left by the hangout sitcom genre, and in *Schitt's Creek*, an instance of the latter queered family sitcom, I suggest we can begin to speculate on masculinities' possible futures in the sitcom.

Note

1 There is a fun range of YouTube videos of, in particular, *Friends* clips without the laugh track, which leaves uncomfortable silences and quite dramatically shifts the affective reactions from the dialogue.

Filmography

Friends: The Reunion. 2021. [TV movie] Winston, Ben, Creator, HBO Max: USA.
All in the Family. 1971–1979. [TV] Lear, Norman, Creator, CBS: USA.
The Big Bang Theory. 2007–2019. [TV] Lorre, Chuck, and Bill Prady, Creator, CBS: USA.
The Bob Newhart Show. 1972–1978. [TV] Davis, David, and Lorenzo Music, Creator, CBS: USA.

Brooklyn Nine-Nine. 2013–2021. [TV] Goor, Dan, and Michael Schur, Creator, Fox, NBC: USA.
Buffy the Vampire Slayer. 1997–2003. [TV] Whedon, Joss, Creator, The WB, UPN: USA.
Cheers. 1982–1993. [TV] Charles, Glen, Les Charles, and James Burrows, Creator, NBC: USA.
Coupling. 2000–2004. [TV] Moffat, Steven, Creator, BBC: UK.
Days of Our Lives. 1965–present. [TV] Cordray, Ted, and Betty Cordray, Creator, NBC: USA.
Dharma & Greg. 1997–2002. [TV] Dartland, Dottie, and Chuck Lorre, Creator, ABC: USA.
Dream On. 1990–1996. [TV] Kauffman, Marta, and David Crane, Creator, NBC: USA.
Forgetting Sarah Marshall. 2008. [Movie] Stoller, Nicholas, Creator, Universal: USA.
Friends. 1994–2004. [TV] Crane, David, and Marta Kauffman, Creator, NBC: USA.
Gilmore Girls. 2000–2007. [TV] Sherman-Palladino, Amy, Creator, The WB, The CW: USA.
Happy Endings. 2011–2013. [TV] Caspe, David, Creator, ABC: USA.
How I Met Your Mother. 2005–2014. [TV] Bays, Carter, and Craig Thomas, Creator, CBS: USA.
I Love Lucy. 1951–1957. [TV] Oppenheimer, Jess, Madelyn Davis, and Bob Carroll Jr., Creator, CBS: USA.
Joey. 2004–2006. Silveri, Scott, and Shana Goldberg-Meehan, Creator, NBC: USA.
Mad About You. 1992–1999. [TV] Reiser, Paul, and Danny Jacobson, Creator, ABC: USA.
The Mary Tyler Moore Show. 1970–1977. [TV] Brooks, James L., and Allan Burns, Creator, CBS: USA.
Modern Family. 2009–2020. [TV] Lloyd, Christopher, and Steven Levitan, Creator, ABC: USA.
New Girl. 2011–2018. [TV] Meriwether, Elizabeth, Creator, Fox: USA.
Parks and Recreation. 2009–2015. [TV] Daniels, Greg, and Michael Schur, Creator, NBC: USA.
Peep Show. 2003–2015. [TV] O'Connor, Andrew, Jesse Armstrong, and Sam Bain, Creator, Channel 4: UK.
Roseanne. 1988–1997. [TV] Williams, Matt, Roseanne Barr, Marcy Casey, and Tom Werner, Creator, ABC: USA.
Scrubs. 2001–2010. [TV] Lawrence, Bill, Creator, NBC, ABC: USA.
Seinfeld. 1989–1998. [TV] David, Larry, and Jerry Seinfeld, Creator, NBC: USA.
Spaced. 1999–2001. [TV] Pegg, Simon, and Jessica Stevenson, Creator, Channel 4: UK.
Twin Peaks. 1990–1991. [TV] Frost, Mark, and David Lynch, Creator, CBS: USA.
Young Sheldon. 2017–present. [TV] Lorre, Chuck, and Steven Moralo, Creator, CBS: USA.

References

Abstract, Nicky James. 1989. "Emotional labour: Skill and work in the social regulation of feelings." *Sociological Review* 27 (1):15–42. doi: 10.1111/j.1467-954X.1989.tb00019.x.

Adamson, Maria. 2016. "Postfeminism, neoliberalism and a 'successfully' balanced femininity in celebrity CEO autobiographies." *Gender, Work and Organization* 24 (3):314–327. doi: 10.1111/gwao.12167.

Albrecht, Michael Mario. 2015. *Masculinity in Contemporary Quality Television*. Oxford: Routledge.

Alter, Rebecca. 2020, "Every blackface episode and scene that's been pulled from streaming so far." *Vulture*, Retrieved 14 September 2021, from https://www.vulture.com/2020/06/blackface-tv-episodes-scenes-removed-streaming.html.

Anderson, Eric. 2009. *Inclusive Masculinity: The Changing Nature of Masculinities*. London: Routledge.

Arxer, Steven L. 2011. "Hybrid masculine power: Reconceptualizing the relationship between homosociality and hegemonic masculinity." *Humanity & Society* 35 (4):390–422. doi: 10.1177/0160597611035004040404.

Attallah, Paul. 2003. "The unworthy discourse: Situation comedy in television." In *Critiquing the Sitcom: A Reader*, edited by Joanne Morreale, 91–115. Syracuse, NY: Syracuse University Press.

Attallah, Paul. 2010. "Television discourse and situation comedy." *Canadian Review of American Studies* 40 (1):1–24. doi: 10.3138/cras.40.1.1.

Banet-Weiser, Sarah, Rosalind Gill, and Catherine Rottenberg. 2020. "Postfeminism, popular feminism and neoliberal feminism? Sarah Banet-Weiser, Rosalind Gill and Catherine Rottenberg in conversation." *Feminist Theory* 21 (1):3–24. doi: 10.1177/1464700119842555.

Boutang, Yann Moulier. 2011. *Cognitive Capitalism*. Translated by Ed Emery. London: Polity.

Brabon, Benjamin A. 2013. "'Chuck Flick': A genealogy of the postfeminist male singleton." In *Postfeminism and Contemporary Hollywood Cinema*, edited by Joel Gwynne, and Nadine Muller, 116–130. Basingstoke: Palgrave Macmillan.

Bridges, Tristan, and C.J. Pascoe. 2014. "Hybrid masculinities: New directions in the sociology of men and masculinities." *Sociology Compass* 8 (3):246–258. doi: 10.1111/soc4.12134.

Brook, Vincent. 2010. "Virtual ethnicity: Incorporation, diversity, and the contemporary 'Jewish' sitcom.." *Sociology Compass* 11 (2):269–285. doi: 10.1080/10457220120098991.

Brown, Carol. 1981. "Mothers, fathers and children: From private to public patriarchy." In *Women and Revolution: A Discussion of the Unhappy Marriage of Marxism and Feminism*, edited by Lydia Sargent, 239–268. Montréal: Black Rose Books.

Brown, Robert S. 2016. "*Cheers*: Searching for the ideal public sphere in the ideal public house." In *The Sitcom Reader: America Re-viewed, Still Skewed*, edited by Mary M. Dalton, and Laura R. Linder, 177–184. Albany, NY: SUNY Press.

Brown, Wendy. 2006. "American nightmare: Neoliberalism, neoconservatism, and de-democratization." *Political Theory* 34 (6):690–714. doi: 10.1177/0090591706293016.

Brown, Wendy. 2015. *Undoing the Demos: Neoliberalism's Stealth Revolution*. Cambridge, MA: MIT Press.

Butler, Judith. 1990. *Gender Trouble*. 2nd ed. Oxford: Routledge.

Chidester, Phil. 2008. "May the circle stay unbroken: *Friends*, the presence of absence, and the rhetorical reinforcement of whiteness." *Critical Studies in Media Communication* 25 (2):157–174. doi: 10.1080/15295030802031772.

Clough, Patricia Ticineto, ed. 2007. *The Affective Turn: Theorizing the Social.* Durham, NC: Duke University Press.
Cobb, Shelley, Neil Ewen, and Hannah Hamad. 2018. "*Friends* reconsidered: Cultural politics, intergenerationality, and afterlives." *Television & New Media* 19 (8):683–691. doi: 10.1177/1527476418778426.
Collins, Jim. 1992. "Postmodernism and television." In *Channels of Discourse, Reassembled: Television and Contemporary Criticism*, edited by Robert C. Allen, 246–265. Oxford: Routledge.
Colwell, Sally. 2014. "From playboy penthouse to high-rise playboy: The bachelor's evolution." *The Word Hoard* 3 (1):96–107.
Connell, R.W. 2005. *Masculinities.* 2nd ed. Cambridge: Blackwell.
Connell, R.W., and James W. Messerschmidt. 2005. "Hegemonic masculinity: Rethinking the concept." *Gender and Society* 19 (6):829–859. doi: 10.1177/0891243205278639.
Cooper, Melinda. 2016. *Family Values: Between Neoliberalism the New Social Conservatism.* New York: Zone.
Cornwall, Andrea, Frank G. Karioris, and Nancy Lindisfarne, eds. 2016. *Masculinities under Neoliberalism.* London: Zed Books.
Dalton, Mary M., and Laura R. Linder. 2016. *The Sitcom Reader: America Re-viewed, Still Skewed.* 2nd ed. Albany, NY: SUNY Press.
Davies, William, and Nicholas Gane. 2021. "Post-neoliberalism? An introduction." *Theory, Culture & Society* 38 (6):3–28. doi: 10.1177/02632764211036722.
Demetriou, Demetrakis Z. 2001. "Connell's concept of hegemonic masculinity: A critique." *Theory and Society* 30 (3):337–361. doi: 10.1023/A:1017596718715.
Desjarlais, Stevie K. Seibert. 2018. "How I met your masculinity: Contrasting male personas portrayed on *How I Met Your Mother.*" *Journal of Popular Film and Television* 46 (3):169–178. doi: 10.1080/01956051.2018.1476833.
Dow, Bonnie. 2006. "The traffic in men and the *Fatal Attraction* of postfeminist masculinity." *Women's Studies in Communication* 29 (1):113–131. doi: 10.1080/07491409.2006.10757630.
Duggan, Lisa. 2004. *The Twilight of Equality?: Neoliberalism, Cultural Politics and the Attack on Democracy.* Boston, MA: Beacon Press.
Eagleton-Pierce, Matthew. 2016. "On individualism in the neoliberal period." PSA 66th Annual International Conference, Brighton.
Enderstein, Athena-Maria. 2018. "(Not) just a girl: Reworking femininity through women's leadership in Europe." *European Journal of Women's Studies* 25 (3):325–340. doi: 10.1177/1097184X15576203.
Ewen, Neil. 2018. "'If I don't input those numbers… it doesn't make much of a difference': Insulated precarity and gendered labor in *Friends.*" *Television & New Media* 19 (8):724–740. doi: 10.1177/1527476418778425.
Faludi, Susan. 1991. *Backlash: The Undeclared War Against American Women.* New York: Three Rivers Press.
Feuer, Jane. 1992. "Genre study and television." In *Channels of Discourse, Reassembled: Television and Contemporary Crticism*, edited by Robert C. Allen, 104–120. London: Routledge.
Fiske, John. 2010. *Television Culture.* 2nd ed. Oxford: Routledge.
Frank, Thomas. 1998. *The Conquest of Cool: Business Culture, Counterculture, and the Rise of Hip Consumerism.* Chicago, IL: University of Chicago Press.

Freeman, Elizabeth. 2010. *Time Binds: Queer Temporalities, Queer Histories*. Edited by Jack Halberstam and Lisa Lowe, *Perverse Modernities*. Durham: Duke University Press.

Garlick, Steve. 2020. "The nature of markets: On the affinity between masculinity and (neo)liberalism." *Journal of Cultural Economy* 13 (5):548–560. doi: 10.1080/17530350.2020.1741017.

Genz, Stephanie. 2009. *Postfemininities in Popular Culture*. Basingstoke: Palgrave Macmillan.

Genz, Stephanie, and Benjamin A. Brabon. 2009. *Postfeminism: Cultural Texts and Theories*. Edinburgh: Edinburgh University Press.

Gill, Rosalind. 2007. "Postfeminist media culture: Elements of sensibility." *European Journal of Cultural Studies* 10 (2):147–166. doi: 10.1177/1367549407075898.

Gill, Rosalind. 2014. "Powerful women, vulnerable men and postfeminist masculinity in men's popular fiction." *Gender and Language* 8 (2). doi: 10.1558/GENL.V8I2.185.

Gill, Rosalind. 2017. "The affective, cultural and psychic life of postfeminism: A postfeminist sensibility 10 years on." *European Journal of Cultural Studies* 20 (6):606–626. doi: 10.1177/1367549417733003.

Gill, Rosalind, and Christina Scharff, eds. 2011. *New Femininities: Postfeminism, Neoliberalism and Subjectivity*. Basingstoke: Palgrave Macmillan.

Gray, Jonathan, and Amanda D. Lotz. 2019. *Television Studies*. Cambridge: Polity.

Griffin, Louise. 2020. "*Friends* superfans reveal worst and most problematic storylines – from Rachel and Joey romance to Ross's toxic masculinity." *Metro*, 27 September. Accessed 7 July 2021.

Hakim, Jamie. 2016. "'The spornosexual': The affective contradictions of male body-work in neoliberal digital culture." *Journal of Gender Studies* 27 (2):231–241. doi: 10.1080/09589236.2016.1217771.

Hall, Stuart. 1993. "Encoding, decoding." In *The Cultural Studies Reader*, edited by Simon During, 90–103. London: Routledge.

Hall, Stuart. 2017. *Selected Political Writings: The Great Moving Right Show and Other Essays*. Durham, NC: Duke University Press.

Hamad, Hannah. 2018. "The one with the feminist critique: Revisiting millenial postfeminism with *Friends*." *Television & New Media* 19 (8):692–707. doi: 10.1177/1527476418779624.

Hamamoto, Darrell Y. 1989. *Nervous laughter: Television situation comedy and liberal democratic ideology*. Edited by J. Fred MacDonald, *Media and Society*. London: Praeger.

Hardt, Michael. 1999. "Affective labour." *boundary* 26 (2):89–100.

Harris, Malcolm. 2017. *Kids These Days: Human Capital and the Making of Millenials*. London: Little, Brown and Company.

Harvey, David. 2007. "Neoliberalism and the city." *Studies in Social Science* 1 (1):1–13. doi: 10.1080/21622671.2016.1166982.

Hearn, Jeff. 2009. "Patriarchies, transpatriarchies and intersectionalities." In *Intimate Citizenships: Gender, Sexualities, Politics*, edited by Elzbieta H. Olesky, 177–192. London: Routledge.

Hearn, Jeff. 2015. *Men of the World: Genders, Globalizations, Transnational Times*. London: Sage.

Hill, Mike. 2004. *After whiteness: Unmaking an American majority*. Edited by Michael Bérubé, *Cultural Front*. London: New York University Press.

Hilmes, Michelle. 1990. "Where everybody knows your name: *Cheers* and the mediation of cultures." *Wide Angle* 12 (2):64–73.
Horn, Rob Van, and Philip Mirowski. 2009. "The rise of the Chicago School of economics and the birth of neoliberalism." In *The Road From Mont Pèlerin: The Making of the Neoliberal Thought Collective*, edited by Philip Mirowski, and Dieter Plehwe, 139–179. London: Harvard University Press.
İçli, Gönül, and Kaya Özçelik. 2012. "Urban renewal as an urban hegemony project." *International Journal of Social Sciences and Humanity Studies* 4 (1):161–174.
Ihnat, Gwen. 2014. "How *Friends* changed the sitcom landscape." *The A.V. Club*, 18 August.
Illouz, Eva. 2007. *Cold Intimacies: The Making of Emotional Capitalism*. Cambridge: Polity.
Jahromi, Neima. 2019. "How '*The Big Bang Theory*' normalized nerd culture." *The New Yorker*, 18 May, Retrieved 29 January 2021, from https://www.newyorker.com/culture/culture-desk/how-the-big-bang-theory-normalized-nerd-culture.
Jenner, Mareike. 2014. "Is this TVIV? On Netflix, TVIII and binge-watching." *New Media & Society* 18 (2):257–273. doi: 10.1177/1461444814541523.
Jhally, Sut, and Justin Lewis. 1992. *Enlightened Racism: The Cosby Show, Audiences, and the Myth of the American Dream*. Boulder, CO: Westview Press.
Kanai, Akane, and Rosalind Gill. 2020. "Woke? Affect, neoliberalism, marginalised identities and consumer culture." *New Formations* 102:10–27. doi: 10.3898/NewF:102.01.2020.
Keyes, Daniel. 1999. "The imaginary community of the live studio audience of television." *Studies in Popular Culture* 21 (3):65–78.
Knox, Simone, and Kai Hanno Schwind. 2019. *Friends: A Reading of the Sitcom*. London: Palgrave Macmillan.
Kutulas, Judy. 2016. "Liberated women and new sensitive men: Reconstructing gender in 1970s workplace comedies." In *The Sitcom Reader: America Re-viewed, Still Skewed*, edited by Mary M. Dalton, and Laura R. Linder, 121–132. Albany, NY: SUNY Press.
Kutulas, Judy. 2018. "Anatomy of a hit: *Friends* and its sitcom legacies." *The Journal of Popular Culture* 51 (5):1172–1189. doi: 10.1111/jpcu.12715.
Landay, Lori. 2016. "*I Love Lucy*: Television and gender in postwar domestic ideology." In *The Sitcom Reader: America Re-viewed, Still Skewed*, edited by Mary M. Dalton, and Laura R. Linder, 31–42. Albany, NY: SUNY Press.
Lazzaroto, Maurizio. 2006. "Immaterial labour." In *Radical Thought in Italy: A Potential Politics*, edited by Paolo Virno, and Michael Hardy, 142–157. Minneapolis, MN: University of Minnesota Press.
Marc, David. 1997. *Comic Visions: Television Comedy and American Culture*. 2nd ed. Oxford: Blackwell.
Marc, David. 2016. "Origins of the genre: In search of the radio sitcom." In *The Sitcom Reader: America Re-viewed, Still Skewed*, edited by Mary M. Dalton, and Laura R. Linder, 1–12. Albany, NY: SUNY Press.
Maricourt, Clotilde de, and Stephen R. Burrell. 2021. "#MeToo or #MenToo? Expressions of backlash and masculinity politics in the #MeToo era." *The Journal of Men's Studies* [online]. doi: 10.1177/10608265211035794.
McGraw, Peter, and Joel Warner. 2014. *The Humor Code: A Global Search for What Makes Things Funny*. London: Simon & Schuster.
McGuigan, Jim. 2009. *Cool Capitalism*. London: Pluto Books.

McGuigan, Jim. 2014. "The Neoliberal Self." *Culture Unbound* 6 (1):223–240. doi: 10.3384/cu.2000.1525.146223.
McIntosh, Heather. 2014. "Representations of female scientists in *The Big Bang Theory*." *Journal of Popular Film and Television* 42 (4):195–204. doi: 10.1080/01956051.2014.896779.
McIntyre, Anthony P. 2015. "*Isn't she adorkable!* Cuteness as political neutralization in the star text of Zooey Deschanel." *Television & New Media* 16 (5):422–438. doi: 10.1177/1527476414524284.
McRobbie, Angela. 2009. *The Aftermath of Feminism: Gender, Culture and Social Change*. London: SAGE.
Mills, Brett. 2009. *The Sitcom*. Edinburgh: Edinburgh University Press.
Mirowski, Philip, and Dieter Plehwe. 2009. *The Road from Mont Pèlerin: The Making of the Neoliberal Thought Collective*. Cambridge, MA: Harvard University Press.
Mittell, Jason. 2004. *Genre and Television: From Cop Shows to Cartoons in American Culture*. London: Routledge.
Modleski, Tania. 1991. *Feminism Without Women: Culture and Criticism in a "Postfeminist" Age*. London: Routledge.
Morreall, John. 2009. *Comic Relief: A Comprehensive Philosophy of Humor*. Oxford: Blackwell.
Muzellec, Laurent, Christopher Kanitz, and Theodore Lynn. 2013. "Fancy a coffee with *Friends* in 'Central Perk'?" *International Journal of Advertising* 32 (3):399–417. doi: 10.2501/IJA-32-3-399-417.
Neale, Steve. 1980. *Genre*. Chippenham: Antony Rowe Ltd.
Nickles, Shelley. 2002. "More is better: Mass consumption, gender, and class identity in postwar America." *American Quarterly* 54 (4):581–622. doi: 10.1353/aq.2002.0040.
Ortner, Sherry B. 2014. "Too soon for post-feminism: The ongoing life of patriarchy in neoliberal America." *History and Anthropology* 25 (4):530–549. doi: 10.1080/02757206.2014.930458.
Özgün, Aras, and Andreas Treske. 2021. "On streaming-media platforms, their audiences, and public life." *Rethinking Marxism* 33 (2):304–323. doi: 10.1080/08935696.2021.1893090.
Pheasant-Kelly, Fran. 2018. "'And then there were three': Childhood, *Bewitched*, and 1960s America." In *Children, Youth, and American Television*, edited by Adrian Schober, and Debbie Olson, 83–101. Oxford: Routledge.
Phipps, Alison. 2014. *The Politics of the Body: Gender in a Neoliberal and Neoconservative Age*. Cambridge: Polity.
Poster, Winifred R. 2013. "Subversions of techno-masculinity: Indian ICT professionals in the global economy." In *Rethinking Transnational Men: Beyond, Between and Within Nations*, edited by Jeff Hearn, M. Blagojevic, and K. Harrison, 113–133. London: Routledge.
Radloff, Jessica. 2018. "'New girl' was never meant to be 'adorkable'—But we fell for it anyway." *Glamour*, 10 April, Retrieved 13 October 2021, from https://www.glamour.com/story/new-girl-final-season.
Reeser, Todd W., and Lucas Gottzén. 2018. "Masculinity and affect: New possibilities, new agendas." *NORMA* 13 (3):145–157. doi: 10.1080/18902138.2018.1528722.
Roeder, Mark. 2013. *Unnatural Selection: Why the Geeks Will Inherit the Earth*. London: HarperCollins.

Roseneil, Sasha, and Shelley Budgeon. 2004. "Cultures of intimacy and care beyond 'the family': Personal life and social change in the early 21st century." *Current Sociology* 52 (2):135–159. doi: 10.1177/0011392104041798.
Rossi, Ugo. 2017. *Cities in Global Capitalism, Urban Futures*. Cambridge: Polity.
Sandell, Jillian. 1998. "I'll be there for you: *Friends* and the fantasy of alternative families." *American Studies* 39 (2):141–155.
Sedgwick, Eve Kosofsky. 2003. *Touching Feeling: Affect, Pedagogy, Performativity*. Durham, NC: Duke University Press.
Sender, Katherine. 2006. "Queens for a day: Queer eye for the straight guy and the neoliberal project." *Critical Studies in Media Communication* 23 (2):131–151. doi: 10.1080/07393180600714505.
Speich, Megan. 2019. "*Friends* is the epitome of toxic masculinity." *Her Campus*, 11 November, Retrieved 7 July 2021, from https://www.hercampus.com/school/wesco/friends-epitome-toxic-masculinity/.
Spigel, Lynn. 1992. *Make Room for TV: Television and the Family Ideal in Postwar America*. Chicago, IL: University of Chicago Press.
Stratton, Jon. 2016. "Die Sheldon die: The Big Bang Theory, everyday neoliberalism and Sheldon as neoliberal man." *Journal for Cultural Research* 20 (2):171–188. doi: 10.1080/14797585.2015.1123515.
Stratton, Jon. 2015. "The price of love: *The Big Bang Theory*, the family and neoliberalism." *European Journal of Cultural Studies* 19 (2):1–18. doi: 10.1177/1367549415585558.
Thompson, Lauren Jade. 2015. "Nothing suits me like a suit: Performing masculinity in *How I Met Your Mother*." *Critical Studies in Television* 10 (2):21–36. doi: 10.7227/CST.10.2.3.
Thompson, Lauren Jade. 2018. "'It's like a guy never lived here!': Reading gendered domestic spaces of *Friends*." *Television & New Media* 19 (8):758–774. doi: 10.1177/1527476418778414.
van Dijk, Teun A. 1993. "Principles of critical discourse analysis." *Discourse & Society* 4 (2):249–283. doi: 10.1177/0957926593004002006.
Venugopal, Rajesh. 2015. "Neoliberalism as a concept." *Economy and Society* 44 (2):165–187. doi: 10.1080/03085147.2015.1013356.
Walker, Charlie, and Steven Roberts, eds. 2018. *Masculinity, Labour, and Neoliberalism: Working-class Men in International Perspective*. Oxford: Palgrave Macmillan.
Walters, Shannon. 2013. "Cool aspie humor: Cognitive difference and Kenneth Burke's comic corrective in *The Big Bang Theory* and *Community*." *Journal of Literary & Cultural Disability Studies* 7 (3):271–288.
West, Candace, and Don H. Zimmerman. 1987. "Doing gender." *Gender and Society* 1 (2):125–151. doi: 10.1177/0891243287001002002.
Witz, Anne, Chris Warhurst, and Dennis Nickson. 2003. "The labour of aesthetics and the aesthetics of organization." *Organization* 10 (1):33–54. doi: 10.1177/1350508403010001375.
Wolfman, Greg, Jeff Hearn, and Tray Yeadon-Lee. 2021. "Hollow femininities: The emerging faces of neoliberal masculinities." *NORMA* 16 (4):217–234. doi: 10.1080/18902138.2021.1996829.
Wright, Georgie. 2018. "Could *Friends* *be* any more problematic?" *i–D*, 17 January, Retrieved 19 July 2022, from https://i-d.vice.com/en_uk/article/a3nqjj/could-friends-be-any-more-problematic?fbclid=IwAR11f9XZL4prySbTMU1gMBgzuQhMwCdhPt-AX0FMkOCUQGe0Zeuhht8QIWU.

2 A brief historiography of US sitcom masculinities

Despite the conventional wisdom that "at the heart of the American sitcom lies the family" (Kutulas 2016b, 17), the sitcom's casts and communities have proven to be more elastic than just the family; fledgling radio sitcoms focused as much on migration as family, while casts of colleagues and friends displaced the family in the 1970s and 1980s, disregarding blood ties but remaining well within the genre. This chapter argues therefore that the sitcom's mediation of domesticity and the family is a function of a wider mediation of the processes by which modes of collective organization and affective belonging become dominant institutions in relation to ideological conjunctures. As Paul Wells (1998, 178) suggests, the sitcom mediates "the pressures and anxieties of the contemporary world, and suggest the Utopian comforts offered by the collective support of a like-minded community" – in other words, the sitcom asks where individuals find respite from the workplace. Families have predominated the sitcom therefore not because the sitcom mediates domestic ideology per se, but because the strict separation of public and domestic that constructs the nuclear family unit has dominated 20th-century capitalisms (Zaretsky 1976, Mintz and Kellogg 1988).

Yet, whether they reside within the family unit, a friendship group, or a workforce, modes of collective organization and affective belonging are gendered institutions – hence, the sitcom's mediation of gender regimes, too. This is not to say that sitcoms simply reinforce patriarchy. Rather, it would be more accurate to say that sitcoms deal with the "problem of the legitimacy of patriarchy" with which Connell was concerned when unfurling the concept of hegemonic masculinity. The sitcom shows, in fact, that patriarchy's legitimation problems are multiple, and are most often salient in surrounding ideological conjunctures that have the potential to question understandings and practices of men and of masculinities (Demetriou 2001) – at each historical juncture, gender regimes appear threatened. The hangout sitcom addresses the tensions between neoliberalism and masculinities simply because neoliberalism, as a hegemonic ideology, is the moment's salient conjunctural problem of the legitimacy of patriarchy. This chapter therefore constructs a historiography of the US sitcom to unpick and map out how it mediates and negotiates several tangled histories of US masculinities, domesticity, capitalism, and patriarchy. In so doing I aim to both define the

DOI: 10.4324/9781003363538-2

discursive dimensions of the sitcom genre (Mittell 2004, Neale 1980), and to contextualize the moment in which the hangout sitcom's masculinities become possible.

Despite a constant shifting and re-adaptation, US sitcom masculinities from 1945 through to the present day are subject to remarkably few, if some, changes, showcasing a perhaps unsurprising resilience (see Miller 2011, Linder 2005). I explore these variations through the diversification of the genre into numerous subgenres that respond to and explore ideological conjunctural shifts and competing forms of collective organization. From the comfy suburbia of the 1950s, the sitcom transmogrifies along with US society and culture, via dalliances with rurality, the supernatural, the military, high art, US black culture, feminism, the workplace, and all the way into postmodern pastiches. Masculinities remain recognizably stable throughout.

I use a range of sitcoms, beginning in the 1950s with *I Love Lucy*, through to the emergence of *Cheers* and *Seinfeld* in the neoliberal era as the progenitors of the hangout sitcom. This, obviously, is not an exhaustive history of the US sitcom or even of US sitcom masculinities.[1] There are several subgenres missed out, such as the hugely important military sitcom embodied by *M*A*S*H* (1972–1983), as well as shows that still occupy hugely important cultural positions, such as *Happy Days* (1974–1984) and *Roseanne* (1988–1997), as well as several that could have been given more detail. Instead, case studies have been chosen for both narrative and expository purposes, demonstrating insights into the tangled histories mentioned above, as well as marshaled into a historical story that ends with the beginnings hangout sitcom.

On the radio

Consensus states that the 1926 radio show *Sam 'n' Henry* (1926–1928), which two years later became *Amos 'n' Andy* (1928–1960), was what we might call the US's first "proto-sitcom". It followed two black men arriving in Chicago from Alabama as part of the "Great Migration" throughout most of the 20th century, which saw around 6,000,000 black people flee the US Deep South where Jim Crow laws were violently upheld for cities in the northeast of the country. After setting up shop in Chicago, the two men, played initially on the radio by white actors, seek all the promises of the American Dream: family, wealth, and social status. Amos and Andy do not find their journey plain-sailing, facing regular obstacles such as their first car lacking a windscreen, and a series of false starts to their attempts at forming families. The Great Migration was a tense and multifarious sociohistorical event, an optimistic recalibration of a version of the American Dream for black people as well as one that caused large amounts of racialized and class tensions in major US cities (Trotter 1991). Listening to *Amos 'n' Andy*, though, you would not have thought this to be the case. They face problems, but there is nothing they cannot wriggle out of with a little ingenuity and a can-do attitude; the lack of a windscreen, for example, becomes a selling point to customers, an opportunity to feel the open air while driving. The program took complex social problems, boiled them down to piecemeal narratives, and addressed them with humor and warmth.

Though David Marc (2016) points out that it is potentially misleading to label *Amos 'n' Andy* and contemporaneous shows "sitcoms", a term that does not really even enter into common parlance until at least the 1950s if not the 1960s, they laid the foundations for the sitcom's genre boundaries. *Amos 'n' Andy* episodes were 15 minutes long and dealt with one storyline, following a simple narrative that disrupted the main characters' status quo, and finding simple, often heart-warming, resolutions. These simple, short, narrative episodes are perhaps the most defining feature of the sitcom as a genre, which is recognizable in the short length and simplicity of its individual storylines. Even into contemporary postmodern pastiches, the piecemeal narrative format of the sitcom remains constant.

These situational narratives are determined by the characters' social and material circumstances, here following the main themes and clashes of the Great Migration: race, class, and intimacy/sexual problems. Darrell Hamamoto (1989, 9) goes as far as to suggest that the "study of the television situation comedy is an exercise in examining the relationship of popular art to its historically specific setting". Some scholars of television argue that the narrative structure's restoration of the status quo make the sitcom always-already an ideologically conservative mode of story, at least in the sense that it conserves or repairs the beginning state of affairs (Fiske 2010, 141). *Amos 'n' Andy*, for example, recuperates and updates many of the facets of the American Dream. Yet, the clarity of the narrative in the sitcom has simultaneously led many scholars to also argue that the sitcom genre always offers a subversive reading, depending on which element of the narrative is emphasized, precisely because, as Attallah puts it, disruption is the point: "in the situation comedy, disruption and discourse are conflated; it is the discourse itself that is the disruption" (Attallah 2003, 105). Hamamoto (1989, 2) suggests that the sitcom has always "offered oppositional ideas, depicted oppression and struggle, and reflected a critical consciousness that stops just short of political mobilization". Paul Wells (1998, 179) develops this point further, arguing the sitcom performs "small acts of political and ideological 'smuggling', and this is central to the genre's endurance", demonstrates this "smuggling" in *Amos 'n' Andy*:

> humour offered solace to an audience who empathized with the hope that things might improve, and with the implied critique of those who had failed to govern effectively. Simultaneously, however, the programme patriotically foregrounded its fundamental belief in the nation's traditions and its ability to recover through the accepted virtues of family and community.
>
> (Wells 1998, 181)

The consumer family

After the Great Depression of the 1930s followed by World War II, the USA that emerged in 1945 had a very different complexion. A national malaise in the preceding decades combined with the horrors of war had posed enormous social and economic challenges to the USA. In response, the country began a shift to a consumer economy, aided by the nuclear family as its unit of consumption. The onset of consumer capitalism had a problem: consumption had long been considered a feminine activity, and so expecting the masculinized laborer-subject who had just returned from the war to purchase luxury consumer goods contributed to moral panics about a crisis in masculinity. As Elaine May (2008 [1988], 85) puts it, many "feared that returning veterans would be unable to resume their positions as responsible citizens and family men. They worried that a crisis in masculinity could lead to crime, 'perversion', and homosexuality". Such public debates extended to the consumption of mass culture, too, which became associated with the feminine domestic sphere (Huyssen 1986, 44–62). The privatized heteronormative nuclear family offered a solution: simply put, dad earned the money and mom spent it (May 2008 [1988]). Yet the ideal of the post-war nuclear family was not entirely binary, with the barriers between domestic and public, and husband and wife, showing a modicum of porousness. While mom would be a domestic housewife who was offered the possibility of freedom from domesticity via consumption, dad would labor during the day but was expected to take an active role in childcare. Within the family, then, mom and dad had different conjugal roles in the US's post-war consumerism.

The privatized nuclear family interpellated the housewife as its primary consumer, and accordingly women's magazines became saturated with adverts for domestic products, which were frequently advertised as having liberatory potential (see, for example, Frederick 1929). Similarly, initial TV adverts targeted the housewife audience, presumed to be the main group watching TV in the private home (Haralovich 2009). Major consumer fairs across the country gave an aspirational insight into what their new, modern homes might look like (Chambers 2019), such that "whereas in the pre-war and war years a fully mechanized household would have been presented in the popular press as a futuristic fantasy, in the post-war years it appeared that tomorrow had arrived" (Spigel 1992, 46). The private domestic home became the plinth on which consumer goods, coming to occupy a position of symbolic capital, could be showcased.

Additionally, with men on the frontline in WWII many women had taken over manual jobs, and with the return of the troops the government as well as private business wanted to see them return immediately to employment (Haralovich 2009), not just to benefit the economy but also acting as a form of national gratitude for wartime service. With all this in mind, in 1948 President Truman held a "Conference on Family Life" at the White House, where he declared that "children and dogs are as necessary to the welfare of this country as is Wall Street and the railroads", marking a concerted effort by the US establishment to elevate a particular domestic ideology as a mode of collective belonging as the primary goal of post-war reconstruction (Zaretsky 1976). A nostalgic reorganization of normative domesticity around the nuclear family offered a clear organizing principle for domestic life.

Social changes

The post-war years saw an upsurge in births across the USA, unmatched both then and since, resulting in a cohort subsequently dubbed "baby boomer" generation (Weiss 2000). To accommodate this explosion, the US began a major homebuilding initiative funded by a multimillion-dollar program of investment by the government. With insurance programs having been set up pre-war for veterans in WWII, the government's Federal Housing Administration (FHA) established a national policy promoting ownership of hundreds of thousands of homes being built in the outer suburbs of major cities (Hayden 1984, 35–37).

These changes offered little to no relief from existing racialized and class divisions; for the US government and the White House, "an ideal *white* and *middle-class* homelife was a primary means of reconstituting and resocialising the American family after World War II" (Haralovich 2009, 61, emphasis added). For example, new suburban neighborhoods were subject to zoning practices, in which multi-family dwellings were not permitted, as they aimed to ensure working-class families were unable to afford to live in the area. The FHA adopted a policy called "red-lining", which marked out and separated mixed-race neighborhoods, while protective covenants on property ensured that realtors and letting agents had to consider how the appearance of the tenants would make suburban neighborhoods more or less desirable (Wright 1981, 247–248). Protective covenants even existed unofficially after the Supreme Court ruled them unconstitutional in 1968.

The new domestic ideology did oversee a shift in popular constructions of men though, popularizing a more domesticated construction of fatherhood. The new suburban dad was not expected to be absent like his supposed pre-war predecessor, but this post-war period saw the first advent, at least popularly, of the "new man", rejecting domineering or "breadwinner" stereotypes in favor of a more caring, attentive, and present form of fatherhood (Spigel 1992). Margaret Marsh (1988, 167) argues that the post-war period saw a convenient marriage of three conditions that allowed for a growth of masculine domesticity:

> it was not until the power relations within middle-class marriage underwent subtle shifts, until the rise of the corporation provided relatively secure jobs with predictable patterns of mobility, and until suburbs began to be viewed as the appropriate space within which to

create the companionate family, that the development of masculine domesticity was possible.

These new societal ideals were embodied in an emerging literature for these new fathers, such as a series by author T.S. Arthur on "Model Husbands", written for women's magazine *Godey's Lady's Book*.

However, most empirical evidence suggests that the conjugal roles within the domestic sphere did not change in any significant way, but rather intensified public social debates about masculinities, producing a moral panic about the concerning emasculation of these new fathers (Weiss 2000, 88–89) – indeed, these debates would find popular articulation in some of the family sitcoms of the 1960s. While social norms of acceptability shifted for some, the porousness between the domestic and public spheres remained limited – indeed, it should be remembered that any change was precipitated precisely by the return of men into jobs and women back into the home, suggesting any shift was marginal. As Lynne Segal (2007) suggests, substantive change to masculinity was not really on the agenda.

Video killed the radio sitcom

Within this milieu, television very quickly became the must-have commodity. Though the radio at its height was a huge phenomenon (some episodes of *Amos 'n' Andy* secured over 40 million viewers), through the late 1940s and early 1950s, in the space of less than a decade, the television overtook it very quickly. As technological advancements gathered apace, the cost and ease of use of a television set both reduced dramatically so that ownership increased astronomically. In 1946 in the USA, just 0.02% of homes had a television set, a figure that rose to 9% in 1950, and in the next five years by 1955 had risen to a staggering 65%. As ownership increased, prices went the opposite way, with the average set costing $440 in 1948, almost halving to $238 by 1954 (Spigel 1992, 32). However, it was not just the growth of television ownership that was relevant to the development of the sitcom, but the cultural position of the television within the home.

Debates took place in lifestyle magazines over both the physical and social location of the television in the home. Its eventual settlement in the living room bolstered the medium as a key activity of the new private suburban middle-class family, and the TV found its marketing niche here,

> depicted as a panacea for the broken homes and hearts of wartime life; not only was it shown to restore faith in family togetherness, but as the most sought-after appliance for sale in postwar America, it also renewed faith in the splendors of consumer capitalism.
>
> (Spigel 1992, 3)

TV executives lauded its intimacy and immediacy, with one NBC executive stating "TV's greatest attributes are its timeliness and intimacy. By timeliness is meant TV's immediacy, its power of delivering direct presence, of transmitting a living scene into the home – *now*, as it happens" (O'Meara 1955, 228). Though the radio had been previously popular, the moving image made the television broadcast akin to the close intimacy of theatre, except that millions could watch simultaneously.

Despite the family sitcom's later prominence, executives were not initially convinced, as "the suitability of theatrical entertainment for a family environment was often questioned by industry executives, critics, regulators, government officials, and audience members" (Spigel 1992, 142). Some of the very early successes in the late 1940s were variety shows and vaudeville (a non-narrative comedy genre, interspersed with songs, dances, and other entertainment), but by the time television had become ubiquitous, its first few major historical successes were sitcoms in which the new nuclear families of the era could see themselves reflected on-screen, taking advantage of the potent intimacy of the medium.

The sitcom, then, was not a method of social control concocted by the upper echelons of government to proselytize the virtues of family life. Rather, as David Marc (2016, 1) argues, a new medium usually generates new genres that are not planned but "treated as more of an afterthought" dependent on the sociocultural status of the new medium. In short, television not only reproduced, but mediated US domestic ideology. With the advent of mass television ownership and a shift in domestic ideology, the development and huge popularity of the sitcom was not a conscious decision by television networks, but a happy accident.

The first golden age of television

The novelty of television's immediacy and mass audience led to a wide range of experimentation in the 1940s and 1950s, with artists, actors, showmen, and musicians widely considered highbrow dallying with a range of genres. Variety shows, vaudeville, and anthology drama series received critical acclaim, while the late 1940s saw the first broadcasts of canonical Disney movies. This abundance of high culture led to the 1950s being dubbed the "Golden Age of Television" (Slide 1991, 121), a label retroactively applied in the 1960s as the sitcom proliferated into dozens of new shows considered by critics to be "low culture". Though the sitcom today is widely considered a lowbrow medium (Attallah 2003), it developed quite organically from early vaudeville and variety shows, its first hits not considered the same sort of lowbrow culture they often are today.

I Love Lucy **and the family sitcom**

The family sitcom, as well the sitcom in general, took flight in 1951 with *I Love Lucy* (1951–1957), which became a huge cultural phenomenon, drawing in viewing figures in the millions, creating plot-related headlines in US national media, and simultaneously codifying many of the television sitcom's conventions and structures. The laugh track, provided by a live studio audience, was one such genre innovation, borne of a problem present in previous radio productions. Executives had found that not only did performers struggle without an audience, but the audience at home found the idea of laughing without fellow audience members uninviting (Giotta 2017). *I Love Lucy* therefore recorded live audience reactions combined with a multi-camera setup, to mimic the idea of being at the theatre, a "communicative prosthesis" (Peters 1999, 214) that successfully married the intimacy of the television with the collective audience experience of theatre. However, most of *I Love Lucy*'s immense success was built on its similitude to the everyday of US families in the 1950s.

The show followed TV producer Ricky Ricardo and his unsatisfied housewife Lucy in a Manhattan apartment (which would change later as suburban families took over the sitcom), and mostly followed her schemes to pursue a career in television against her husband's wishes. Starring real-life husband and wife couple of well-known comedienne Lucille Ball and her husband Desi Arnaz, *I Love Lucy*'s live studio audience was not the show's only exploitation of the possibilities of television's intimate domestic position. The real lives of Ball and Arnaz were osmotic with their on-screen counterparts, with the birth of their second child not just written into the show but his picture starring on the cover of the first ever edition of the US magazine *TV Guide*, the real and on-screen births made scarcely distinguishable. Even Arnaz's on-screen job of a bandleader on TV scarcely differed from his real-life work.

The show used this porousness between reality and television to demonstrate a remarkable understanding of the domestic experiences of a vast cross-section of the US population in the 1950s. Lori Landay (2016, 33) shows how *I Love Lucy* reflected an ongoing renegotiation of heterosexual marriage in the post-war period, a combination of the unsatisfied housewife's aspiration to escape the drudgery of daily domesticity up against the desires of returning war husbands who wanted a wife to provide domestic comforts, while Pamela Wojcik (2010) demonstrates how it negotiates issues of domestic space familiar to viewers. Though neither Arnaz nor his character were veterans, the nuclear family behind closed doors left the conjugal roles of married parenthood to be renegotiated and reconsidered (May 2008 [1988]); if men could now stay at home and engage in housework, could women continue the wage labor they had done while their husbands were fighting? *I Love Lucy*'s answer was that Lucy's jealousy of Ricky's career only spawned bizarre antics. In one of the show's most well-known storylines, Lucy tricks her way into a gig advertising a fictitious new vitamin supplement, "vitameatavegamin", which has a high enough alcohol content to get her so drunk in rehearsals as to be too inebriated to competently act in the final commercial (*I Love Lucy*, "Lucy Does a TV Commercial"). In the show's pilot, Ricky (then called Larry) longs for heterosexual normalcy, declaring "I want a wife who's just a wife" (*I Love Lucy*, "The Girls Want to Go to a Nightclub").

The message: stick to your conjugal roles. For approaching these problems, the short piecemeal storylines of the sitcom were well-suited.

By 1956, however, the Ricardos' New York apartment was increasingly outdated. As families moved in their droves into the suburbs, so did Ricky, Lucy, and Ricky Jr., the show relocating for its final season to a large country house in Westport, Connecticut. Despite its now established position in the TV canon, it only lasted one season in the suburbs, its ending prefigured by the real-life separation of the lead on-screen couple. A new cluster of suburban family sitcoms took its place.

The suburban family man

As fatherhood moved into the suburbs, patriarchy faced a new problem of legitimization in domestication: how were the military masculinities of a country at war to adapt to quiet, domestic life in the suburbs? *Leave it to Beaver*'s (1957–1963) answer was the managerial fatherhood of Ward Cleaver. Ward, his wife June, and two sons Wally and the eponymous Theodore "Beaver" Cleaver, lived in the fictional Mayfield, a suburban town whose specific origin is left vague enough to embody the new and idealized middle-class white suburb. As suggested by the title, the narrative disruption in the show most frequently (but certainly not always) comes from Beaver, the younger of the two sons, as he didactically learns how to become a man in the suburbs. Though *Leave it to Beaver* was not the only, the most popular, or even the first, suburban family sitcom, it is notable for the harmonious Cleaver family, whose quickly resolved conflicts were considered by the contemporaneous *New York Times* to be "too broad and artificial to be persuasive" (Gould 1957). Nevertheless, the image of the *Leave it to Beaver* family remains a well-grounded myth in the American imaginary (Coontz 1997).

Fatherhood in *Leave it to Beaver*, for Hamamoto (1989, 22), reinscribes a nostalgic "portrayal of the Victorian family patriarch as 'boss'" as a "middle-class modern father as organization man or 'manager'". It adapts the pre-war image of an austere Victorian fatherhood into a more loving, but still defiantly stern, patriarch, thereby hybridizing existing hegemonic masculinity with the new caring father of the 1950s. As Pugh (2018, 31) points out, amid the show's conservative domestic ideology, "traditional gender roles and separate domestic spheres are maintained yet progressively expanded", signified by the frilly apron worn by Ward when he does the washing up; while the apron indicates an expanded set of masculine options, it does so by reinforcing the gendered divisions that had previously existed.

Yet, this idyllic life was one only available to middle-class men and families, both on-screen and in real life (Hayden 1984); working-class families on television struggled to develop the same harmony as the Cleavers, notably in the appearance of a "bumbling father" trope. *The Life of Riley*'s (1953–1958) patriarch, factory-worker Chester Riley, harbors a longstanding status anxiety, having settled in a newly built suburban home in California.

Most of the action in *The Life of Riley* takes place in the home, and the narrative is disrupted when the boundaries of the domestic and public are upset (Hamamoto 1989, 18). For example, in one episode Chester attempts to assist his wife Peg by taking their clothes to the laundromat, only to accidentally wind up engaged to a French woman he meets there for the sake of a green card marriage (*The Life of Riley*, "Riley Gets Engaged"). Seen here is a well-meaning attempt by Chester to engage in the domestic affairs of the household, yet at the same time the gendered boundaries of each sphere are retained. Chester's escapades are perhaps early prototypes of the class-oriented rural sitcoms that emerged in the 1960s.

New frontiers and a dwindling consensus

By the 1960s, with rationing mostly gone and the emergence of America the superpower, living standards had dramatically improved. In particular, the growth of consumerism in tandem with further technological improvements (technicolor television!) enabled the ownership of a vast array of luxuries. These ongoing changes intensified continuing public debates about the moral decay of family values, intergenerational conflicts, and the overall threat of mass culture (Spigel 1992, 50–60). The sitcom had settled into its mediative role, but before the eventual absorption of the liberatory politics of the 1960s into the mainstream (McGuigan 2009) came backlash, and with it a fall into the position of low culture, as critics lamented the end of the Golden Age.

The first "magicoms" emerged, shows in which regular nuclear families were given magical powers, usually as a way of warning the white majority against the dangers of liberation politics. *The Addams Family* (1964–1966) began in 1964, conferring otherness on a Latinx family by giving them a range of magical powers. For instance, Paloma Martinez-Cruz (2020) suggests that patriarch Gomez Addams invokes a domesticized version of the trope of a "Chicano Dracula", a form of Latinx masculinity that she argues adds a supernatural vampiric layer to already othering racialized discourses exaggerating the sexual prowess of Latinx men. Meanwhile, *Bewitched* (1964–1972) warned of the dangers of women's rights, with a harried and nagged husband Darrin Stephens inadvertently married to the witch Samantha Stephens, a fact he only finds out after their wedding, and finds consistently emasculating. As Susan Douglas (1994, 138) argues, it is not a coincidence that "at the moment girls took to the streets in an outpouring of female resistance", and "while their mothers flocked to buy a book demanding equal rights for women, the witch and other women with supernatural powers would reappear on the cultural landscape".

Meanwhile, the "ruralcom" warned of the dangers of mixing the agricultural rural class with urban folk. The first major "ruralcom" was *The Real McCoys* (1957–1963), which followed the story of a farming family who relocate to California and their struggles to adapt to the modern world, setting the standard storyline of a rural farming family who lucked their way into affluent suburban or urban neighborhoods. This formula was followed by the hugely popular *The Beverly Hillbillies* (1962–1971), following the Clampett family who find an oil reserve on their farm and up sticks to Beverly Hills in California. The show is, in short, a comedy of errors about their unsuitability for urban life, particularly for patriarch Jed Clampett who must raise his children on his own following the pre-show death of his wife. Jed's plight is that of most men, and fatherhood in general, in the post-war period, in a struggle to adapt to a new emergent form of domesticated masculinity (Marc 1997, 64–66, see also Eskridge 2019, Worland and O'Leary 2016).

By the 1970s there was a recognition that these changes to the gender order were here to stay, and gradually the sitcom reflected this. Notably, writer Norman Lear contributed to the production of a range of "relevancy sitcoms", such as *All in the Family* (1971–1979), which began to openly and consciously ask questions about a range of social issues, including race and gender politics through the medium of the family sitcom. Meanwhile, as the post-war domestic ideology gradually ebbed, and the 1960s successes of the women's movement in the US were followed by significant increases of the numbers of women in the workplace, many young middle-class baby boomers had a very different experience of intimacy to their parents, relying on fraternal workplace colleagues rather than family for their sense of collective belonging. In this context a separate group of relevancy sitcoms emerged that shifted from the intimate domestic bonds of family to the intimate workplace bonds of friendship. The first of these was *The Mary Tyler Moore Show* (1970–1977), which broke ground by eponymizing a single, sexually liberated, career-focused woman working in television. Several years later, *WKRP in Cincinnati* (1978–1982) emphasized not an eponymous character, but the bonds formed amongst work colleagues. Moving beyond blood ties, "in 1970s workplace comedies, coworkers became family, a metaphor that suited the baby boomers' desire for community on their own terms" (Kutulas 2016a, 124). These workplace sitcoms reflected the mediation of gender in workplaces in which women were becoming more visible. The WKRP network is still dominated and run by men who would be familiar to sitcom viewers of the preceding decades, but, alongside this are a variety of new sensitive men such as program director Andy Travis, who acts as the obvious analogue to the liberated women of *WKRP in Cincinnati* (Kutulas 2016a, 130). These male characters treat their female coworkers with respect, supporting them, promoting them, and defending them, prefiguring postfeminist masculinities in much subsequent popular culture that support and legitimate individual women's successes (Dow 2006). Yet, Andy's sensitivity to the plight of women sees him rewarded heterosexually outside of the workplace, thereby reformulating masculinity within the confines of heteronormativity. Such male sensitivity is therefore unthreatening to the existing gender order as feminist demands are absorbed into the mainstream.

Emergent neoliberalism

By the 1980s, the post-war consensus had taken a beating. The myth of the nuclear family's actual dominance had long been called into question (Mintz and Kellogg 1988), and following the elections of Reagan in the US and Thatcher in the UK, the post-war economic settlement was a thing of the past. In its place was a newly emergent economic proposition, based on an ontology of radical individualism, in which capital and markets were unrestricted and free.

In 1979, Stuart Hall recognized a dominant cultural shift away from collective organization, towards what he calls a "monetarist" (Hall 2017, 179) culture characterized by the extension of individualist economic logic into the social, cultural, and political domains (Duggan 2004). This anti-collectivism informs neoliberal notions of identity, in which historical and material contexts are deemed less relevant to identity formation than individual self-determination. In fact, identity and lifestyle are defined by consumer choice, such that the previously oppositional politics of the 1960s are marketed as consumer products, a phenomenon that McGuigan (2009) calls "cool capitalism" (see also Frank 1998). The disaffection of such politics is cool precisely for its oppositional and anti-mainstream aesthetic, yet this form of cultural individualism is in effect a requirement for the neoliberal subject; not a libertarian principle, but "compulsory individualization" (McGuigan 2014, 233).

This individual self-determination stems from a neoliberal social politics that is divorced from history. If humans are mere individuals, defined only by some inner essence, then the politics of inequality in terms of identity categories that liberatory politics aimed to eradicate, have already been eradicated (Brown 2015). Inequality here is not the product of historical context but of individual failure to act as a responsible neoliberal subject (McGuigan 2014) – a politics that we will see is extremely compatible with the myth of the American Dream (Brown 2006). Such a post-collective politics was quickly legible on screen, across identity categories – gender, class, race, sexuality, and more.

While it took the family sitcom a good decade and a half to catch up with the Civil Rights era, the most-watched show of the 1980s was *The Cosby Show*, named for the now-disgraced but long-revered comedian and sexual predator Bill Cosby, followed the middle-class black Huxtable family in Brooklyn in New York, with Cosby himself playing gynecologist dad Cliff Huxtable. Sut Jhally and Justin Lewis (1992) argue that *The Cosby Show* helped "to cultivate an impression, particularly among white people, that racism is no longer a problem in the United States", and that as racism was therefore "a sin of the past ... *The Cosby Show*, accordingly, represented a new 'freedom of opportunity' apparently enjoyed by black people" (Jhally and Lewis 1992, 71–72), which they call a "post-racial" politics. Marc (1997, 182) even goes as far as to describe it as the "definitive Reagan era sitcom" for the way it embodied Reaganite neoliberal culture and politics. Within the show's post-racial politics, Cliff Huxtable's genteel and caring middle-class masculinity certainly marks a departure from the patronizing images of black Americans in *Amos 'n' Andy*, but even rejects images produced by a cluster of black relevancy sitcoms in the 1970s, such as *Sanford and Son* (1972–1977), a Norman Lear associated venture that had often depicted black men as "loud, conniving and ostentatious" (Cummings 1988, 78), reinscribing black masculinities for the Reagan era.

Cheers and the first post-class hangout

In the workplace sitcoms of the 1970s, it was a joint endeavor of labor that drew communities of colleagues together; ten years later, in *Cheers* (1982–1993), the links were growing flimsier. Though *Cheers* was set most of the time in a workplace, only a small proportion of the main characters worked there, with the show's eponymous bar owned by former baseball player Sam Malone, who employs hapless waitress Carla Tortelli and later bartender Woody Boyd. The rest of the cast are notably and deliberately motley: graduate student Diane Chambers, retired baseball coach Ernie Pantusso, accountant Norm Peterson, postal worker Cliff Clavin, and in later seasons psychiatrists Frasier Crane and Lilith Sternin, as well as Rebecca Howe, who owns the company who purchases the bar as a franchise. It is not work that brings these people together, but the public space of the bar.

Most available scholarship on *Cheers* focuses on the way it levels out public space across class difference (Brown 2016). In *Cheers*, the healthy public debate about issues ranging from low to high culture are fair game for any character, with the storylines resolving on the importance of community and class harmony over class difference. Brown cites a debate in season one about homosexuality, in which Sam's old friend Tom Kenderson schedules a book launch at the bar that documents his story of coming out as gay (*Cheers*, "The Boys in the Bar"). In the ensuing debate, Sam and some of the obviously more working-class bar patrons are reticent with their homophobia – yet, when the middle-class Diane says he should go ahead with the event, Sam does so, and in turn magically convinces all the bar patrons that being gay is, in fact, fine. In this example, class is about cultural taste and social stance, rather than material background, as Hilmes (1990, 69) points out: "here, class allegiance is not predicated on economics or birth but on attitudes; not on the hard facts of life but on the ways in which those facts are interpreted and valued by the characters". *Cheers* might reasonably be described therefore as a post-class sitcom, one in which class is not just deemed to not matter in terms of the social, but one in which material wealth is determined to be irrelevant to happiness and communal belonging, emphasized not just in the harmonious cross-class cast, but also in the reduction of class identity to cultural taste (Bourdieu 2010 [1984]). In this way, *Cheers* builds on the emerging neoliberalism's anti-collectivism, co-opting the communal bonds of friendship as a barrier to the potential of class conflict.

Like the rest of the show, then, masculinity in *Cheers* is post-class. Sam Malone follows the path of many of the baby boomer generation, of a working-class upbringing and residual habitus, toward becoming the owner of a bar. Despite the constant reminders of his working-class background, in fact, Sam would most likely be the wealthiest of the group, despite the upper-class sophistication of Frasier Crane, a professional psychologist. In, for example, the ruralcoms of the 1970s, working-class masculinities were obvious and explicit, and you could tell how much money a character made by how backward and bigoted their views were; in *The Beverly Hillbillies*, Jed's agricultural masculinity was made known via his often-outdated views on social issues. Masculinity in *Cheers*, because of its lesser interest in the material conditions of class, reconfers this position onto Sam Malone, whose working-class habitus is more relevant than his material wealth. Frasier Crane, on the other hand, articulates more progressive views because of his upper-class habitus. In *Cheers*, then, the problem of patriarchy's legitimacy is how to reformulate hierarchies of masculinities without the intersection of class in an emerging neoliberal hegemony.

Figure 2.1 The class differences between Sam Malone (Ted Danson, left), and Frasier Crane (Kelsey Grammer, right), are largely reduced to aesthetic ones, illustrated in the sporty casual attire of Sam and the dandy-like smart attire of Frasier.

Postmodernity and neoliberal hegemony

The sitcoms of the 1980s, then, moved beyond what we might understand as modernist conceptions of both class and race, though remained firmly within modernist conceptions of gender. By "modernist" is simply meant that both class and race exist as real and historical categories that have real and profound material effects on the lives of individuals. In *The Cosby Show* and *Cheers*, class and race are reduced to cultural difference, unrelated to the material position of the individual and instead only conferring a cultural identity. In rejecting such modernist conceptions, then, neoliberal capitalism resembles Jameson's (1991) conception of late capitalism, which he argues is governed by a postmodern logic. For Jameson (1991), the cultural moment of the 1990s and 2000s at least was one in which culture's relationship with history, or more specifically with historicity, is significantly weakened. Where modernist culture therefore sought a relationship with the real, material, world, postmodern cultural artefacts instead can only refer to the real world in a series of pastiches or parodies – as an example, "nostalgia films restructured the whole issue of pastiche and project it onto a collective and social level, where the desperate attempt to appropriate a missing past is now refracted through the iron law of fashion change" (Jameson 1991, 19). Baudrillard (1988) goes as far as to argue that television is itself the ideal postmodern cultural form, the visual offering a riper field for parody or pastiche than audio or the written word. Postmodern television, then, is notable for its self-referential nature, for its self-aware intertextual acknowledgement of canonical tropes rather than unconscious discursive perpetuation (Collins 1992).

Even the family is up for grabs in this cultural landscape – animated sitcom *The Simpsons* (1989–present), follows a stereotypical, culturally white (though stylized as yellow due to early design necessity) working-class family, and rarely misses an opportunity to parody, starting with an animated format that eschews a fixed temporal setting, parodying the relative stability of characters in the sitcom, a genre in which conservative narrative resolution precedes, and thereby precludes the possibility of, character development (Davis et al. 2015). Even the Simpson patriarch Homer, being by all accounts selfish, boorish, rude, and uncaring to both his family and the wider Springfield community, serves as a parodic critique of the sitcom's bumbling father trope (Malin 2005, 73), even though this regularly works out as much an affectionate tribute rather than full critique. As Jonathan Gray (2006, 58) points out,

> while family-affirming endings are nearly always undercut, they are not denied altogether. Rather, in offering a sweet ending, then a sarcastic, parodic pull of the rug, as is their common technique, *The Simpsons* still gives us that sweet ending, if in modified form.

A brief historiography of US sitcom masculinities 55

On the face of it, then, the postmodern sitcom appears to offer subversion over ideological hegemony, even if deeper and more specific readings threaten this possibility. Such a phenomenon makes *Seinfeld* (1989–1998) all the more interesting.

Seinfeld's anxious masculinities

Developing the hangout format of *Cheers*, *Seinfeld* was developed by already known stand-up comedian Jerry Seinfeld, playing a fictional version of himself, and a group of his friends: ex-girlfriend Elaine Benes (Julia Louis-Dreyfus), best friend George Costanza (Jason Alexander), and wacky neighbor Cosmo Kramer (Michael Richards). George's pitch to TV executives for a "sitcom about nothing" might be seen as a pastiche of the postmodern itself, (*Seinfeld*, "The Pitch"). A "sitcom about nothing" was what many viewers and critics had labeled *Seinfeld* itself beforehand, and to a great extent they were right; there was nothing to link the characters in the show apart from the fact they hang out together. They were neither colleagues nor family members and the show had multiple frequent locations – even in *Cheers*, almost every episode took place at the bar, which acted as an organizing point. In *Seinfeld*, the specific form of collective organization is much looser and more ephemeral. A constant anxiety about affective belonging thereby pervades the show, cutting across gender boundaries.

In the words of co-creator Larry David, in *Seinfeld* there is "no hugging, no learning" (Reed 2016). It not only lacks a clear community, but rarely offers a didactic message on any moral issue. This postmodern disregard for morality does not, however, mean that the show was alien to its contemporaneous society, or that it frequently explored contemporary social issues. In fact, the lack of moral lessons is indicative of surrounding societal norms. Pierson (2004) describes *Seinfeld* as a "modern comedy of manners" concerned with contemporary social norms in the US, such that, "through its comical concern with social manners and customs, [it] seems to assert not the decline of civility but rather its preponderance in American society" (Pierson 2004, 54). C. Wesley Buerkle (2011) further argues that this decline of civility harked the hegemonic emergence of a new form of capitalism, in which behavior is not regulated from the outside, but an act of self-regulation (McGuigan 2014). He cites one of *Seinfeld*'s most infamous episodes, in which all four characters engage in a competition to determine who can go the longest without masturbating (*Seinfeld*, "The Contest"), a contest that relies on personal confession rather than direct oversight. The characters are all convinced that George will lose the bet first, but he manages to hold on, despite the fact that his mother walking in on him "alone" and being sent to hospital after she falls over triggers the episode. George then spends most of episode extremely anxiously on the receiving end of a series of stern admonishments from his mother, who asks whether he has anything better to do on a weekday afternoon, implicitly critiquing a perceived solipsism of both George and contemporary society.

Seinfeld foregrounds three anxious men. Jerry and George are frequently anxious about their masculinities, while the unhinged Kramer is only not anxious because of his detachment from reality; to be a socially aware man in *Seinfeld* is to be anxious. If this chapter so far has shown anything, it is that sitcom masculinities have always been anxious, that patriarchy always has a problem of legitimacy – in this moment,

> with the decline of the self-made man and the gradual disappearance of the "other directed" male personality models of the 1950s, and especially with the Vietnam War and the rise of feminism in the 1960s and 1970s, the traditional guideposts to male maturity and masculinity seemed to have disappeared or were in disrepute.
> (Auster 2016, 193)

Anxiety is not new to masculinities in the US sitcom, but in *Seinfeld* and the hangout sitcom genre it heralded, anxiety is heavily accentuated, preceded by a half century of televisual exploration of the limits of the socioeconomic position of US masculinities.

Community, family and TV masculinities in the 21st century

If the sitcom is about collective organization and affective belonging, three modes of collective organization have and continue to predominate the genre in the 20th century: the family, the workplace, and the friendship group. Neoliberalism's relationship with the family is a confused, complex, and contradictory one, neither mutually harmonious nor dissonant (Brecher 2012, Cooper 2016). It is at least clear is that the nuclear family is certainly not in any mortal danger, neither as a Western institution nor as a sitcom community. The recent *Modern Family* (2009–2020), for example, was at various points the most-watched sitcom on television, following three nuclear families encompassing two generations of an extended family. However, its hegemony is at least under threat following a series of cultural, historical, and legal changes over the course of the century – while *Modern Family* follows one traditional nuclear family, the other two households consist of the grandfather patriarch of the show with his much younger Colombian wife and her son from a previous marriage, as well as two gay men who adopt a young Vietnamese girl. It is certainly difficult to envision *Modern Family* being made even 30 years ago.

While the incorporation of queer sexualities into the family sitcom is a novel development, the stepfamily is well-trodden ground; yet, neither really pose a threat to the nuclear family, as opposed to adapting it to social conditions. Perhaps the bigger threat is the increasing difficulty of demarcating the boundaries between domestic and public spheres. The private family home in real life is spilling out into the public realm, and vice versa. In the past, capitalist relations separated a cold emotionless and importantly masculinized workplace from a warm, emotional, comforting, and importantly feminized domestic space (Hayden 1984). Indeed, this is entirely the point of the dominance of family sitcoms of the 1950s and 1960s – *I Love Lucy* resonated with millions because it offered literal emotional respite from the workplace despite contemporary social contradictions, thanks to television's newfound ubiquity, while the ruralcoms and magicoms of the 1960s acted as a bulwark against threats to the middle-class nuclear family from feminists and rural folk. Illouz (2007) argues that this porousness between public and private constructs "emotional capitalism" – she argues both that intimacies are becoming ever colder, and that capitalism and labor requires ever more emotion from workers. In the hangout sitcom, we see these two phenomena complement one another in the formation of an insular group of friends who find harmony in one another's company as shelter from the tribulations of neoliberalism, a role to which the nuclear family with its generational differences is less well-suited.

The coldness of neoliberal intimacy is partially determined by the extension of monetary logic into the private sphere, with notions of friendship treated socially as transactional rather than subjective. Neoliberal individualism plays a part too, and it is no coincidence therefore that the hangout sitcom invariably takes place in the city – neither in suburbia nor in the rural. The city's dense population, fast pace and industrial origins make it the ideal conditions for neoliberalism's self-responsible subject, making the forming of bonds more difficult and encouraging a normative individualism (Rossi 2017). In this situation, the public sphere becomes the location for intimate relations, outside of the family – a café or a bar become the organizing points. The family, however, does not go away.

While collective belonging has shifted, the nuclear family remains the reference point, with the hangout sitcom frequently offering pastiches of family relations, implying that various characters adopt the roles of mother or father. This tendency should probably be read as an intertextual reference to the TV sitcom's origins, demonstrating the family's ongoing hegemony under capitalist relations. Another way in which the family remains important is as the telos of the hangout sitcom, a show that normally ends with most of the characters coupling off. This heteronormative pressure is a key motive of the anxious masculinities of the hangout sitcom. However, this anxiety does not play out uniformly among the men of the hangout sitcom, as I will explore in the next chapter.

Note

1 For a more extensive history, David Marc's *Comic Visions* (1997) offers a narrative history of comedy on US television, Darrell Hamamoto's *Nervous Laughter* (1989) systematically examines the ideological debates that take place within the sitcom and its subgenres, and Mary Dalton and Laura Linder's *Sitcom Reader* (2016) offers a condensed and varied history of specific subgenres and shows.

Filmography

The Addams Family. 1964–1966. [TV] Levy, David, Creator, ABC: USA.
All in the Family. 1971–1979. [TV] Lear, Norman, Creator, CBS: USA.
Amos 'n' Andy. 1928–1960. [Radio] Correll, Charles, and Freeman Gosden, Creator, WMAQ AM: USA.
The Beverly Hillbillies. 1962–1971. [TV] Henning, Paul, Creator, CBS: USA.
Bewitched. 1964–1972. [TV] Saks, Sol, Creator, ABC: USA.
Cheers. 1982–1993. [TV] Charles, Glen, Les Charles, and James Burrows, Creator, NBC: USA.
Happy Days. 1974–1984. [TV] Marshall, Garry, Creator, ABC: USA.
I Love Lucy. 1951–1957. [TV] Oppenheimer, Jess, Madelyn Davis, and Bob Carroll Jr., Creator, CBS: USA.
Leave it to Beaver. 1957–1963. [TV] Connelly, Joe, and Bob Mosher, Creator, CBS, ABC: USA.
The Life of Riley. 1953–1958. [TV] McKnight, Tom, Creator, NBC: USA.
M*A*S*H. 1972–1983. [TV] Gelbart, Larry, Creator, CBS: USA.
The Mary Tyler Moore Show. 1970–1977. [TV] Brooks, James L., and Allan Burns, Creator, CBS: USA.
Modern Family. 2009–2020. [TV] Lloyd, Christopher, and Steven Levitan, Creator, ABC: USA.
The Real McCoys. 1957–1963. [TV] Pincus, Irving, Creator, ABC, CBS: USA.
Roseanne. 1988–1997. [TV] Williams, Matt, Roseanne Barr, Marcy Casey, and Tom Werner, Creator, ABC: USA.
Sam 'n' Henry. 1926–1928. [Radio programme] Gosden, Freeman, and Charles Correll, Creator, WGN: USA.
Sanford and Son. 1972–1977. [TV] Lear, Norman, and Bud Yorkin, Creator, NBC: USA.
Seinfeld. 1989–1998. [TV] David, Larry, and Jerry Seinfeld, Creator, NBC: USA.
The Simpsons. 1989–present. [TV] Groening, Matt, Creator, Fox: USA.
WKRP in Cincinnati. 1978–1982. [TV] Wilson, Hugh, Creator, CBS: USA.

References

Attallah, Paul. 2003. "The unworthy discourse: Situation comedy in television." In *Critiquing the Sitcom: A Reader*, edited by Joanne Morreale, 91–115. Syracuse, NY: Syracuse University Press.
Auster, Albert. 2016. "*Seinfeld*: The transcendence of the quotidian." In *The Sitcom Reader: America Re-viewed, Still Skewed*, edited by Mary M. Dalton, and Laura R. Linder, 189–197. Albany, NY: SUNY Press.
Baudrillard, Jean. 1988. *The Ecstasy of Communication.* Cambridge, MA: MIT Press.
Bourdieu, Pierre. 2010 [1984]. *Distinction: A Social Critique of the Judgement of Taste.* Translated by Richard Nice. London: Routledge.
Brecher, Bob. 2012. "The family and neoliberalism: Time to revive a critique." *Ethics and Social Welfare* 6 (2):157–167. doi: 10.1080/17496535.2012.682503.
Brown, Robert S. 2016. "*Cheers*: Searching for the ideal public sphere in the ideal public house." In *The Sitcom Reader: America Re-viewed, Still Skewed*, edited by Mary M. Dalton, and Laura R. Linder, 177–184. Albany, NY: SUNY Press.

Brown, Wendy. 2006. "American nightmare: Neoliberalism, neoconservatism, and de-democratization." *Political Theory* 34 (6):690–714. doi: 10.1177/0090591706293016.
Brown, Wendy. 2015. *Undoing the Demos: Neoliberalism's Stealth Revolution*. Cambridge, MA: MIT Press.
Buerkle, C. Wesley. 2011. "Masters of their domain: *Seinfeld* and the discipline of mediated men's sexual economy." In *Performing American Masculinities: The 21st Century Man in Popular Culture*, edited by Elwood Watson, and Marc E. Shaw, 9–34. Bloomington, IN: Indiana University Press.
Chambers, Deborah. 2019. "Designing early television for the ideal home: The roles of industrial designers and exhibitions, 1930s–1950s." *The Journal of Popular Television* 7 (2):145–159. doi: 10.1386/jptv.7.2.145_1.
Collins, Jim. 1992. "Postmodernism and television." In *Channels of Discourse, Reassembled: Television and Contemporary Criticism*, edited by Robert C. Allen, 246–265. Oxford: Routledge.
Coontz, Stephanie. 1997. "*Leave it to Beaver* and *Ozzie and Harriet*: American families in the 1950s." In *Undoing Place? A Geographical Reader*, edited by Linda McDowell, 13–21. Oxford: Routledge.
Cooper, Melinda. 2016. *Family Values: Between Neoliberalism the New Social Conservatism*. New York: Zone.
Cummings, Melbourne S. 1988. "The changing image of the black family on television." *The Journal of Popular Culture* 22 (2):75–85. doi: 10.1111/j.0022-3840.1988.2202_75.x.
Dalton, Mary M., and Laura R. Linder. 2016. *The Sitcom Reader: America Re-viewed, Still Skewed*. 2nd ed. Albany, NY: SUNY Press.
Davis, Amy M., Jemma Gilboy, and James Zborowski. 2015. "How time works in *The Simpsons*." *Animation* 10 (3):175–188. doi: 10.1177/1746847715602403.
Demetriou, Demetrakis Z. 2001. "Connell's concept of hegemonic masculinity: A critique." *Theory and Society* 30 (3):337–361. doi: 10.1023/A:1017596718715.
Douglas, Susan. 1994. *Where the Girls Are: Growing Up Female with the Mass Media*. New York: Three Rivers Press.
Dow, Bonnie. 2006. "The traffic in men and the *Fatal Attraction* of postfeminist masculinity." *Women's Studies in Communication* 29 (1):113–131. doi: 10.1080/07491409.2006.10757630.
Duggan, Lisa. 2004. *The Twilight of Equality?: Neoliberalism, Cultural Politics and the Attack on Democracy*. Boston, MA: Beacon Press.
Eskridge, Sara K. 2019. *Rube Tube: CBS and Rural Comedy in the Sixties*. Columbia, MO: University of Missouri Press.
Fiske, John. 2010. *Television Culture*. 2nd ed. Oxford: Routledge.
Frank, Thomas. 1998. *The Conquest of Cool: Business Culture, Counterculture, and the Rise of Hip Consumerism*. Chicago, IL: University of Chicago Press.
Frederick, Christine. 1929. *Selling Mrs. Consumer*. New York: Business Bourse.
Giotta, Gina. 2017. "Sounding live: An institutional history of the television laugh track." *Journal of Communication Inquiry* 41 (4):331–348. doi: 10.1177/0196859917713760.
Gould, Jack. 1957. "Radio-TV: Outer space." *New York Times*, 5 October.
Gray, Jonathan. 2006. *Watching with the Simpsons: Television, parody, and intertextuality*. Edited by David Morley, *Comedia*. Oxford: Routledge.

Hamamoto, Darrell Y. 1989. "Nervous laughter: Television situation comedy and liberal democratic ideology." In *Media and Society*, edited by J. Fred MacDonald. London: Praeger.

Haralovich, Mary Beth. 2009. "Sitcoms and suburbs: Positioning the 1950s homemaker." *Quarterly Review of Film and Video* 11 (1):61–83. doi: 10.1080/10509208909361287.

Hayden, Dolores. 1984. *Redesigning the American Dream: The Future of Housing, Work, and Family Life*. London: W.W. Norton & Company.

Hilmes, Michelle. 1990. "Where everybody knows your name: *Cheers* and the mediation of cultures." *Wide Angle* 12 (2):64–73.

Huyssen, Andreas. 1986. *After the Great Divide: Modernism, Mass Culture and Postmodernism*. London: Macmillan Press.

Illouz, Eva. 2007. *Cold Intimacies: The Making of Emotional Capitalism*. Cambridge: Polity.

Jameson, Fredric. 1991. *Postmodernism or, the Cultural Logic of Late Capitalism*. London: Verso.

Jhally, Sut, and Justin Lewis. 1992. *Enlightened Racism: The Cosby Show, Audiences, and the Myth of the American Dream*. Boulder, CO: Westview Press.

Kutulas, Judy. 2016a. "Liberated women and new sensitive men: Reconstructing gender in 1970s workplace comedies." In *The Sitcom Reader: America Re-viewed, Still Skewed*, edited by Mary M. Dalton, and Laura R. Linder, 121–132. Albany, NY: SUNY Press.

Kutulas, Judy. 2016b. "Who rules the roost? Sitcom family dynamics from the Cleavers to *Modern Family*." In *The Sitcom Reader: America Re-viewed, Still Skewed*, edited by Mary M. Dalton, and Laura R. Linder, 17–30. New York: SUNY Press.

Landay, Lori. 2016. "*I Love Lucy*: Television and gender in postwar domestic ideology." In *The Sitcom Reader: America Re-viewed, Still Skewed*, edited by Mary M. Dalton, and Laura R. Linder, 31–42. Albany, NY: SUNY Press.

Linder, Laura R. 2005. "From Ozzie to Ozzy: The reassuring nonevolution of the sitcom family." In *The Sitcom Reader: America Viewed and Skewed*, edited by Mary M. Dalton, and Laura R. Linder, 61–72. Albany, NY: SUNY Press.

Malin, Brenton J. 2005. *American Masculinity under Clinton: Popular Media and the Ninetie "Crisis of Masculinity"*. New York: Peter Lang.

Marc, David. 1997. *Comic Visions: Television Comedy and American Culture*. 2nd ed. Oxford: Blackwell.

Marc, David. 2016. "Origins of the genre: In search of the radio sitcom." In *The Sitcom Reader: America Re-viewed, Still Skewed*, edited by Mary M. Dalton, and Laura R. Linder, 1–12. Albany, NY: SUNY Press.

Marsh, Margaret. 1988. "Suburban men and masculine domesticity, 1870–1915." *American Quarterly* 40 (2):165–186. doi: 10.2307/2713066.

Martinez-Cruz, Paloma. 2020. "Chicano Dracula: The passions and predilections of Bela Lugosi, Gomez Addams, and Kid Congo Powers." In *Decolonizing Latinx Masculinities*, edited by Arturo J. Aldama, and Frederick Luis Aldama, 185–197. Tucson, AZ: University of Arizona Press.

May, Elaine Tyler. 2008 [1988]. *Homeward Bound: American Families in the Cold War Era*. 3rd ed. New York: Basic Books.

McGuigan, Jim. 2009. *Cool Capitalism*. London: Pluto Books.

McGuigan, Jim. 2014. "The neoliberal self." *Culture Unbound* 6 (1):223–240. doi: 10.3384/cu.2000.1525.146223.

Miller, Diana. 2011. "Masculinity in popular sitcoms, 1955–60 and 2000–2005." *Culture, Society & Masculinities* 3 (2):141–159. doi: 10.3149/CSM.0302.141.

Mintz, Steven, and Susan Kellogg. 1988. *Domestic Revolutions: A Social History of American Family Life*. New York: The Free Press.

Mittell, Jason. 2004. *Genre and Television: From Cop Shows to Cartoons in American Culture*. London: Routledge.

Neale, Steve. 1980. *Genre*. Chippenham: Antony Rowe Ltd.

O'Meara, Carroll. 1955. *Television Program Production*. New York: Ronald Press.

Peters, John. 1999. *Speaking into the Air: A History of the Idea of Communication*. Chicago, IL: University of Chicago Press.

Pierson, David. 2004. "A show about nothing: *Seinfeld* and the modern comedy of manners." *The Journal of Popular Culture* 34 (1):49–64. doi: 10.1111/J.0022-3840.2000.3401_49.X.

Pugh, Tison. 2018. *The Queer Fantasies of the American Family Sitcom*. New Brunswick, NJ: Rutgers University Press.

Reed, Ryan. 2016. "Jerry Seinfeld: 'Show about nothing' tag is 'nonsense'." *Rolling Stone*, 29 August, Retrieved from https://www.rollingstone.com/tv/tv-news/jerry-seinfeld-show-about-nothing-tag-is-nonsense-248863/.

Rossi, Ugo. 2017. *Cities in Global Capitalism, Urban Futures*. Cambridge: Polity.

Segal, Lynne. 2007. *Slow Motion: Changing Masculinties, Changing Men*. 3rd ed. London: Palgrave Macmillan.

Slide, Anthony. 1991. *The Television Industry: A Historical Dictionary*. New York: Greenwood Press.

Spigel, Lynn. 1992. *Make Room for TV: Television and the Family Ideal in Postwar America*. Chicago, IL: University of Chicago Press.

Trotter, Joe William Jr., ed. 1991. *The Great Migration in Historical Perspective*. Bloomington, IN: Indiana University Press.

Weiss, Jessica. 2000. *To Have and to Hold: Marriage, the Baby Boom and Social Change*. Chicago, IL: University of Chicago Press.

Wells, Paul. 1998. "'Where everybody knows your name': Open conviction and closed contexts in the American situation comedy." In *Because I Tell a Joke or Two: Comedy, Politics, and Social Difference*, edited by Stephen Wagg, 178–199. Oxford: Routledge.

Wojcik, Pamela Robertson. 2010. *The Apartment Plot: Urban Living in American Film and Popular Culture, 1945 to 1975*. Durham, NC: Durham University Press.

Worland, Rick, and John O'Leary. 2016. "The rural sitcom from *The Real McCoys* to relevance." In *The Sitcom Reader: America Re-viewed, Still Skewed*, edited by Mary M. Dalton, and Laura R. Linder, 59–74. Albany, NY: SUNY Press.

Wright, Gwendolyn. 1981. *Building the Dream: A Social History of Housing in America*. London: MIT Press.

Zaretsky, Eli. 1976. *Capitalism, the Family and Personal Life*. New York: Harper & Row.

3 A typology of straight white men in the hangout sitcom

Like many others, I took part in and witnessed many times in my childhood and teenage years the game "which *Friends* character are you?". This formulation, rather than "which *Friends* character are you most like?", is indicative of the extent of empathy and familiarity several generations have had toward *Friends* and its characters. More recently, online quizzes have asked this question – a search for "which *Friends* character are you?" returns over 150,000 results, seemingly with a new version of the quiz every day on a new website. The questions can be broadly split into three categories: direct references to the show, general character idiosyncrasies, and, of course, romance. *Buzzfeed* need to know which popular culture character you would most like to date, or what you will be doing on New Year's Eve (Lewis 2013), with many of the options revolving around a romantic partner. *Brainfall* go straight in with your ideal honeymoon destination (Brainfall 2015), UK radio station *heart* your ideal date (heart 2015).

The hangout sitcom's relation to heterosexual romance is beyond an incidental feature, with entire characters and character types defined in relation to their heterosexuality. The subgenre is organized around a series of normative life events with the definitive teloses of marriage, and, even if we do not always see it, the family. Elizabeth Freeman (2010, 3) uses the concept of *chrononormativity* to describe these temporal societal norms, which she defines as "the use of time to organize individual human bodies toward maximum productivity". It is a way of asking, what is the expected journey of bodies over time in relation to the existing structural demands? Following Dana Luciano, she further suggests that bodies are incorporated into chrononormativity via socio-politically contextual forms of "chronobiopolitics" – "teleological schemes of events or strategies for living such as marriage, accumulation of health and wealth for the future, reproduction, childrearing, and death and its attendant rituals" (Freeman 2010, 4). These schemes, which are not just heteronormative, but also tend to be aligned with capitalist subjectivity and, in the Global North, whiteness, underline the importance the hangout sitcom places on hegemonic masculinity's ultimate telos – the nuclear family, whose shadow remains present despite its conspicuous absence and sometimes implicit critique. Of 23 main characters in the four sitcoms, 18 end up married, with only 5 with some ambiguity

DOI: 10.4324/9781003363538-3

regarding their heterosexual futures. Of those five, one had a spin-off cancelled prematurely (Joey), one is a single father (Barney), and it is strongly implied two of them will end up together anyway (Ted and Robin), leaving just one non-white character, Raj, single. The hangout sitcom is certainly organized around straight time. Yet, this leaves us with a range of questions about what neoliberal chrononormativity looks like. Neoliberalism's relation to the family and gender politics contains significant contradictions, such as an often-feminized ideal subject against the continuing domination of men, the collective organization of the family against radical individualism, and the sense that legal advances in women's rights will leave men behind.

The hangout sitcom negotiates these tensions, producing a range of characters, both male and female, whose paths of heterosexual chrononormativity vary. *Friends* is an obvious example. Chandler and Monica are married by season five; Ross and Rachel are both in constant fear of commitment and are on-and-off frequently; Joey is a ladies' man apparently happy to avoid settling down through most of the show; and Phoebe seems happy having casual sex without the same vanity as Joey, until she finds a husband in the show's latter seasons. Following the male characters here, there is then striking similarities between the three in *Friends* and the three in *How I Met Your Mother*. Marshall, like Chandler, settles down early; Ted, like Ross, has an on-off relationship with another main character that is resolved in the final episode; Barney, like Joey, lives a bachelor lifestyle. These male character tropes, defined in relation to how they perform heterosexuality, become de rigueur throughout the subgenre.

The hangout sitcom's typology of man

In reflecting and mediating what are familiar intimate social problems, US sitcom characters resonate when their personalities, social dilemmas, and idiosyncrasies are both familiar and sympathetic. It is a genre that is deeply socially contextual and works when audiences see themselves reflected onscreen. The sitcom is therefore not written to have vaguely defined or esoteric characters. Rather, because subgenres reflect a grouping of temporally specific discourses, sitcom characters tend to strongly resemble and build on character tropes from older sitcoms, and not just among a subgenre either, but spanning the full genre. It is possible in the sitcom to trace a broad character genealogy, between different characters from different shows (in the postmodern era, scripts even directly acknowledge the intertextuality of the sitcom), which is not accidental.

These character types are therefore defined by their relation to discourse. John Fiske (2010) shows that the important distinction between characters is not personality, but their relation to narrative structure, where character is merely a function of narrative. He talks not of character types, but of "character roles", which are "concerned only with what a character *does* in the narrative structure, not with whom he or she *is* as an individual" (Fiske 2010,

137). These character roles become codified as character-related tropes, ones with which most people who watch TV will be extremely familiar.

Character roles, then, are variable locations within discursive negotiation, taken up as a particular way or method for resolving discursive tension. This is not to say that most of the time the characters adopt the same positions throughout, but that they do vary, and that I am not here identifying some sort of formula for writing a hangout sitcom, as opposed to what it is that, narratively, characters are trying to achieve. Considering this variation, it would be more accurate to define these as "subject positions", a term borrowed from the method of discursive psychology that usually refers to the positions taken up by interview participants in relation to social scenarios (Edwards and Potter 1992, Potter and Edwards 1993); in watching these sitcoms, I found a similar phenomenon of character roles that vary according to the demands of narrative.

So, if hangout sitcoms negotiate the ideological dilemmas produced by neoliberal contradictions between collective family and individualization, and, for men, the attendant concerns of socioeconomic demotion, some indications of a feminized subjectivity, and the relative decline of the patriarchal institution of the nuclear family, then their narrative trajectories are marked by an often ambiguous and contradictory neoliberal form of chrononormativity. The result is that straight white masculinities in the hangout sitcom are riddled with insecurities and time panics, male characters who struggle to perform versions of masculinity suitable for both patriarchal and neoliberal subjectivities. I therefore argue that hangout sitcoms frequently feature three main male subject positions defined by their relations to this complex form of chrononormativity, negotiating its problems in different ways. All three encode notions of fragility and insecurity that arise from the difficulties of traversing neoliberal chrononormativity.

The three straight white male subject positions I outline within the hangout sitcom are the postfeminist male singleton (PMS) (borrowed from Ben Brabon 2013), the douchebag, and the househusband. These three subject positions reference and rearticulate previous character tropes from a range of sitcom and other diverse genre and media lineages to find narrative resolutions to the problems of the legitimacy of patriarchies and masculinities in a neoliberal era. Table 3.1 details the subject positions, with notes about their discursive backgrounds, behaviors, and typical job associations, and lists the characters who most often adopt each position in each show.

Perhaps the first thing to note from this table is that the three non-white characters, Raj, Winston, and Coach, do not occupy any of these three positions with much clarity or regularity. These subject positions, then, are white; not off limits to the occasional occupation by a non-white man, but it is at least clear that non-white masculinities still struggle in the hangout sitcom to shake off a sense of marginalized or othered masculinity. Hegemonic masculinity, in short, in the hangout sitcom, remains white – more on this in Chapter 5.

Table 3.1 The three male subject positions in the US hangout sitcom.

	Postfeminist male singleton	Douchebag	Househusband
Family background	Emotionally stunted parents with academic support over love	Often at least one absent parent	Mixed – character often evolves from other positions
Discursive background	Fear of unsuitability to patriarchy and capitalism	Campy overperformance of masculinity and neoliberal subjectivity	Successful performance of masculinity and neoliberal subjectivity
Behaviors	Heterosexual time panic, unadulterated anxiety and neurosis	Misogyny and womanizing	Domestic emasculation overcome by heterosexuality
Labor	Often creative, poetic, or intellectual	Usually corporate and/or office-based	Usually corporate and/or office-based
Friends	Usually Ross, fairly typically embodied	Usually Joey, mostly typical despite acting career	Usually Chandler, though not married until season five of ten
How I Met Your Mother	Usually Ted, very typically embodied	Usually Barney, very typically embodied	Usually Marshall, very typically embodied
The Big Bang Theory	Usually Leonard, though career is different	Sheldon usually performs this atypically, along with Howard for the first few seasons	Howard adopts this position in most later seasons
New Girl	Usually Nick, though not always typical	Schmidt, very typically embodied until he's married	Schmidt adopts this position in most later seasons

The postfeminist male singleton (PMS) spends the duration of the show desperately searching for "the one", a female soulmate who he must (and in every case here, does) marry at the end of his narrative arc. This arc is characterized by a series of fleeting sexual encounters with women, often used to highlight anxiety that he, and by implication contemporary masculinity, is unfit for familial life. He is a hopeless romantic, frequently motivated by a family upbringing financially secure but emotionally lacking. He is, as Ben Brabon (2013, 117) puts it, "unable to fulfil his patriarchal duties due to the incapacitating social and economic topography of late capitalism".

Concerned about a variety of social, cultural, and economic pressures, then, the PMS performs pure and unadulterated anxiety and time panic.

The douchebag faces the same set of concerns, but his solution is not to be anxious, but to overcompensate for both patriarchal and neoliberal expectations. Where forms of patriarchy inculcate an extreme heteronormativity and a conservative gender order, neoliberalism demands new forms of bodily discipline and individual determination; the douchebag usually constructs both performances to excess, with both an aesthetic obsession either around fashion or the body, combined with womanizing and misogynistic behaviors and attitudes. His constant desire to live up to expectations is regularly made literal by one or more absent parents, and thereby a lack of familial role models.

Finally, the househusband, a descendant of the comedic straight man, demonstrates to the other two characters their aspirational goals: he marries a woman early on, and usually has a young family before the show's end. He also has a stable, professional, technical middle-class job – in other words, he performs both masculinity and neoliberal subjectivity perfectly, even to the extent that his potential feminization from his domestic identity is overcome by the stability of his work and heterosexual marriage.

They are three positions defined by heterosexuality and organized around "straight time"; the postfeminist male singleton is on his search for his destined female partner, the douchebag is either a womanizer or a misogynist, and the househusband is in a stable married relationship with a woman. It is the househusband who performs heterosexuality correctly, complying with a range of subjective demands and hitting his chrononormative goals in good time. As such, it is toward the hegemonic position of the househusband that both insufficient positions, the PMS and the douchebag, move.

The postfeminist male singleton

The PMS can find his genealogy as the offspring of two archetypes, first in the postfeminist female singleton of chick lit and romantic comedy fame, typified by Bridget Jones, a modern woman caught between her career and her love life, constantly worried she is unfit for love. As Diane Negra (2006, online) describes it: "in a (perverse) spirit of gender egalitarianism, deficient/dysfunctional single femininity is now increasingly matched by deficient/dysfunctional single masculinity in several high-profile films and television series". The PMS combines these tropes, though, with the bachelor archetype, a heterosexual and marriageable single man whose lack of heterosexual commitment is a shame, but not pathologized like the female singleton. But the PMS differs from both these archetypes. His single status is not pathologized to the same extent as the female singleton; where the female singleton's problems have in the past been framed as personal faults, the PMS is a victim of circumstance. At the same time, where the bachelor often revels in his single status, the PMS is in a constant time panic over it. Approaching his

30s, worried that he is unfit for family and for romance, he is desperate to find "the one".

Ted in *How I Met Your Mother* occupies the PMS subject position probably more typically than any other character, closely followed by Ross in *Friends*, and Leonard in *The Big Bang Theory*. Nick is the clearest example in *New Girl*, but differs significantly from the others – Nick's malaise extends beyond his marriageable status and into other realms of his life, and, I argue, is what happens to the PMS when societal pressures have all become too much for masculinity.

Nostalgia and neo-traditionalism

The PMS is a romantic, frequently found pining for an idealized historical moment in which the poetics of love and marriage were easy for men to negotiate. Ted is moved by the poems of Pablo Neruda, enjoys renaissance fairs, and is described often as the "father of the group", not because of parental-like care for his friends, but more for a nostalgic disposition for romance. Indeed, the PMS's job is often a function of this. Ross's work as a paleontology professor may be scientific, but he teaches as well as studies an otherworldly, romanticized past. Similarly, Ted's architecture career revolves around a grand artistic vision until he too becomes a university lecturer, teaching his romanticized vision of architecture. I suggest that the PMS's romantic masculinity works, following Peter Redman (2001, 189), as a "discipline of love", "to assert and validate a particular and socially powerful kind of masculinity – white, heteronormative, and professional or middle class – that simultaneously contest[s] (and in some cases, punishe[s]) those forms of masculinity and femininity that failed to complement it". Romance is a necessary pre-requisite of the white, professional, and middle-class masculinities of the hangout sitcom, a form of masculinity articulated as a progressive update that nevertheless rearticulates in the hangout sitcom a gender neo-traditionalism (Hamad 2018).

The PMS's family background and parents' attitudes follow the hangout sitcom's tendency to question the nuclear families of the past. Parental imperfections tend to underline his romantic disposition, usually one of an academically supportive and financially stable upbringing, shielding an almost complete emotional aloofness such that he seeks love and neediness. Ross's parents were materially generous but stirred competition between him and Monica, like Leonard's parents who fostered competition between him and his older brother, did not celebrate birthdays or Christmas, and for the latter even forced him and his siblings to write research papers for which they would be graded. The first time we meet Ted's parents they announce a divorce, a split that they imply would have happened much earlier were it not for Ted's presence (*How I Met Your Mother*, "Brunch").

This resultant romanticism leads him to frequently clash with paternal figures whose masculinities are framed as outdated and emotionless. Ted has a work run-in with his boss, Hammond Druthers (Bryan Cranston), who designs a bank skyscraper that looks unambiguously like a penis and scrotum (*How I Met Your Mother*, "Aldrin Justice"). When the bankers who commissioned the building reject Druthers' pitch, Ted, against Druthers' wishes, pitches a different idea. Druthers' design draws on already obvious associations between skyscrapers, phallic imagery, and masculinity, and in being rejected by city bankers, is rejected by an obvious representative of neoliberalism. The building's phallogocentrism is maintained through Ted, even while it is cosmetically different, indicating continuity via evolution; Ted's design differs from Druthers, but not the structures in which Druthers works. Far from dismantling or deconstructing masculinities, the PMS's romantic masculinity is fundamentally conservative, a cosmetic modification on existing structures.

Hannah Hamad (2018, 695) suggests that Monica in *Friends* "embodies and articulates a discourse of neo-traditionalism that is centered on (white) heteronormative romantic love, and the fetishization of the domestic sphere". Her obsessive attitude to the orderliness of her home, combined with her clear and constant desire to find the Ward to her June Cleaver, marks out a gender politics more traditional than it might look cosmetically. The PMS is the same, his romantic, nostalgic disposition culminating in a neo-traditional gender politics. He treats marriage and heterosexual romance as a process of possession and exchange (Rubin 1975), often articulated as a sense of entitlement to a romantic partner. Ross at one point hides the phone number of a man Rachel met at a bar from her, even though they are not dating (*Friends*, "The One With Rachel's Phone Number"), while Ted, upon the engagement of Robin and Barney, informs Lily, "Robin shouldn't be with Barney, she should be with me" (*How I Met Your Mother*, "Band or DJ?"). When Penny attends community college, Leonard encourages her to invite a friend over to study with, but becomes outwardly difficult with her when Penny, with no sexual intent implied, invites over a handsome male classmate (*The Big Bang Theory*, "The 43 Peculiarity"). Similarly, he tries to forbid a friend of Penny's sleeping on her couch, even though he has nowhere else to go (*The Big Bang Theory*, "The Guitarist Amplification"). The PMS's neurotic possessiveness of his partner orients his own insecurities derived from a perceived loss of power towards the retention of established, conservative, cultural norms of gender.

Will they, won't they?

The postfeminist male singleton usually has a "will they, won't they", on-off relationship with his future partner clearly set up from the beginning, a female co-star who is "the one" right before his eyes, except that he does not see it yet. Ross has Rachel, who he knew from school; Ted has Robin, who he meets in the pub in the pilot episode; Leonard has Penny, who moves in to live opposite them in the pilot; Nick has Jess, who moves into his flat in the pilot. Ross and Rachel first kiss in season one (*Friends*, "The One With the East German Laundry Detergent"), first date in season two (*Friends*, "The One Where Ross and Rachel ... You Know"), then breaking up after several episodes following a now-infamous relationship "break" with ill-defined boundaries, during which Ross sleeps with someone else (*Friends*, "The One Where Ross and Rachel Take a Break"), after which they get together and break up several times. The other PMSs have similar dating patterns – Ted and Robin go on a date in the pilot episode where Ted declares he loves her (*How I Met Your Mother*, "Pilot"), and they get together toward the end of the season (*How I Met Your Mother*, "Come On"), are together through season two, and then on and off as both romantic partners and "friends with benefits" at various points, until the finale, when it is strongly implied they rekindle their romance (*How I Met Your Mother*, "Last Forever – Part Two"). There is no pattern to the character or subject position of the female love interest – Rachel is not dissimilar to Penny, but Robin and Jess are very different characters from the other two.

Love stories in Western cultures have typically followed a "romantic hero" narrative, in which a male hero undergoes a trial or set of trials to win the heroine (see Frye 1996–2012). We see this in romance novels to the present day (Belsey 1994, Allan 2020), but also in Hollywood cinema (Funnell 2018), as well as television dramas (Leggott et al. 2018) – notably the romantic comedy and period genres. As Catherine Belsey notes, this typical storyline emerges from and reinforces a gendered binary of active/passive – in short, the woman is a thing that happens to the man. The "will they, won't they" trope in sitcoms (perhaps popularized by Sam and Diane in *Cheers*) appears to upset this, introducing some uncertainty to the male romantic partner's journey, as well as a sense of peril to its presumed conclusion due to his passivity. The PMS is often as passive throughout various stages of his relationship as his love interest, such as when Rachel makes the first move. It emerges in an episode where they look at some old video footage that Ross, two years older than Rachel and her best friend Monica's brother, was ready to take her to her high school prom after she was stood up, which she did not know at the time (*Friends*, "The One With the Prom Video"). Rachel only learns of this when they are both adults, which triggers their romantic relationship as she rewards him for his chivalry with a kiss.

Such uncertainty to the PMS's destination appears to underline the neoliberal weakening of straight chrononormativity, its distinctions between public and private, work and domestic space, or the active hero and the passive heroine. With the conclusion in jeopardy, the PMS appears to indicate the sequences and life events constructed via heteronormative time are under threat (see Pellegrini 2022). In fact, this jeopardy is the mechanism by which the PMS's masculinity itself makes sense – without it, the narrative would not exist. The PMS's eventual happiness and his getting-the-girl narrative resolution therefore extend the typical love story, ultimately organizing the PMS's aspirations around a patriarchal and capitalist chrononormativity.

70 *A typology of straight white men in the hangout sitcom*

Figure 3.1 The heartbreak of teenage Ross's failed but noble pursuit of Rachel ultimately leads to a happy ending.

As such, placing the focus on the physical action from Rachel masks the affective dimensions of the wider interaction, in which nerdy, lonely Ross has had to watch Rachel date countless men while he nobly watches and pines for her from afar. At the center of their first kiss is a storyline about Ross's happiness and desire, treating Rachel as a storyline that happens to him, marking and re-entrenching that gendered active/passive binary, and establishing the subject position within the lineage of a typical romantic hero, even if this involves a move toward affective initiation rather than physical initiation. This continues into *How I Met Your Mother*, where Ted does not approach women himself, but instead is introduced by Barney to potential love interests – including Robin in the pilot episode – with his regular line "have you met Ted?". This instead works as a male proxy activity, underlining the PMS's inactivity yet retaining a gendered binary.

Nick's extended malaise

Popular culture has more recently demonstrated an unwillingness to pathologize single women, and a determination to celebrate single status. A series of chick flicks through the early 2010s follow not one single woman, but a group of them striking out on their own, choosing whether they want to find a partner, movies such as *Bridesmaids* (2011) and the all-female remake of *Ghostbusters* (2016). Jess in *New Girl* is such a character, a woman who inherits the less-pathologized elements of the PMS. Her lack of settling down is not due to her own flaws, but because of a society that prevents her from doing so. She, like the PMS, is single, but not inadequate. Perhaps to therefore avoid making two characters to similar, Nick, who most clearly and most often embodies the PMS role in the most recent hangout sitcom studied here, *New Girl*, does so slightly differently. He is single and wants love, but he does not search for "the one" in the same way as do other iterations. He aspires to a career as a creative auteur, longing to be a novelist, bringing a certain romance to the character, but he is in a dead-end job as a bartender until later seasons, having dropped out of law school prior to the show's beginning. Unlike Ted, whose declarations of love are an ongoing joke throughout *How I Met Your Mother*, Nick is often unable to express any sort of emotion.

Nick, I argue, is a jaded PMS, for whom all the promises of neoliberal self-improvement and the patriarchal dividend have seemingly evaporated. Nick's suburban, decidedly non-middle-class, Chicago family had money problems, as we learn when he is put in charge of organizing his father's funeral in season two (*New Girl*, "Chicago"), a man who never successfully passed down to him the rules of manhood and its benefits. He abandoned his law degree as he struggled to accept its interpellation of him as a functioning professional neoliberal subject. Instead, owing to a lack of self-esteem combined with impostor syndrome, Nick is apparently happy as a bartender. Instead of the time panic, anxiety, and neo-traditionalism, Nick has mostly all but given up on adapting to the demands of neoliberal subjectivity, and of chrononormativity – mostly, but not completely. Nick remains nostalgic in ways that are often less immediate and obvious, and particularly in his dealings with his father and future father-in-law.

We meet Nick's father Walt once, in season two, before he dies later in the season, played by Dennis Farina. After learning his career is that of a "con man", the main thrust of the narrative is that Nick is furious at him turning up unannounced, while Jess attempts to restore their relationship (*New Girl*, "A Father's Love"). When Nick and Walt get down to brass tacks, Nick invokes notions of responsibility and biopolitics, angrily telling his dad, "I am not a successful adult – I don't eat vegetables and/or take care of myself, and it's because of you". Nick's extended malaise, and subsequent inability to chrononormatively self-responsibilize is down to insufficiently learned masculinity. However, Walt can be seen as a proxy for moment in which a prior generation of men find themselves unable to adapt to the demands of neoliberal subjectivity, producing a significant generational gap between masculinities. However, even despite the differences between Nick's PMS and older forms, there remains certain neo-traditional assumptions.

When he dates Jess, *New Girl* foregrounds the similarities and relationship between Nick and his future father-in-law Bob, who is played by Rob Reiner. Reiner in the 1970s played Mike Stivic on the Norman Lear sitcom *All in the Family* (1971–1979), a young Polish American whose left-leaning politics and resultant exaggerated laziness cause him to clash with his conservative father-in-law Archie Bunker. Yet, in *New Girl*, Bob Day, played by a baby boomer-generation actor known best for an emasculated and humiliated man in a 1970s sitcom, is presented as the more successful masculinity than Walt Miller, played by Dennis Farina, a baby boomer-generation actor known for a series of highly masculinized mobster and police officer roles. Masculinities are evaluated in the hangout sitcom here differently to their televisual predecessors, with caring forms placed somewhere in the dominant position. Even with Bob, though, there are some suggestions that heterosexuality remains a process of possession and exchange, highlighted by the way Nick and Bob often talk about their relationship without Jess present. Jess's dad has as much say in the relationship as the two of them, such that when he informs Nick that he is, verbatim, not "good enough" (*New Girl*, "Winston's Birthday") to be Jess's boyfriend, and forbids their relationship, the idea that Bob's – and importantly only, Bob, not Jess's mom's – take on their relationship matters is taken as common sense.

The douchebag

The next subject position I call the *douchebag*, a word taken from *New Girl*, in which Schmidt's character has a "douchebag jar", as opposed to a swear jar, into which he must drop money when he behaves like a douchebag. Embodied by Joey in *Friends*, Barney in *How I Met Your Mother*, and Schmidt in *New Girl* (2011–2018), and shared in interesting and different ways by Howard and Sheldon in *The Big Bang Theory*, the douchebag responds to the same concerns that the PMS does – perceived socioeconomic demotion, changes to chrononormativity, and the contradictory messaging of masculine and neoliberal subjectivities. Instead of anxiously struggling to perform any of these effectively, as the PMS does, the douchebag constructs a performance of excess. His fumbled resolution overcompensates and thereby overperforms, to an almost campy extent, both the heterosexuality of the masculine subject and the bodily self-discipline of the neoliberal subject.

Of all three male subject positions, the douchebag is the most exclusive to the hangout sitcom, as we see similar characters of the househusband and PMS in other genres and media – his combination of tragedy and misogyny is, as far as I have found, unique to the subgenre. Despite his clearest ancestors being the jock, loudly heterosexual and typically attractive, and the bachelor, the douchebag is written as more likeable and more three-dimensional than either of these two. In fact, he frequently exemplifies the hangout sitcom's genre-mixing focus on character development with an explicit arc based on the complexity of his psychology. Such psychology, put simply, is that his misogyny and womanizing are merely a façade covering major insecurities.

This combination – psychological insecurity married to a verging on campy hypermasculinity – regularly reads as a public critical commentary on 21st-century masculinity. Though my choice of the word "douchebag" has been questioned on several occasions for the strength of the word choice and the evaluative work it does, I suggest that it is the writers and creative teams behind the sitcoms who do this evaluative work. "Douchebag" represents a reasonable description of a character whose behaviors are clearly written to be evaluated negatively (while simultaneously reflecting the gen X, Y, and millennial colloquial vernacular of the hangout sitcom). However, the tragedy of the douchebag is that he is haunted by past specters of masculinity and contemporary challenges to chrononormativity, challenges he must overcome. As such, his narrative-discursive role is to sympathize with those who mourn changes to masculinities and "straight time" that the hangout sitcom exemplifies. In short, insofar as each show presents their douchebag as sympathetic and continues to organize sexuality chrononormatively – even offering them all paths to redemption – it falls short of a structural critical commentary on masculinity.

Bodily discipline and aesthetic labor

Attempting to marry masculine performance with neoliberal capacities for aesthetic labor, the douchebag produces an artificially constructed male body, reflecting a 21st-century masculinity whose loss of power leads to a desire for the creation of "erotic capital" (Hakim 2020). Toward the beginning of the conjuncture, we see this play out in the first season of *Friends*, where Joey lands a role in an Al Pacino movie, to discover that it is not quite the opportunity he had expected. Instead of a speaking role, Joey is hired to be a body double for Pacino in a shower scene from behind where Pacino, representative of a baby boomer masculinity, does not want to expose his backside, such that Joey is his "butt double" (*Friends*, "The One With The Butt"). The shoot goes awkwardly as Joey over-acts, clenching his buttocks excessively, and he is fired from the job. The contrast between Al Pacino's Hollywood masculinity and Joey's bodily masculinity, directly plays with a perceived reversal of the male gaze onto the male body (Neale 1983), simultaneously commodifying it for Joey's monetary gain. Nudity accentuates the bodily discipline required of the neoliberal subject (Bartky 1998, Young 2005), while reducing masculinity to the male body.

Schmidt accentuates the douchebag's bodily discipline with a masculinized update on "Fat Monica" in *Friends* – both characters are shown in flashback episodes, with their regular actors in makeup and prosthetics, to have been overweight until they became versed in bodily discipline in their early 20s. Drawing on fat studies scholarship, Amy Gullage (2014) shows how "Fat Monica" articulates that fat people are poor capitalist subjects, lazy, gluttonous, and sexually undesirable. By 2012, these strict lessons about bodily discipline have become lessons for men, too, emphasizing the importance of men's bodies' desirability in the neoliberal era. Indeed, it is important that neoliberal bodily discipline remains heterosexualized.

In season two, for example, Schmidt's cousin who is also known by their shared surname (Rob Riggle) visits. Challenged by Cece, the two of them compete in several challenges to decide who should be called "the one true

74 *A typology of straight white men in the hangout sitcom*

Figure 3.2 Schmidt, in the season one episode "Cece Crashes", waits outside the shower for Cece with his top off, using his carefully preened, moisturized body toward heterosexual success.

Schmidt" (*New Girl*, "Parents"). The first round of contests draws on associations between the male body and labor, such as weightlifting and press-ups, before the original Schmidt argues that masculinity has changed, declaring "Your caveman ideas about manhood are so over. Manhood today is about exfoliation, and cheese courses, and emotional honesty, and Paxil" (*New Girl*, "Parents") (Paxil is a prescribed antidepressant). The second part of the competition is culinary, as they attempt to create the better plate of food. Finally, Cece tells them that to truly establish who is more masculine, they need to show that they are comfortable in their masculinity, and that the winner will be the Schmidt who kisses their housemate, Winston. The second Schmidt (Rob Riggle's Schmidt) does this, but immediately regrets it, and in the final scene the two of them let each other know they do not mind the other one using the same name.

The first set of contests proposes that masculinity is a bodily property, and the second disrupts this theory via Schmidt's speech "caveman" masculinity, with the final resolution proposing that masculinity is about being "comfortable in your own masculinity", suggesting a form of masculinity that can be individualized beyond a structural norm. Masculinity is disrupted by the neoliberal bodily discipline of cosmetic exfoliation and the notion of emotional honesty, both of which challenge the initial equilibrium. Yet, this disruption occurs within existing masculine structures, only challenging the association of masculinity with competition using homophobia. As such, the douchebag's masculinity demonstrates a somewhat superficial change to masculinity.

A different form of gaze on the douchebag's body, in *How I Met Your Mother*, Barney's tailored suits construct a foppish obsession with fashion that verges on camp, intensified by the fact that the extremely heterosexual Barney Stinson is played by Neil Patrick Harris, who, as well as being openly gay, is known for musical theatre and LGBTQI+ activism. Barney was never fat, but he did used to belong to an almost equally unproductive subculture: the hippy. The obvious artifice of Barney's suited performance, read next to the openly gay Harris, as well as frequent comeuppance for his womanizing, certainly suggests that *How I Met Your Mother* is performing evaluative work, that his gender performance is not a desirable one (Lotz 2014, Thompson 2015). However, there remains a distinct pathos to the haunting of Barney's present. A season one flashback reveals that Barney's suit obsession derives from being romantically rejected by a woman who chose to date a man with an unspecified corporate job instead of Barney the hippy barista (*How I Met Your Mother*, "Game Night"), who starts wearing them to imitate and emulate his love rival. Barney's suits become a campy costume to elicit audience sympathy, due to his being haunted by not only his past, but by masculinities of the past. In Judith Butler's words, the suits do not "implicitly [reveal] the imitative structure of gender itself—as well as its contingency" (Butler 1990, 187) as a subversive drag performance might, but rather they mourn the impossibility of Barney living up to an unquestioned original masculinity. Though presenting as a character role whose personal masculine crisis stimulates significant pathos, the douchebag character thereby falls short of a critical commentary on masculinity.

Nerdy douchebags and "toxic geek masculinity"

The Big Bang Theory marries aspects of often marginalized nerd masculinities with the tropes of the hangout sitcom, resulting in male subject positions that are certainly recognizable as instances of the genre, but transplanted by setting, tone, humor, and cultural references. The show has a clear PMS in Leonard, who trades in tropes most like his fellow characters in other shows, perhaps as the PMS is a subject position that shares with nerds and geeks stereotypes about neurosis and bookishness. However, the douchebag's hypersexuality and virility are a problem for the typically desexualized male nerd. As such, *The Big Bang Theory* translates the douchebag's campy overperformance of neoliberal and masculine subjectivity in two different ways, in the characters Sheldon and Howard.

Sheldon, like Joey, Schmidt, and Barney, has some questionable ideas about gender (see also Salter and Blodgett 2017), for example blaming Penny's choice of clothing for Howard upskirting her (*The Big Bang Theory*, "The Cooper-Hofstadter Polarization"). The show suggests that Sheldon's sexism emerges from a vulnerability and fear of loneliness. Like Schmidt and Barney, Sheldon was an outsider from a young age, with parents who did not understand their son's prodigal abilities, and a father who died during his childhood. Further, in an episode of prequel *Young Sheldon*, his younger self cries upon receiving a physics award, believing he will be friendless for the rest of his life (*Young Sheldon*, "A Swedish Science Thing and the Equation for Toast"). He certainly encodes, then, a form of backlash script like douchebag character roles in other shows. Yet, where Joey, Barney, and Schmidt's iterations of the douchebag are all overtly and painfully heterosexual, however, Sheldon is almost entirely asexual, at least until his relationship with Amy, and is not particularly interested in his appearance.

Like Neil Patrick Harris and his character Barney, Sheldon's actor Jim Parsons is a gay man known for his activism, and the show deliberately plays on this with an excessive, campy performance, but of asexuality. I suggest that asexuality allows Sheldon to, on a personal level, resolve the discursive tensions that inhere between the masculine and neoliberal subjects, producing masculinity by rejecting the long-lasting bonds required by the family as an obstacle to the neoliberal ends of self-entrepreneurship and self-determination, a similar logic to "volcels", a phenomenon related to online alt-right spaces where men voluntarily choose celibacy because they find women a distraction. His automaton-like rationality produces a skepticism toward friendship and romance that he has a literal, codified, and legally binding roommate/friendship contract with Leonard. This leads Stratton (2016) to suggest Sheldon performs neoliberal subjectivity in its purest, most ideal form, unadulterated by ideological or discursive tensions (Garlick 2020), where human bonds and intimacy are transactional, all enabled by the desexualized nerd stereotype (Stratton 2016). However, Sheldon's unadulterated neoliberal subjectivity is played as autism, suggesting that the neoliberal subject requires some level of contradiction to be considered normal enough for everyday life. To be purely neoliberal is to not fully understand the social world, and by the end, we see Sheldon more willing to face complexity and contradiction in the social world up front, as he comes to accept a neoliberal chrononormative future.

While he is not asexual, Howard is not a typical douchebag either, despite some typical signification, such as a father who left the family when Howard was 11, and an overbearing Jewish mother not dissimilar to Schmidt. Howard instead sees the douchebag role as an aspiration, attempting constantly to be the kind of ladies' man he sees on television, but, being a nerd, unable to actualize his sexual desires. The first season features an extended gag about a formula he develops to calculate how likely it is a woman will sleep with him, involving the "Wolowitz co-efficient", determined by "neediness times dress size squared" (*The Big Bang Theory*, "The Hofstadter Isotope"). Penny addresses him directly about his sexism in season two, after he makes several advances toward her, a criticism that he brushes off and blames on women who he believes have mistreated him. Misreading Penny's sympathy as attraction, he attempts to kiss her, and is greeted with a punch in the nose, which he later describes cheerfully as getting "halfway to pity sex" (*The Big Bang Theory*, "The Killer Robot Instability"). His dress reflects his douchebag aspirations, recognizing and understanding the associations of douchebag behavior and the body, but his attempts to keep up with such fashions can be reasonably described as dated, with a bowl cut, bright shirts with large collars, skintight colorful pants, and a belt with a large buckle (there are some suggestions that his dress is modeled after scientist Carl Sagan). He is not typically handsome or attractive like the douchebags in the other shows. Despite all these behaviors, we are implored to understand Howard as tragic and sympathetic. And, like Sheldon, he graduates from his douchebag role as he begins to strike off chrononormative heterosexual achievements, getting married first of the group, and having children before any other, too.

Familial redemption

It is via the family that the douchebag redeems himself, having rarely come from a stable nuclear family – in fact, part of the reason for the douchebag's inability to perform a reasonable and acceptable form of masculinity is often that his father was not there to teach him how. Schmidt and Howard's fathers left the family during their childhoods, while Barney was raised by his lone mother, finding out later in life that the man he called "Uncle Jerry" was his biological father. While Sheldon's father is shown in prequel *Young Sheldon* (2017–present) to be emotionally supportive, he is also shown to not understand his intellect, and dies when Sheldon is 14 years old. In *Friends*, Joey's relationship with his father is less tragic, but still troubled due to disagreements about career choices. In short, all of them, for at least a significant portion of their childhood, were raised mostly by their mothers.

Only child Schmidt's New Yorker Jewish mother fulfills all the stereotypes: she overbears, over-mothers, and when they meet, tries to control her son. She competes Oedipally with Schmidt's at-the-time fiancée Cece over who can better take care of an upset Schmidt (*New Girl*, "Homecoming"), and when Schmidt asks his mom for money for an investment, she denies the money until he finishes writing thank you cards for his bar mitzvah presents (*New Girl*, "The Right Thing"). She is the typical "all engulfing nurturer who devours the very soul with every spoonful of hot chicken soup she gives" (Duncan 1983, 27) that has represented Jewish mothers on US television for several decades – indeed, it is implied that this is what created "fat Schmidt". Schmidt's father, who it seems is probably not Jewish, left the family when Schmidt was very young. The two reconnect in later seasons, but Schmidt is wary of his father's ability to remain present in his life.

All of this appears to be a commentary not just on masculinity, but specifically on the nuclear family. However, even the douchebag's struggles with his family background become re-oriented around "straight time" – though the family is the source of his problem, it is also his salvation. In season three of *The Big Bang Theory*, Howard meets Bernadette, at the time a graduate student, and the two marry a season later; Sheldon settles down with Amy; Barney does find some redemption with Robin, but we also learn he settles down, finding his calling in becoming a single father. Though Joey never finds happiness in the family, his story in spin-off *Joey* remains unfinished.

For Schmidt, it is not paternal reconnection that sees his narrative arc resolved, but his eventual commitment to Cece, a winding narrative that incorporates themes of bodily discipline, care, identity, and the family. He and Cece begin a relationship in season one (*New Girl*, "Valentine's Day"), until Schmidt drops in on her at work and cannot overcome inadequate possessive and jealous feelings watching her pose suggestively with another male model, and the two break up at the end of season one (*New Girl*, "See Ya"). Soul-searching, Schmidt soon rekindles a romance with an ex-girlfriend of his, Elizabeth (*New Girl*, "Bachelorette Party"), who dated Schmidt when he was overweight, the two sharing a love of food. While Elizabeth is the subject of a variety of jokes about eating, such as flashbacks where the two of them incorporate food into their sex life, she is not exclusively defined by her weight. Instead, she serves a didactic lesson for Schmidt, teaching him to be defined beyond his body and instead by his character – Max Greenfield, for example, wears a fat suit to play Schmidt, while Elizabeth's actor Merritt Wever has no prosthetics. Elizabeth informs Schmidt that it was not the weight loss that led to their split, but, as she says, "you were the greatest boyfriend, and then you lost weight, and you got mean" (*New Girl*, "Bachelorette Party"). The douchebag has mis-learned a contradictory lesson from neoliberal subjectivity, in which cold calculation, similarly to Sheldon, should apply in every sphere. There is perhaps the possibility of a reparative reading here, hidden behind the prosthetic fat suit and weight jokes, such that *New Girl* offers a critique of bodily discipline, offering in its place an argument for the positives of care.

However, while Schmidt takes on this lesson, Elizabeth is gone within the next set of episodes, and does not appear on *New Girl* again. After Cece tells Schmidt she still loves him in the season two finale (*New Girl*, "Elaine's Big Day"), believing himself to be in love with both women, he tells each woman that he has dumped the other woman. This inevitably reaches an explosive conclusion several episodes into season three when the two women both find out he has been dating both (*New Girl*, "Double Date"), and with Elizabeth out of the picture, a break-up that it does not take him long to get over, Schmidt returns to pining for former model Cece. They marry in season five, during a ceremony when Schmidt symbolically smashes the douchebag jar in place of a wine glass as goes the traditional Jewish ceremony (*New Girl*, "Landing Gear"), the next chrononormative event ticked off. Completing his arc, by the time *New Girl* wraps up in season seven, Schmidt has chosen to leave his job and become a full-time stay-at-home dad. It remains in reference to the family and heterosexuality, albeit perhaps a slightly modified version of the nuclear family, that the douchebag eventually becomes the aspirational househusband.

The househusband

The househusband gets married and has children before anyone else, usually has the most settled job (though is often less happy with it), and is often positioned as a comedic straight man. He is what Ward Cleaver and his fellow middle-class managerial fathers might look like in a prequel show, prior to their settling down in the suburbs. He is as chrononormative as it gets – professional career, proposal, marriage, family, children, all usually well before the show's finale. The time panic that defines the other two positions evaporates. As far as the hangout sitcom might have a neoliberal "hegemonic masculinity", the househusband is it, and yet his presence in the genre is far less assured than the other two positions. Only *How I Met Your Mother* has a househusband from the beginning, and although for *Friends* we might reasonably attribute this to its early experiments with the genre (even if Chandler and Monica marry in season five of ten) both *The Big Bang Theory* and *New Girl* only have characters that frequently occupy the househusband position after they achieve enough life goals to do so, as explored in each previous section.

The househusband reflects the contradictions that emerge from combining neoliberalism and masculinity in any way that is "successful", often echoing the perceived turn-of-the-century crisis in the middle-class masculinities of unhappy office workers in texts such as *Fight Club* (Brabon 2007) or *American Beauty* (Arthur 2004). However, where these texts produce frustrated masculinities that lash out with violence or borderline pedophilic

Figure 3.3 Marshall and Lily get married in season two episode "Something Borrowed", with Marshall's besotted look here somewhat typical.

sexual desire, for the hangout sitcom's more family friendly unhappy office worker, this results in a continual feminization and questioning of sexuality. Therefore, while he is often presented as the "straight man", the househusband is frequently the subject of mistaken sexuality jokes as a result of both his domestic and work situations – we see this particularly with Chandler. However, he leaves a range of ambiguous readings open here, potentially exposing some of the discursive clashes between neoliberalism and the family.

Bullshit labor

The househusband tends to have a professional career – the two most explicit iterations of the position, Chandler does something involving "statistical analysis and data reconfiguration", while Marshall works for a corporate law firm, with the function of both workplaces to construct in each character an unfulfilled and insecure masculinity; the former is emasculated by apathy toward a job he finds unfulfilling, and the latter emasculated by his hatred of a job that he finds far too masculine for him.

The exact nature of Chandler's dead-end job is the constant butt of jokes – at times, Chandler himself seems unsure what it is he does. Contrasted against Joey's enthusiasm for acting and Ross's candid love of dinosaurs, the househusband's labor directly acknowledges the "bullshit" part of David Graeber's (2018, xxi) notion of responsible "bullshit jobs", jobs where "huge swathes of people spend their days performing tasks they secretly believe do not really need to be performed"; Chandler's line, "If I don't input those numbers ... it doesn't make much of a difference", could be lifted from Graeber's thesis. Neil Ewen (2018) argues that Chandler's dissatisfaction with his work is inseparable from the constant jokes about his masculinity, and his sexuality that is regularly mistaken for gay. In season one, the other main characters admit to mistaking him for gay, and unable to say exactly why they think so, Monica offers a vague explanation: "I dunno, you—you just—you have a quality" (*Friends*, "The One Where Nana Dies Twice"). As Ewen (2018, 736) observes, "the problems the friends have in pinning down this 'quality' in Chandler mirrors their inability to remember what he does for a job". Chandler's bullshit job, and specifically its neoliberalized lack of manual labor, competition, and productive elements, emasculate him, a commentary on the discourses about the "crisis in masculinity" throughout the 1990s in a way that appears to lament or mourn masculinity's stability in the current era. However, there is a theme of personal sacrifice for the sake of wife and family that begins to emerge from Chandler following his marriage in season five, which becomes more emblematic of Marshall as the hangout sitcom subgenre develops.

Sacrifice is the overriding theme of Marshall's corporate law job, one he does not really want, but accepts that he needs the money following Lily's accidental spoiling of an $8,000 dress (*How I Met Your Mother*,

"Cupcake"), in stark contrast to Barney's apparent rapacious enthusiasm for corporate labor. He is reluctant to take the work on moral grounds, more interested in environmental law than what he sees as immoral corporate law. His first few days working in corporate law are charted in the episode "Life Among the Gorillas", named after a fictional work of anthropology that becomes a palpable metaphor for his experience in corporate law, where his colleagues are rude and misogynistic, counting the women they have slept with and rating them numerically. Marshall's corresponding emasculation, while the butt of jokes, is also portrayed as a positive; we are not supposed to think much of the boorish jocks in his office. They mock Marshall when he opens his lunchbox, assembled by Lily, with crusts cut off and an affectionate note inside. Marshall determines that the best strategy for negotiating his new workplace is to conform and join in the misogynistic banter. He subsequently sees himself in the mirror as a gorilla, acting to fit in with the natives like the fictional anthropologist author of the eponymous book/episode title. The metaphor is obvious: the misogynistic masculinity of those who work in Marshall's office is literally less evolved than Marshall's, whose masculinity is further down the evolutionary line. In the end, Marshall gives up on the masculine performance, and decides he wants to be himself, demonstrated by the final scene of the episode where he and Lily duet the Elton John and Kiki Dee song "Don't Go Breaking My Heart" at karaoke, a performance camped up comedically. The househusband is shown to be happier in the home than at work.

Domesticity and mistaken sexuality

Despite being more at home in the domestic sphere than the work sphere, though, the hangout sitcom continues to demonstrate discomfort with this idea. The "mistaken for gay" plot became extremely common in the 1990s to mediate men's anxieties about their own masculinities in light of the increasing visibility and acceptance of gay men in the USA (Becker 2014). For Chandler, the most frequent butt of such jokes, such anxiety was amplified by his family background. Chandler's parents are divorced after his dad came out as a gay man who not only used to have frequent rendezvous with their pool boy, but is now either a drag queen, transvestite, or trans woman named Helena Handbasket – a departure from his birth name Charles – in a show called "Viva Las Gay-Gas". The writers (knowingly or unknowingly) constantly conflate and confuse the distinction between drag and trans woman identities, to the extent their gender identity is not entirely clear, what pronouns might be appropriate, or even what name to use. Chandler is extremely embarrassed by this and does not talk to his father for several years, but it is also used as a point of continuity between a father and son who, it is implied, both present non-heteronormatively, perhaps an odd set of circumstances for a character who in many ways is the show's best example of hegemonic masculinity.

While Neil Ewen (2018) suggests that Chandler's precarity is "insulated" by class privileges, I further suggest here that his perceived homosexuality is insulated by his successful heterosexuality; Chandler is both *Friends'* arbiter of fatherhood as well as the most emasculated of the male characters, made possible precisely because his masculinity is insured by fatherhood, as well as a direct result of his suitability to domesticity. This is driven not just by anxiety about what might be considered a "post-closeted" culture (Dean 2014) in which heteronormativity is not quite as strong as it once may have been, but also inseparable from emasculation by the same surrounding social and economic circumstances that drive the PMS and douchebag's anxieties. In particular, what is the position of a domesticated househusband in an increasingly individualized urban work culture?

Though Marshall's family background is rather different, and he is rarely questioned over his sexuality, he remains somewhat emasculated in such environments, more suited to the domestic sphere. He grew up in a large household as the smallest and weakest of his three large rural Minnesota brothers, an ongoing joke considering actor Jason Segel is by some way the tallest and broadest of the main characters. As such, he frequently expresses disdain for city life, and by proxy, post-industrial life: "I'm too big for New York, okay? I'm always trying to fit into cramped little subway seats or duck under doorways that were built 150 years ago" (*How I Met Your Mother*, "I Heart NJ").

The divide between urban and rural here is reflected in the mind/body binary, recalling existing research on rural masculinities. Stenbacka (2011) argues that rural men on Swedish television are constructed as backward, opposite the modern forward-thinking urban man, part of which is achieved by attaching the rural men to machines and physical labor. The male body is equally important to Marshall's family's heavy rural masculinity and Barney's carefully coiffed urban version, but where the former is constructed via physical wage labor, the latter is constructed by artifice. The hangout sitcom certainly paints Marshall the househusband as the aspirational hegemonic ideal to which Barney and Ted aspire; and yet, it also questions the possibility of achieving that hegemonic ideal within a neoliberal framework, not only constructing misogynistic and boorish masculinities as backward, but to a great extent, rural and domesticated masculinities, too.

Caring hegemonic man?

Peter Redman's (2001) research on the links between romantic heterosexuality and middle-class professional masculinity are as important to the househusband as the PMS. He suggests that romance provides school boys "with a route into a new form of masculinity, one that in validating academic prowess and individualism orientated the boys toward a professional and middle-class future" (Redman 2001, 189). It is within these discourses that any discussions about the househusband's hegemony belongs.

Marshall reverts to his romantic self mostly because he believes his time as a "gorilla" denies the internal essence of his identity, rather than because he objects to the morality of misogynistic culture in the office; meanwhile, for Schmidt and Howard, moving from douchebag to househusband involves "greater levels of mutuality, commitment, intensity of emotion, and sexual activity" (Redman 2001, 190). So, if hegemonic masculinity is generally considered a widely dispersed grouping of performances and discourses rather than a single, palpable, idea, then what the househusband suggests is that heterosexuality is best performed romantically. In the hangout sitcom, the type of man all the male characters seem to aspire to is the househusband. The PMS and the douchebag are both in various stages of achieving his position, gaining further narrative rewards the closer they get, and it is when they begin to adopt what those in the field of critical studies on men and masculinities have called "caring masculinities" (Eisen and Yamashita 2019, Elliott 2016, Hughson 2019) marked by romance that they achieve it.

In *New Girl*'s season seven, set three years after season six, when we are reintroduced to the cast, we learn that Schmidt has been on paternity leave since the birth of his and Cece's daughter Ruth. Although he does return to work, we also witness the full completion of his narrative arc – after he gets home from his first day back, Cece asks him how it was, and he replies, "frickin' crushed it", very quickly following that with, "and I think I want to quit. I just kept wishing that I was here, taking care of Ruth. It's the best job I've ever had. What would you think if I was home full-time?" (*New Girl*, "Godparents"). Schmidt's full conversion from womanizing boor to stay-at-home dad is the most marked chrononormative journey, perhaps best exemplifying male heterosexuality in the hangout sitcom, thematically combining time panic, both socioeconomic and emotional insecurity, chrononormativity, romance, and care via two different subject positions. He shows us that despite the wider range of positions made available for men on-screen, thanks to masculine adaptation to neoliberal subjectivity, resulting in an oftentimes ambiguous and contradictory encoding of neoliberal masculinity, sitcom masculinities remain in thrall to a modified nuclear family. Still, it is in the househusband that we find the clearest indication of forms of care that undermine older forms of masculinity. What, though, about Cece? Schmidt can only afford to give up paid work with the financial support of Cece's successful business managing male models – does the hangout sitcom instead present us with female masculinities more successful than their male counterparts?

The limits of heterosexuality

In *Female Masculinities*, Jack Halberstam suggests that the most successful performance of masculinity in James Bond is Judi Dench's iteration of the MI5 boss known only as M. He writes:

masculinity, in this rather actionless film, is primarily prosthetic and, in this and countless other action films, has little if anything to do with biological maleness signified more often as a technical special effect. In *Goldeneye* it is M who most convincingly performs masculinity, and she does so partly by exposing the sham of Bond's own performance.

(Halberstam 1998, 3–4)

Such an analysis opens an intriguing area of inquiry in the hangout sitcom: amid three male subject positions that are all some version of neutered, insecure, uncertain, excessive, what if we can read more successful masculinities in the hangout sitcom from the women? Robin is more ruthless and more grounded than any of the men; Penny's street-smarts pull the clueless nerds out of many scrapes; Cece is Schmidt's physical protector far more often than the other way around; and when Monica and Chandler are trying to pick out a sperm donor to get pregnant, she euphemistically calls her organizing efforts *her* erection (*Friends*, "The One Where Rachel Goes Back to Work"). Certainly, a part of the hangout sitcom is that the female characters often perform gender in a way that "exposes the sham" of the artificiality of neoliberal masculinities. In the *New Girl* storyline of the contest between the two Schmidts, Cece spends the episode attempting to expose the performative nature of each Schmidt's gender performance.

However, female masculinities in the hangout sitcom are also often as performative as the men's: *How I Met Your Mother* goes to great lengths to detail Robin's gendered family background. She is the only child of a father who desperately wanted a son, to the extent that she is actually Robin Scherbatsky Jr., named after her father. Growing up, Robin Sr. forced a whole swathe of masculinized activities on his daughter, indoctrinating her with favorite sports teams and, invoking and parodying Robert Bly and the men's movements' preoccupations with pre-agricultural masculinities, teaching her to be a hunter-gatherer (*How I Met Your Mother*, "Happily Ever After"). Such a troubled relationship with her father places Robin less in the category of exposing the sham of masculinity by a more convincing and less artificial performance of it, as opposed to something that perhaps resembles the douchebag and his troubled father–son relationship. Some of these lessons have stuck, and are why, for example, Robin and Barney have a "bro's night out" in season one, where they both "suit up", smoke cigars and drink Scotch whisky (*How I Met Your Mother*, "Zip, Zip, Zip"), or why Robin's defining arc involves her constantly choosing between career and domestic life.

In fact, women in the hangout sitcom are commonly said to perform postfeminist femininities (Genz 2009, Gill and Scharff 2011, Hamad 2018), which is, like masculinities in the current era, doubly encoded, containing "paradoxes of contemporary femininity that references both traditional narratives of feminine passivity and more progressive scripts of feminine agency" (Genz 2009, 17). Monica's "neo-traditionalism" exemplifies the former, while Robin's masculinized habits exemplify the latter. Often, the women in the sitcom *are* more masculine than their male co-stars, but they are also still bound by the strictures of patriarchal femininities. So, while such postfeminist femininities do indeed prescribe some form of subjective agency to women in ways that family sitcoms may not have done, they do so while largely following neoliberal scripts, remaining in thrall to naturalized notions of chrononormative and patriarchal femininities.

Even on women, then, masculinities in the hangout sitcom remain resolutely heteronormative as they attempt to resolve the tensions between neoliberal and masculine subjectivities. While the postfeminist male singleton fails to conform to either, the douchebag exaggerates both neoliberal and masculine subjectivities. Meanwhile, the househusband comes closest to representing neoliberal hegemonic masculinity, but still does so with a host of contradictions pertaining to neoliberalism's family values.

Masculinities here also remain resolutely middle-class, defined by professionalized careers, and telling the stories of aspirational middle-class white men and women working in law, architecture, science, corporations, and IT. Even when they are not in managerial professions, like Joey in *Friends*, they are insulated by class background (Ewen 2018). Earning money is the good life, and good masculinities are available to those who have aspiration. *New Girl*'s homeless comedy relief character, "outside Dave", sits on the bench outside the gang's apartment and is permanently drunk, incoherent, and lecherous toward women.

Where the family sitcom guarantees men their place as family patriarch, the hangout sitcom offers less certainty, fatherhood both guaranteed and not. It is nearly always the final narrative resolution for most male characters, but this ending is constantly in jeopardy, with its unfulfillment the main panic of most men in these shows. Like neoliberalism, the hangout sitcom refigures the family, replacing it with a closed-off friendship circle (Roseneil and Budgeon 2004), even as it chrononormatively deploys the family's nerve endings (Ludwig 2016, Duggan 2002). The househusband, meanwhile, as the hegemonic man of the hangout sitcom, reveals more explicitly that neoliberal masculinities exist in a tension between holding down an individualized neoliberal job, and being caring enough to produce the affective commitment required by the nuclear family. If it is via care and affection that the hangout sitcom offers its most significant lessons on changed masculinities, what happens when such care moves beyond hetero-relationships, and into homosocial ones?

Filmography

All in the Family. 1971–1979. [TV] Lear, Norman, Creator, CBS: USA.
The Big Bang Theory. 2007–2019. [TV] Lorre, Chuck, and Bill Prady, Creator, CBS: USA.
Bridesmaids. 2011. [Movie] Feig, Paul, Creator, Universal Pictures: USA.
Ghostbusters. 2016. [Movie] Feig, Paul, Creator, Sony Pictures Releasing: USA.

How I Met Your Mother. 2005–2014. [TV] Bays, Carter, and Craig Thomas, Creator, CBS: USA.
New Girl. 2011–2018. [TV] Meriwether, Elizabeth, Creator, Fox: USA.
Young Sheldon. 2017–present. [TV] Lorre, Chuck, and Steven Moralo, Creator, CBS: USA.

References

Allan, Jonathan A. 2020. "Men, Masculinities, and Popular Romance." Edited by John Mercer, and Clarissa Smith, *Masculinity, Sex and Popular Culture* Oxford: Routledge.
Arthur, Erica. 2004. "Where Lester Burnham falls down: Exposing the facade of victimhood in *American Beauty*." *Men and Masculinities* 7 (2):127–143. doi: 10.1177/1097184X03257512.
Bartky, Sandra Lee. 1998. "Foucault, feminization and the modernization of patriarchal power." In *The Politics of Women's Bodies: Sexuality, Appearance and Behaviour*, edited by Rose Weitz, 25–45. Oxford: Oxford University Press.
Becker, Ron. 2014. "Becoming bromosexual: Straight men, gay men, and male bonding on US TV." In *Reading the Bromance: Homosocial Relationships in Film and Television*, edited by Michael DeAngelis, 233–254. Detroit, MI: Wayne State University Press.
Belsey, Catherine. 1994. *Desire: Love Stories in Western Culture.* Oxford: Blackwell.
Brabon, Benjamin A. 2013. "'Chuck Flick': A genealogy of the postfeminist male singleton." In *Postfeminism and Contemporary Hollywood Cinema*, edited by Joel Gwynne, and Nadine Muller, 116–130. Basingstoke: Palgrave Macmillan.
Brabon, Benjamin A. 2007. "The spectral phallus: Re-membering the postfeminist man." In *Postfeminist Gothic: Critical Interventions in Contemporary Culture*, edited by Benjamin A. Brabon, and Stephanie Genz, 56–67. London: Palgrave Macmillan.
Butler, Judith. 1990. *Gender Trouble.* 2nd ed. Oxford: Routledge.
Dean, James Joseph. 2014. *Straights: Heterosexuality in Post-closeted Culture.* London: New York University Press.
Duggan, Lisa. 2002. "The new homonormativity: The sexual politics of neoliberalism." In *Materializing Democracy: Toward a Revitalized Cultural Politics*, edited by Russ Castronovo, and Dana D. Nelson, 175–194. Durham, NC: Duke University Press.
Duncan, Erika. 1983. "The hungry Jewish mother." In *On Being a Jewish Feminist: A Reader*, edited by Susanna Heschel, 27–39. New York: Schocken Books.
Edwards, Derek, and Jonathan Potter. 1992. *Discursive Psychology.* London: Sage.
Eisen, Daniel B., and Liann Yamashita. 2019. "Borrowing from femininity: The caring man, hybrid masculinities, and maintaining male dominance." *Men and Masculinities* 22 (5):801–820. doi: 10.1177/1097184X17728552.
Elliott, Karla. 2016. "Caring masculinities: Theorizing an emerging concepts." *Men and Masculinities* 19 (3):24–259. doi: 10.1177/1097184X15576203.
Ewen, Neil. 2018. "'If I don't input those numbers… it doesn't make much of a difference': Insulated precarity and gendered labor in *Friends*." *Television & New Media* 19 (8):724–740. doi: 10.1177/1527476418778425.
Fiske, John. 2010. *Television Culture.* 2nd ed. Oxford: Routledge.

Freeman, Elizabeth. 2010. *Time Binds: Queer Temporalities, Queer Histories*. Edited by Jack Halberstam, and Lisa Lowe, *Perverse Modernities*. Durham: Duke University Press.
Frye, Northrop. 1996–2012. *Collected Works of Northrop Frye*. Toronto: University of Toronto Press.
Funnell, Lisa. 2018. "Reworking the Bond girl concept in the Craig era." *Journal of Popular Film and Television* 46 (1):11–21. doi: 10.1080/01956051.2018.1423205.
Garlick, Steve. 2020. "The nature of markets: On the affinity between masculinity and (neo)liberalism." *Journal of Cultural Economy* 13 (5):548–560. doi: 10.1080/17530350.2020.1741017.
Genz, Stephanie. 2009. *Postfemininities in Popular Culture*. Basingstoke: Palgrave Macmillan.
Gill, Rosalind, and Christina Scharff, eds. 2011. *New Femininities: Postfeminism, Neoliberalism and Subjectivity*. Basingstoke: Palgrave Macmillan.
Graeber, David. 2018. *Bullshit Jobs: A Theory*. London: Allen Lane.
Gullage, Amy. 2014. "Fat Monica, fat suits, and *Friends*." *Feminist Media Studies* 14 (2):178–189. doi: 10.1080/14680777.2012.724026.
Hakim, Jamie. 2020. *Work That Body: Male Bodies in Digital Culture*. London: Rowman & Littlefield.
Halberstam, Jack. 1998. *Female Masculinity*. London: Duke University Press.
Hamad, Hannah. 2018. "The One With The Feminist Critique: Revisiting millenial postfeminism with *Friends*." *Television & New Media* 19 (8):692–707. doi: 10.1177/1527476418779624.
Hughson, Marina. 2019. "Caring men and masculinities on the Balkan semiperiphery: Transformation through hybridisation and contradictions." *Teorija in Praksa* 56 (4):1001–1016.
Leggott, James, Julie Anna Taddeo, and Katherine Byrne, eds. 2018. *Conflicting Masculinities: Men in Television Period Drama*. Oxford: Bloomsbury.
Lewis, Jen. 2013. "Which 'friends' character are you?" BuzzFeed. https://www.buzzfeed.com/jenlewis/which-friends-character-are-you. Accessed 21 July 2022.
Lotz, Amanda D. 2014. *Cable Guys: Television and Masculinities in the 21st Century*. New York: NYU Press.
Ludwig, Gundula. 2016. "Desiring neoliberalism." *Sexuality Research and Social Policy* 13 (3):417–427. doi: 10.1007/s13178-016-0257-6.
Neale, Steve. 1983. "Masculinity as spectacle." *Screen* 24 (6):2–17. doi: 10.1093/screen/24.6.2.
Negra, Diane. 2006. "Where the boys are: Postfeminism and the new single man." FLOW.tv. http://www.flowjournal.org/2006/04/wedding-crashers-failure-to-launch-feminism-postfeminism-masculinity/. Accessed 7 September.
Pellegrini, Chiara. 2022. "Anticipating the plot: Overdetermining heteronormative destiny on the twenty-first century screen." *Textual Practice* [online]:1–23. doi: 10.1080/0950236X.2022.2043932.
Potter, Jonathan, and Derek Edwards. 1993. "Discursive social psychology." In *The New Handbook of Language and Social Psychology*, edited by Peter Robinson, and Howard Giles, 103–118. London: Wiley.
Redman, Peter. 2001. "The discipline of love: Negotiation and regulation in boys' performance of a romance-based heterosexual masculinity." *Men and Masculinities* 4 (2):186–200. doi: 10.1177/1097184X01004002006.

Roseneil, Sasha, and Shelley Budgeon. 2004. "Cultures of intimacy and care beyond 'the family': Personal life and social change in the early 21st century." *Current Sociology* 52 (2):135–159. doi: 10.1177/0011392104041798.

Rubin, Gayle. 1975. "The traffic in women: Notes on the political economy of sex." In *Toward and Anthropology of Women*, edited by R. Rayna, 157–210. New York: Monthly Review Press.

Salter, Anastasia, and Bridget Blodgett. 2017. *Toxic Geek Masculinity in Media: Sexism, Trolling, and Identity Politics*. London: Palgrave Macmillan.

Stenbacka, Susanna. 2011. "Othering the rural: About the construction of rural masculinities and the unspoken urban hegemonic ideal in Swedish media." *Journal of Rural Studies* 27 (1):235–244. doi: 10.1016/J.JRURSTUD.2011.05.006.

Stratton, Jon. 2016. "Die Sheldon die: The Big Bang Theory, everyday neoliberalism and Sheldon as neoliberal man." *Journal for Cultural Research* 20 (2):171–188. doi: 10.1080/14797585.2015.1123515.

Thompson, Lauren Jade. 2015. "Nothing suits me like a suit: Performing masculinity in *How I Met Your Mother*." *Critical Studies in Television* 10 (2):21–36. doi: 10.7227/CST.10.2.3.

"Which Friends character are you." 2015. Brainfall. https://brainfall.com/quizzes/which-friends-character-are-you/. Accessed 21 July.

"Which Friends character are you?" 2015. Heart. https://www.heart.co.uk/lifestyle/which-friends-character-are-you/. Accessed 21 July.

Young, Iris Marion. 2005. *On female experience: Throwing like a girl and other essays*. Edited by Cheshire Calhoun, *Studies in Feminist Philosophy*. Oxford: Oxford University Press.

4 Bromantic comedy

Male homosociality, heterosexuality, and relationships

"I love that guy".
Matt LeBlanc, responding to questions about
Matthew Perry on a press tour in 2016 (Yandoli 2016)

Bromance, men's friendships, and neoliberal affects

Todd Migliaccio (2010, 227) argues that "when men interact with friends, they are 'doing masculinity'" – rather than gender shaping what friendships look like, it is in friendship that gender is performed and achieved. Within this framework, he cites two principles by which male friendships construct masculinities. The first, a matter of how friendship is achieved, follows Scott Swain's (1989) conception of "closeness in the doing", sharing activity to sustain intimacy, rather than the use of expression or self-disclosure. The second, concerned with telos, argues that male friendships are largely instrumental, defined by transaction and use-value rather than as ends in themselves. However, if Migliaccio is right that doing friendship is doing gender, it is perhaps in homosocial men's friendships that we are seeing some of the most significant shifts in performances of masculinities. A flurry of recent research output has indicated that men's friendships have become significantly more expressive, at least among certain demographics (Robinson et al. 2017, Scoats and Robinson 2020, Goedecke 2018, McQueen 2017),[1] resulting in ongoing questions about general developments in men's senses of emotionality (Reeser and Gottzén 2018, de Boise and Hearn 2017).

There is an attendant sense, Amanda Lotz (2014, 6) suggests in her own study of the "bromance", of "'something going on' with the male characters and depictions of masculinity" in popular media, films, and TV shows, too. Scholars have, for a while now, been interested in such male friendships, ones with strikingly intimate dimensions, unafraid of accusations of emasculation or homophobic boundary policing, as they appear in scripted television and movies (Brabon 2013, DeAngelis 2014b, Alberti 2013). They tend to get called "bromances", a portmanteau of the heterosexualized "bro" and the feminized notion of "romance". Lotz (2014, 146) suggests that they "push boundaries of homosocial masculinities in these friendships", and mark a

DOI: 10.4324/9781003363538-4

shift away from homoerotic subtext toward explicit homoerotic text. She cites, for example, *Scrubs* (2001–2010), a workplace sitcom heavily influenced by *Friends* (1994–2004), in which two of the main characters, JD and Turk, famously declare their "guy love" for each other in song (*Scrubs*, "My Musical"). Yet, as Lotz points out, in the same song, the characters protect against gay anxieties with lines such as "it's like I married my best friend, but in a totally manly way".

Here, the limits and contradictions of the bromance are demonstrated, a concept which is anyway paradoxical, as Michael DeAngelis (2014b, 1) points out: "bromance involves something that must happen (the demonstration of intimacy itself) on the condition that other things do not happen (the avowal or expression of sexual desire between straight men)". DeAngelis's (2014b) edited volume contains a variety of essays about the bromance on-screen that tend toward this conclusion: that the homoerotic textual elements of male intimacy on-screen appear continually limited, even while occasionally representing potentialities for the disruption of heteronormativity (particularly DeAngelis 2014a).

The hangout sitcom bromance

All four shows in this book feature close homosocial male friendships that are at least as central to the show as any given heterosexual coupling. These friendships – these "bromances" – construct, à la Migliaccio (2010), the hangout sitcom's masculinities in different ways over a 20-year period. Despite the limits of the word "bromance", the sense of "something going on" in such an apparently clear fashion – collective care, queer-presenting affection, and textual homoeroticism – is not what one might expect from the hangout sitcom considering how, so far, the book has explored how its masculinities teeter between a neoliberal feminizing compulsion and a continuing complicity from performing masculinity.

As I argued in Chapter 2, the hangout sitcom represents a dominant mode of affective collective belonging in a neoliberal moment that is characterized by a lack of long-lasting bonds or intimacies (Anderson 2016, Illouz 2007); the nuclear family here has its hegemony challenged (Roseneil and Budgeon 2004, Brecher 2012). Instead, young groups of attractive twentysomethings in the hangout sitcom have rather different relationships with one another than those within the family. For homosocial male bonding, this would appear to produce a dilemma: do you write male friendship that remains in thrall to fears of emasculation and homophobic policing and to "closeness in the doing", or do you write ones loving and supporting enough to appear to provide sanctuary from the alienation of neoliberal work? This dilemma, however, is paid little heed by the hangout sitcom's male friendships, which, certainly by the broadcast of *New Girl* in 2012, unashamedly construct homosocial cultures of non-sexual, though often homoerotic, male love.

With the bromance so key to the hangout sitcom throughout, this chapter argues that it is in homosocial friendship, rather than heterosexuality, that the hangout sitcom offers its most ambiguous and hopeful portrayals of masculinity, ones that can be convincingly read as, if not substantive changes to masculinity, then at least moments of fluctuation, despite a range of limitations relating particularly to class and race. In constructing friendships and bonds between like-minded young people in response to neoliberalism's complex family politics, the hangout sitcom inadvertently, and over time, challenges existing hegemonic discourses surrounding homosocial male friendships.

Standalone narratives and relationship maintenance

In the last few decades of sociological inquiry, scholars have turned attention to affect in new ways, bringing suggestions of a sociological "affective turn", following other "turns" such as the linguistic and the cultural. Patricia Clough (2007, ix) identifies this affective turn in two linked phenomena: "the focus on the body, which has been most extensively advanced in feminist theory, and the exploration of emotions, conducted predominantly in queer theory".

This chapter focuses on the latter, examining one homosocial friendship from each show, via a narrative analysis of a particular storyline concerned with each male pairing, contextualized by the backgrounds of each couple. Throughout, I consider the possibilities of queer readings and the ways in which viewers decode individual moments, lines, and character traits with rather different ideas than perhaps the writers intended. These pairings are outlined in Table 4.1.

The narratives were chosen as ones that featured "relationship maintenance" between the friends, a concept Lotz (2014, 150) also uses to analyze the bromance, and one that is regularly used by psychologists. For this chapter, relationship maintenance refers to moments of threat or jeopardy to the dyadic relationship that are narratively resolved by communication, bonding, or joint reflection. Here, it is worth again reflecting on the sitcom as a genre, which is that of piecemeal narratives that discursively address surrounding social and intimate dilemmas. For the bromance or homosocial male friendship, relationship maintenance is how the narrative is resolved; the narrative of each episode here begins with stable homosocial friendship (of some form or other), which is disrupted by outside events that are indicative of wider cultural social discourses and resolved by some form of maintenance.

The aim of this chapter, then, is to identify and characterize the initial stability, the moment of disruption, and the way in which the relationship is maintained or transformed, and in so doing, identify the discourses relating to men, masculinities, and neoliberalism. I have selected four standalone "narratives" – with the emphasis on narrative as classically defined and clearly identifiable, rather than individual episodes per se. In *Friends*, for example, relationship maintenance between Joey and Chandler is not all that

92 *Bromance, homosociality, heterosexuality, and relationships*

Table 4.1 The four bromances and narratives selected.

Show	Couple	Background	Narrative/episode
Friends	Joey and Chandler	Joey responded to Chandler's advert looking for a roommate.	From "The One Where Joey Moves Out" to "The One where Eddie Won't Go" from season two, 1996 – Joey, having moved out two episodes prior, finds himself bankrupt and wants to move back in with Chandler, but Chandler cannot evict his new flatmate, Eddie.
How I Met Your Mother	Ted and Marshall	Roommates since college.	"Duel Citizenship" from season five, 2009 – after finding out that a pizza place he and Marshall used to go is closing down, Ted proposes a road trip for the two of them, except Marshall invites Lily.
The Big Bang Theory	Leonard and Sheldon	Leonard answered Sheldon's advert looking for a roommate.	"The Friendship Contraction" from season five, 2012 – Sheldon's antics become too much for Leonard, and the two break off their binding friendship contract.
New Girl	Schmidt and Nick	Roommates since college.	"Road Trip" in season five, 2016 – after feeling emasculated, Schmidt organizes a typically manly bachelor party.

common, so that the narrative selected for *Friends* covers four episodes from season two, while the other three shows all consist of one narrative confined to one episode.

Roommates, opposites, and queer road trips

The analysis in this chapter drew out several thematic continuities between bromances, some of which apply across bromances, despite not being part of the selection criteria – much of this can be seen in Table 4.1.

The ways in which each meet and know each other, in every instance, is that they share an apartment or college dormitory – not that they grew up together, or that they shared a house, but specifically that they share the domestic space of an apartment. In *How I Met Your Mother* and *New Girl*, it begins at college, and in *Friends* and *The Big Bang Theory*, one of the two responds to a roommate advert from the other. Homosocial male friendships in the family sitcom were not part of the domestic space, but most often in the workplace – Ward Cleaver's friend Fred Rutherford was a workmate, just like Archie Bunker's friend Stretch Cunningham. Yet, there is some indication of continuity here, too, in the shift from workplace to university or college dormitories, reflecting wider patterns of professionalization and human capital among post-1980 generations in the Global North (Harris 2017). Such dorm rooms blurring hard and fast public and private spheres, the location of male intimacy does not always adhere to strict rules in the hangout sitcom, often intertextually referencing family sitcoms by producing dialogue between male characters that would not look out of place were it written for Ward and June Cleaver.

In the hangout sitcom bromance, opposites attract. Though all the characters here are straight white men, within this framework their family backgrounds often could not be much more dissimilar in terms of class, geography, and parenting. Much of this seems to reflect a heteronormative framework, as the ways in which the differences manifest are constructed along gendered lines: Chandler's mistaken sexual identity against Joey's uber-heterosexuality, or Schmidt's domestic cleanliness opposite Nick's slovenliness. However, these do not always adhere to the same side, such that while Joey takes the "masculine" side on sexuality, his preoccupation with grooming and appearance places him aesthetically on the feminine side in comparison to Chandler's relative lack of care.

By chance, two of the episodes chosen here, from *How I Met Your Mother* and *New Girl*, are road trip episodes that reference the road movie genre, and I read them as instances of that genre as well as the hangout sitcom genre. The road movie is an important part of the American cultural imaginary when it comes to masculinity, associated with a kind of frontier masculinity of mobility and discovery (Cohan and Hark 1997) that emerges from and intertextually references the Western (Roberts 1997), and harks back to the country's roots as a diversity of colonial settlements. It is also a genre that has tended to follow two masculinized heterosexual men faced by a series of obstacles as they address their friendship. It is, in short, a genre about male homosociality, with, according to most readings, more than its fair share of underlying homoeroticism – a homoeroticism that has in more recent years been made more textual than subtextual (Lang 1997).

Like the road movie, though, the most interesting and relevant finding of this chapter is how, between 1994 and 2018, the hangout sitcom bromance becomes more textually queer, more expressive, and more critical of instrumental friendship. *How I Met Your Mother* and *New Girl* in particular revel far more in making explicit any queer subtext and bringing to the forefront relationship maintenance. Chandler and Joey's friendship in *Friends* deploys an outward appearance of instrumentality, of being roommates before friends, and of "closeness in the doing", with the nature of those "doings" often masculinized, with elements of love and care that begin to challenge typical male friendships. By *New Girl*'s release, however, the hangout sitcom's bromance is openly critical of "closeness in the doing", and the narrative explored here appears a direct critique of this via affective expressiveness. This gradual change is made possible by neoliberalism's affective contradictions, but offers a potential radical reading that uses bromance to upset some elements of existing masculinities.

Chandler and Joey

Ross and Chandler's friendship predates Joey and Chandler's – while the former friendship was forged when the two were roommates at college, Joey moved into Chandler's apartment after responding to an advert several years prior to the show's beginning (*Friends*, "The One With the Flashback"). Their friendship is defined by a constant anxiety about their sexualities, manifesting in countless jokes where either Chandler or the two of them together have their sexuality misread as gay – Joey for instance, upon viewing Chandler's apartment in his roommate search, reads Chandler as gay, telling him, "don't worry, I'm okay with the gay thing". In general, I agree with Ron Becker (2014, 236) that "these narratives negotiated growing anxieties about the legibility of sexual identity and the pitfalls of male homosociality at a time when widespread gay visibility and the social acceptance of homosexuality were relatively new". As such, Chandler and Joey's "bromance" is far less explicitly "bromantic" than any of the other couples explored, with more management of heteronormative expectations for them than for other friendships. In the same episode as we see this mistaken sexual identity, the backbone of their friendship is quickly established as a platonic homosocial one when Chandler walks in on Joey in the living room watching *Baywatch* (1989–1999) and is mesmerized by the sight of Nicole Eggert and Pamela Anderson in bikinis. The dilemma between a supportive friendship that offers bonds and affective belonging, and the strictures of masculine behavior, is very carefully trodden in *Friends*, a stark difference with subsequent hangout sitcoms. I argue, as Hannah Hamad (2018, 702) suggests, that

> the ironic mode through which this remediation takes place, and Chandler's ultimate refusal of Joey's embrace, evinces ambivalent anxiety about the potential challenge to the hegemony of normative masculinity posed by their intimacy, and which is distilled into his curt refusal of it on becoming conscious of the frequency of its recurrence.

This means that relationship maintenance is less verbalized or obvious between Chandler and Joey, which makes it more difficult to identify a significant episode or narrative.

The One Where Eddie Won't Go

The narrative string of episodes chosen, therefore, accounts for the importance of shared domestic space to Chandler and Joey's relationship, mostly acknowledged via intertextual references to family sitcoms while protecting against accusations of homosexuality by giving them dialogue that imitate an old, bickering, married couple. In "The One Where Eddie Won't Go", there is little to no relationship maintenance until the episode's coda, which is the resolution to a narrative that begins four episodes earlier in "The One Where Joey Moves Out". The two of them attend a party hosted by one of Joey's slightly more successful co-stars, where they both express a liking of the co-star's apartment. When Joey finds out his co-star is moving out soon, he suggests Joey should move in. This leads to an argument between Chandler and Joey that reads, as above, as if it were between a married couple in a family sitcom.

Joey: Can we drop this? I am not interested in the guy's apartment.
Chandler: Oh please, I saw the way you were checking out his moldings. You want it.
Joey: Why would I want another apartment, huh? I've already got an apartment that I love.
Chandler: Well, it wouldn't kill you to say it once in a while.
Joey: Alright, you want the truth? I'm thinkin' about it.
Chandler: What?
Joey: I'm sorry. I'm 28 years old, I've never lived alone, and I'm finally at a place where I've got enough money that I don't need a roommate anymore.
Chandler: Woah, woah, woah. I don't need a roommate either, OK? I can afford to live here by myself.

Chandler's accusation that Joey is "checking out" the co-star's moldings assigns Chandler a feminized expressive "wife" role in the relationship, further underpinned by his complaint that "it wouldn't kill you to say it once in a while", a clear reference toward an expression of love. The potential for male homosocial love here is therefore undermined not once, but three times over – first by the refusal to directly acknowledge it, and then by heteronormatively assigning one male character the expressive role, which in turn is enabled by the marked absurdity and laugh track demonstrating how ridiculous it might be for a male character to express love for another male character.

Yet, the episode does also then hint at real intimacy between the two of them. In the final scene, the two are unable to express that they will miss one another, and after an exchange where Joey says "I don't know when I'm gonna see you again", and tells Chandler to "take care", Joey walks out of the apartment, then after several seconds walks back in, and hugs Chandler from behind hard for several seconds, while Chandler smiles, and Joey rushes straight back out, leaving Chandler to survey the now empty flat. This largely wordless, but nevertheless affecting, exchange suggests to audiences a deep and real friendship, but at the same time is preceded by a constant undermining of close homosocial male friendship by earmarking it as absurd, through a contrast with the heterosexual couples of family sitcoms. Queer subtext remains subtext – readable, but still marked as othered.

The next episode, "The One Where Eddie Moves In", starts with a scene that, in isolation, presents the possibility of a subversive reading. In a pastiche of a 1990s chick flick, Chandler hovers over the phone, wondering aloud if he should call Joey. Eventually he does, and after skirting around their feelings, they watch *Baywatch* on the phone together, gossiping about it like a masculinized soap opera, presenting two diametric cultural gendered reference points. It is possible to read this scene in isolation as drawing an equivalence between the campy excess of *Baywatch*'s male gaze and the chick flick, thus highlighting the performative and iterative nature of gender. But in the context of an episode that rejects several opportunities for the characters to express affection for one another, such a reading is difficult to justify.

When Chandler finds a new roommate named Eddie at a supermarket, a well-groomed man with an Italian American New York accent and an obvious resemblance to Joey, he is described later by Rachel as a "rebound roommate", suggesting there is something gay about close male friendship. Similarly, when returning to Chandler and Eddie's apartment to "pick up his mail", he enters as Eddie serves Chandler some "eggs a la Eddie", which Joey notices do not match the way he had previously cooked eggs for Chandler, Joey takes umbrage. When Chandler insists that he likes "both eggs equally", and Joey scoffs, saying "nobody likes two different kinds of eggs equally – you like one better than the other, and I wanna know which", what is nominally about eggs is about with whom they want to share a domestic space. In short, affection comes in metaphors and indirect hints only. After Eddie's habits begin to irritate Chandler, in the final, humorous, scene of the episode, the song "All by Myself" by Eric Carmen plays, with a montage that moves between the two of them watching *Baywatch* alone, staring longingly at the empty chair beside them, then Chandler playing foosball by himself, and Joey playing ping-pong by himself, and finally the two of them staring longingly out of their separate flat windows as it rains.

There are reprieves in *Friends*, though, moments in which Chandler and Joey move beyond "closeness in the doing" and show affection for its own sake. When Joey's character on *Days of Our Lives* is killed off in the following episode, and Chandler is at Joey's apartment with the other friends, Chandler tells him, "It's gonna be okay, you know that?" (*Friends*, "The One Where Dr. Ramoray Dies"). Further, by the next episode, "The One Where Eddie Won't Go", Chandler and Joey's tender moment appears to have repaired their relationship. Yet, *Friends* chooses to articulate this by contrasting Joey and Chandler's friendship with the less bromantic relationship between Joey and Ross. When the latter assists Joey in looking over his finances, a role usually fulfilled by Chandler, he offers little to no comfort as opposed to realism and harsh words. When Ross returns to apologize, his pep talk is characterized by too much obvious effort and falls flat, even

Bromance, homosociality, heterosexuality, and relationships 97

if it appears well-intentioned. The episode thereby highlights significant differences between a supportive and loving domestic relationship and a more standard dyadic public one, but it does so in a way that means the characters do as little as possible to directly acknowledge this.

Back at Chandler's apartment, Eddie has not gone, and Chandler comes home from work to find Eddie has still not moved out. The narrative is resolved when Eddie attempts to unlock the apartment, only to find that Chandler has changed the locks. When he knocks, Chandler pretends like Eddie has never lived at the apartment, instead introducing him to his roommate Joey, who coolly reveals himself by an armchair swivel to audience cheers and applause. Eddie very quickly accepts that he never lived there. The door closes, and then this exchange unfolds:

Chandler: So you want me to help you unpack your stuff?
Joey: Nah. Nah, I'm ok. Oh and uh, just so you know, I'm not movin' back in 'cause I have to. Well, I mean, I do have to. It's just that that place wasn't really, I mean, this is …
Chandler: Welcome home man. [As they hug and jump around, the audience applaud and cheer.]
Joey: A little foos[ball]?
Chandler: Absolutely.

Season six clip show episode "The One with Mac and C.H.E.E.S.E." features a montage of Joey and Chandler's hugs that, as above, demonstrates

Figure 4.1 Joey's largely one-sided hug protects against queer subtext bubbling too close to the surface.

98 *Bromance, homosociality, heterosexuality, and relationships*

anxiety about actual closeness as opposed to closeness in the doing. Above, Chandler cuts Joey off to prevent any verbalized affection, and Joey follows suit as the two revel in their "closeness in the doing" via the foosball table. The clip show episode, meanwhile, documents Chandler's habit of rejecting physical affection from his friend. This model of presenting the opportunity for affection only for the characters to reject it serves as a template for Ted and Marshall.

Ted and Marshall

Following the recurring theme, Ted and Marshall's backgrounds are dissimilar – a middle-class urban only child from upper New York state, and a rural youngest of four boys perhaps less well-moneyed from Minnesota, each of them occupying an expressive role in different scenarios. These different backgrounds are reflected in their relationship when the two meet at college as roommates (*How I Met Your Mother*, "How I Met Everyone Else"), Marshall describing Ted as "a little bit pretentious", and Ted describing Marshall as "a total slob" (*How I Met Your Mother*, "Arrivederci, Fiero"). They overcome their differences on a lengthy road trip, the premise of which is that Marshall has offered to drop Ted home from college while driving back home himself, but the trip is waylaid by a snowstorm. The ensuing peril brings the two close such that, as Ted states, "that trip is when Marshall and I became best friends".

There is a silliness that distinguishes Ted and Marshall's relationship from Joey and Chandler's. While the *Friends* bromance occasionally abandons a masculine barrier to excitement and fun, when together, Ted and Marshall almost regress to childhood – their favorite song is not a rock and roll anthem, but "500 Miles" by The Proclaimers; indicating at some early signs of the mainstreaming of geek masculinities, they both love the *Star Wars* franchise; and, importantly, they frequently cry and hug when expressing their feelings for one another. This explicit emotionality begins to mark a break with homosociality in *Friends*, coming alongside references to them being "married" – not "like" they are married, but the characters saying they *are* married.

Duel Citizenship

Season 5's "Duel Citizenship" begins with Ted entering MacLaren's and announcing to Marshall that "Gazzola's is closing". Queried by Robin, Ted responds that Gazzola's is "a filthy mecca of spectacular if undercooked pizza located at 316 Kinzie Street, Chicago, Illinois". Marshall adds: "Back in college, Ted and I used to take these crazy road trips from Connecticut all the way to Chicago just for a Gazzola's pizza", and then speculates "those Gazzola trips, that's … that's when we really became bros". Without much hesitation, and despite describing the trips as "brutal" and unpleasant, they very quickly decide they are going to leave at 9am the next day to drive to Gazzola's. Here the status quo is established, an instrumental male friendship, built on shared activities described in masculinized terms.

The next morning, prior to leaving, Ted enthuses to Barney, telling him, "I am so psyched! Marshall and I haven't done something, just the two of us, for so long. Ever since he got married, he's turned from an I to a we". We are shown a flashback to support Ted's concern, a phone call from Ted where Marshall's use of the first-person plural while gazing lovingly at Lily only get more bizarre, finishing with "we no longer have a hemorrhoid problem", forewarning of the narrative disruption. Marshall enters the room, and the two share some excitement before Lily enters declaring, "all right, let's hit the road!". Ted, obviously disappointed, asks Marshall "you invited Lily?", to which he responds, "we most certainly did!". The rest of the episode unfolds as Ted grows increasingly impatient with Lily acting as what he sees as an interloper in his and Marshall's friendship, while Marshall tries to continually ensure that relations between the three of them remain positive.

Read as a road movie, "Duel Citizenship" demonstrates that male friendships are at least as central to the thrust of *How I Met Your Mother* as are heterosexual relationships. As Robin Wood (2003, 228) observes, in buddy movies, of which the road movie is a form, "the emotional center, the emotional charge, is in the male/male relationship, which is patently what the films are *about*". Lily's role here is therefore as an interloper and disrupter who tries to impose domestic feminine home life onto a public masculine road trip. Femininity remains unwelcome in the public space of the road trip. However, while the public/private divide remains explicitly gendered, the substance of the public sphere undergoes a significant change here, disrupted by the caring bonds of Ted and Marshall's friendship throughout.

The three of them – Ted, Marshall, and Lily – enter the car, and at first Ted tries to hide his disappointment, but soon struggles when Lily reveals a rather large 2–3-liter bottle of water and saying, "I just pee a lot. You'll see!" After Marshall attempts to reassure him, "don't worry, we'll get out on the road, it'll be just like old times", future Ted's voiceover responds, "it wasn't". A series of flashbacks contrasting past fun-filled trips to Gazzola's and the present toilet-trip-filled one follow. In the first, Ted and Marshall are driving to Gazzola's, dressed in era- and age-appropriate clothing, happily singing "500 Miles" by The Proclaimers; in the present day, the three sit in silence, and Lily happily offers Ted a sugar-snap pea from a large bag of them, which reminds her that she "has to pee" – this is contrasted with the masculinized meaty beef jerky the two used to snack on while driving to Gazzola's. In the past, Marshall drives as Ted covers his eyes, instructing him where to drive, while the two giggle excitedly; in the present, Ted naps, Marshall drives, and Lily sees a yellow car, which triggers her to punch Ted, and request another toilet break. In the past, Ted drives topless while Marshall sips fizzy drinks at a toll gate; in the present, Lily returns to the car

100 *Bromance, homosociality, heterosexuality, and relationships*

Figure 4.2 The contrast between the old road trips (above) and the new road trip (below) emphasizes the importance that *How I Met Your Mother* puts on male homosocial affect.

with a shopping bag, and offers to put music on – Ted suggests nerdy comic duo the Jerky Boys, but instead Lily puts on an audiobook called "Goodbye Sparky", narrated by Kenny Rogers, about a "boy and his dog".

It is difficult to read "Goodbye Sparky" as anything other than a reference to John Grogan's autobiographical book, *Marley & Me: Life and Love with the World's Worst Dog* (Grogan 2005), released two years prior to this episode, and later made into a feature film with A-listers Owen Wilson and, coincidentally, Jennifer Aniston (2008). It tells the story of a beloved family dog who dies at the end of the book, much like "Goodbye Sparky". The intense emotional bond between dog and owner represented in each is initially scoffed at by Ted, irritated by Lily's, and femininity's, interloping. After the show cuts to the end of "disk seven" of "Goodbye Sparky", future Ted declares "it was the worst trip ever, but then it got worse". The three of them check into a hotel, which they are told has "catered to couples" since they opened in 1881. Ted is, currently, single – unfit, as we quickly see, for the couple's activities, such as the cornmeal body scrub spa treatment.

That evening, Ted goes to Marshall and Lily's room and convinces Marshall to join him for a "light beer". Once on the road, though, Ted, determined to get his friend back from this romantic interloper, essentially kidnaps Marshall to drive to Chicago. Marshall, initially distressed, thinks he will be unable to "have some fun", as Ted suggests, telling him "I just abandoned my wife. How am I supposed to have fun?". The next shot, we are told four minutes later, is the two of them gleefully singing "500 Miles", as they did on past trips to Gazzola's, Marshall apparently having forgotten his anxieties, declaring "if she's pissed, she's pissed!".

Finally at Gazzola's, Marshall still in his spa bathrobe, and enjoying their "rubbery" pizza, the chef informs them that the secret ingredient in the crust is cornmeal, reminding Marshall of the cornmeal body scrub they seem to have shared, and to suddenly pine for Lily. After Marshall accuses Ted of being entirely to blame for his abandoning Lily, the following exchange ensues:

Marshall: We were having a perfectly nice trip, and then you kidnapped me. You didn't even let me put on underwear!
Ted: We never used to put on underwear! That was the fun of a bro's trip to Gazzola's! We left everything, and everyone behind. It was just you and me! But now it's like you've disappeared into Lily.
Marshall: That is not true.
Ted: It is true. You're not upset because you're worried she's mad. You're upset because you'd rather be with her, eating muffins than here with me, eating this delicious— I think one of my mushrooms just crawled away.
Marshall: Well, you know what? That mushroom's not the only thing that's leaving. Car keys, please.

The old married couple gag that we might expect from Joey and Chandler has gone – Ted and Marshall confront their feelings for one another by talking about them, a far cry from what Chandler and Joey are ever willing to do, and something we only see in *Friends* between heterosexual couples. Perhaps this exchange is dogged by the fact that the argument is over a woman interloping in their space, and the fact that Marshall, the househusband who defends the invasion of femininity, is sat in what might be reasonably called an emasculating bathrobe that does not quite cover his knees, a visual gag about how ridiculous the tall man looks in the too-short, feminized clothing. However, it still does not suffer from the same undercutting as the bromance in *Friends*; Marshall and Ted's love for one another is not the subject of innuendo, and nor is it the object of ridicule. As the next scene unfolds, their emotions are directly acknowledged.

Driving back toward the hotel, the two initially sit in silence listening to the end of "Goodbye Sparky", which quickly emerges as a parable for Ted and Marshall's relationship. Sparky's owner recounts how the dog began to feel left out after he got married, and laments that he never let Sparky know that he had room in his heart for both his wife and his dog before the dog was run over by a car. This leads them each to both recognize the other's hurt feelings, and repair the obvious bromance with a short but affecting exchange.

Marshall: I'm sorry, Ted!
Ted: I'm sorry! No, I'm sorry. I never should have been mad at you!
Marshall: No, I never should have brought Lily. She pees all the time, even at the apartment. Still bros?
Ted: Best bros. Hey, you want to crank some Van Halen just like old times?
Marshall: Hells, yeah!
Ted: Or listen to the Sparky book again?
Marshall: Let's listen to the Sparky book again!

In the end, the public/private divide is upheld as Marshall opines, to no objection, that he "never should have brought Lily", yet this narrative resolution also transforms the public space at the beginning of the episode from one that is "brutal" to one in which directly acknowledged homosocial love can thrive – indeed, it is one where "Goodbye Sparky" occupies a more hallowed position than the rock music of Van Halen. This is a bromance in the limiting sense of the term, as the two agree to continue to be "bros", not "friends" or another similar term. It is not a bromance, as Michael DeAngelis (2014a) suggests of the main characters in *Superbad*, that we can reasonably say offers the notion of a queer future, as we know that both of them are hurtling toward an unrelentingly heteronormative future. It would also be difficult to claim that Ted and Marshall offer a bromance with a remotely queer present. Yet, the resolution of their friendship here does not restore the masculinized status quo that was offered at the beginning of the episode, despite the retention of public and private spheres, instead offering a modified one that presents some ambiguity about a contemporary blurring of public and private spheres.

Leonard and Sheldon

Leonard and Sheldon have almost identical lives; they are nerds who enjoy comics and science fiction, and both work in the physics department at the California Institute of Technology. Yet, like the other friendships in this chapter, the two men are in their upbringings quite different – whereas the former's family did not just support, but actively pushed and pushed, his academic endeavors, the latter's either did not understand or care.

Prior to the show beginning, Leonard gets a job at Caltech, where Sheldon already works, and, seeking somewhere to live, responds to an advert by Sheldon looking for a roommate. When he arrives, he is subjected to a series of tests on his scientific knowledge, opinions on sci-fi characters, and importantly his practical suitability as a roommate (*The Big Bang Theory*, "The Staircase

Implementation"). The last of these tests is the most grueling, as Leonard becomes familiar with Sheldon's obsessive idiosyncrasies – having the same spot on the sofa, his compulsive refusal to try a different take-out restaurant than the one he knows he likes, and, of course, the roommate/friendship contract.

The contract is particular to *The Big Bang Theory*, and to Sheldon and Leonard's friendship, a codification of homosocial relations that eliminate any form of affect or emotion from it. I argue that the roommate contract offers two equally viable but contradictory readings of male friendship in a neoliberal moment; it either reflects and reproduces a form of male homosociality sapped of affect and emotionality, or it offers a critical commentary on the instrumentality of male homosociality. This, I argue, is because of the liminal space between hegemony and subordination occupied by the nerd masculinities in the show. In examining neoliberal and masculine affects through the prism of nerd masculinities, then, bromance in *The Big Bang Theory* leaves an ambiguous set of meanings.

The Friendship Contraction

Season five episode "The Friendship Contraction" begins with Sheldon entering a sleeping Leonard's bedroom wearing a hard hat and high visibility jacket, loudly sounding a klaxon on his phone. Startled awake, Leonard bolts up, screams and exclaims "what the hell!?". Sheldon responds, business-like, "emergency preparedness drill", which, "once a quarter", he says, is part of their roommate agreement. He informs Leonard that this drill will imitate a statewide earthquake, and as Leonard reluctantly but voluntarily rouses, Sheldon pushes him on the floor, shouting "hypothetical aftershock!".

The next morning in their work cafeteria, Sheldon offers Leonard feedback: "Readiness: unsatisfactory. Follows direction: barely. Attitude: a little too much. Overall: not only will he probably die in a fiery inferno, his incessant whining would most certainly spoil everyone else's day". Leonard, irritated and tired from the drill, decides to go home. Sheldon tells him he cannot, as he needs to take Sheldon to the dentist later. When Leonard tells him he is too exhausted, Sheldon cites "section 37b of the roommate agreement", which stipulates that Leonard must take him. Leonard responds: "I am sick of the roommate agreement. It's ridiculous. I'm your roommate, not your chauffeur". He declares "I'm done", and Sheldon asks if he wants to "invoke clause 209", which "strips down the roommate agreement to its bare essentials" – rent, utilities, and minor social acknowledgement of one another. An exasperated Leonard responds, "where do I sign?". Once signed, Sheldon declares, "All right. That's it. We are now no longer companions, boon or otherwise. We are now merely acquaintances".

So, in the contract, homosociality is fully instrumentalized to the point of codification, in a way that reflects both the performance of male friendship in general, as well as the neoliberal compulsion to introduce rational economic logic into private relations. This is the status quo of male homosociality in

The Big Bang Theory, disrupted by Leonard's breaking of the contract, at which point homosociality becomes untenable. If one were to imagine this plot in another hangout sitcom, say, between Chandler and Joey, we would be immediately inclined to read it as a critique: how absurd is it that male friendships, already instrumentalized, are becoming increasingly transactional in this era? However, Sheldon's heavily implied autism presents him as an outlier, and, combined with the indicated subordination of all the male characters' nerd masculinities, offers the possibility of reading such a form of friendship as outlier too. By this latter reading, nerdy male homosociality is constructed as the "other" to normal male homosociality. These two readings continue to be present as the contract is negotiated in the episode.

Later, entering the apartment, Sheldon addresses "friends, and Dr. Hofstadter", before implying that he has assumed his girlfriend Amy will take him to the dentist tomorrow, which she says she cannot do. He then reads a list of favors he needs to the rest of the group, mostly involving giving him lifts to various places, hoping that one of them will help. He gets no positive responses. When his friends' collective reluctance becomes clear, he attempts to finagle his favors from the store owner and peripheral friend to the cast, Stuart (Kevin Sussman), damaging his case by greeting Stuart as his "ninth favorite person", who also refuses. Through the rest of the episode, Sheldon's actions indicate he is desperate to have Leonard back in his life, though his efforts revolve around making the transaction of re-signing the roommate agreement more materially appealing, rather than just apologizing. Geeky, autistic, othered Sheldon continues to outwardly see friendship as a transactional exchange, but his more emotional desperation is made extremely clear to the viewer – if transactional value were all he gained, Sheldon would immediately apologize to regain Leonard's signature, which he is too prideful to do.

Later that night, the apartment block experiences a power cut, leading Sheldon to implement his "power-failure protocol", which mostly involves a headtorch, the light from which he makes explicit Leonard is not allowed to use to see. He also pulls out a short green glowstick, and in an obvious moment of phallogocentric imagery, Leonard unveils a long green toy lightsaber, recognizable from the *Star Wars* movies, at least four times as long as Sheldon's, saying, "You call that a glowstick? That is a glowstick". As he and Penny begin to leave back to her flat (the two are dating at the time), Sheldon, again revealing emotional attachment, desperately offers him "all 61 episodes of the BBC series *Red Dwarf* and *Fiddle Faddle*", both cult British sci-fi shows. Penny offers Leonard wine and "some bubble wrap we could pop".

In Penny's apartment, Leonard and Penny begin to kiss. Sheldon abruptly enters, offering s'mores but only if Leonard re-signs the roommate agreement. Leonard, with the prospect of a night with his girlfriend, declines. When Sheldon says he will eat them by himself, leaving the room, Penny shows some sympathy with a pitying "aww". Leonard responds "don't aw him! He brought this on himself". She says "I think he misses his little

Bromance, homosociality, heterosexuality, and relationships 105

Figure 4.3 Leonard and Sheldon in "The Friendship Contraction".

buddy", to which Leonard responds "fine", and reluctantly leaves the apartment to make amends. For the first time in the episode, Leonard begins to show some of the pride Sheldon has demonstrated throughout. The following exchange ensues:

Leonard: Listen, Sheldon, this is stupid. I don't see why we can't be friends. And I'm willing to drive you around and help you out with stuff. I just don't want to do it because of some silly roommate agreement.
Sheldon: What are you proposing?
Leonard: That we go back to the way things were. But when I do something for you, you show a little appreciation.
Sheldon: And how would I do that?
Leonard: You say thank you.
Sheldon: Every time?
Leonard: It's not crazy.
Sheldon: Counter-proposal. We reinstate the full roommate agreement with the following addendum, in the spirit of Mother's Day or Father's Day, once a year, we set aside day to celebrate all your contributions to my life, both actual and imagined by you. We could call it Leonard's Day.
Leonard: I kind of like the sound of that.
Sheldon: Of course you do. It's about you, like everything else. [Lights come back on.] Oh, thank goodness. I don't think I had it in me to make another glass of water.
Leonard: So, do I get breakfast in bed on Leonard's Day?

Sheldon: No.
Leonard: Can I sit in your spot?
Sheldon: No.
Leonard: Can I control the thermostat?
Sheldon: No.
Leonard: Do I get a card?
Sheldon: Of course you get a card. It's Leonard's Day.

Leonard begins the exchange by suggesting the codification of friendship is fine, but it needs to be inflected with some form of affect – specifically, appreciation. Sheldon then attempts to codify such appreciation, once again turning friendship into a transaction that massages Leonard's ego, offering him "Leonard's Day" in return for re-signing the contract, a formal day in which the focus will be on Leonard. Leonard quickly agrees, re-consenting to the status quo disrupted at the beginning of the episode, an instrumental friendship. However, what happens next is the opposite to the way that Chandler and Joey's bromance would present emotionality and closeness, undercut by a sarcastic joke. Here, the sarcastic joke of the entire episode is undercut by the presentation of serious and real friendship. Penny enters the room and reveals that the reason for the power cut was that someone had actively pulled the main breaker switch in the basement of the block. Via Sheldon's poor acting, it is implied that it was he who pulled the main breaker switch, engineering a situation in which he could get his friend back. Such an about-turn leaves the possible readings of the situation open to the viewer, as despite Sheldon's othering, he also demonstrates that he understands the absurdity of a contractual friendship, demonstrating the neoliberal contradictions between the necessary bonds formed by friendship groups, and the desire to turn love and sociality into a transaction. *The Big Bang Theory* offers both readings.

Schmidt and Nick

Par for the course, Schmidt and Nick had markedly different childhoods – the former with a single, stereotypical middle-class New York Jewish overbearing mom, the latter a boisterous suburban Chicago extended family. They meet as roommates at college in Los Angeles, Nick studying law and Schmidt studying business, bonding over their shared lack of a father, and resultantly fall into something of a co-dependent relationship with each acting parentally for the other in certain arenas, in quite gendered ways. Nick mostly adopts the role of Schmidt's dad on the numerous occasions where Schmidt is abandoned by his father, demonstrated in a series of flashbacks in which Nick appears with a milkshake to soothe his friend (*New Girl*, "Return to Sender"). Schmidt at different moments both mothers and fathers Nick, a man who is unprepared for the adult world because of an often-absent, unreliable, and morally dubious father.

Nick and Schmidt's relationship and love for one another is a matter of public and explicit record. Long gone are the days where a wordless hug was enough to cement male friendship. In *New Girl*, the men's love for one another is apparent, even if Nick struggles to say it up front. They, along with Winston, bond on an emotional bros' night in, with words of unconditional support for one another (*New Girl*, "Teachers"); Schmidt's neediness for closeness to Nick leads him to spend an entire episode trying to catch a glimpse of Nick's penis after he discovers he is the only person in the flat not to have seen it (*New Girl*, "Naked"); and in the episode explored here, *Road Trip*, Nick offers loving encouragement when Schmidt worries he will not be a good enough husband to Cece.

Perhaps the most interesting is that Schmidt and Nick, albeit in very minor ways, rarely fall out substantively – in the very final episode of the show, Schmidt grows frustrated when he discovers that the peppermint foot lotion he has been getting Nick for his birthday every year has been sat, unused, in a box in Nick's room (*New Girl*, "Engram Pattersky"), but a more serious disagreement over a house move, new girlfriend, or roommate politics, is nowhere to be found. As such, relationship maintenance is rare. The chosen episode therefore demonstrates their unconditional support for one another when Schmidt's heterosexual relationship breaks down, indicating at the stark differences between bromance in the hangout sitcom in *Friends* in the 1990s, and in *New Girl* in the 2010s.

Road Trip

The season five episode "Road Trip" charts Schmidt's bachelor party before his marriage to Cece. At the beginning of the episode, Schmidt and Cece are in their car, discussing their upcoming wedding, and Schmidt laments that his initial desire to have a bachelor party in Tokyo will not be possible, and that instead the plan is for a Japanese-themed party including a spa, "hot springs", and "cherry blossoms". Schmidt, wearer of kimonos, is from the beginning of *New Girl* enamored by an Orientalist construction of Japanese culture (Said 2003 [1978]). Japan is also signified by another form of Orientalism, in a working culture signified by "self-immolation, total self-sacrifice – whether it is killing oneself for one's feudal lord or for the company by overwork" (Rosen 2000), diligent, self-responsible, and fully committed, and in many ways an idealized capitalist, though perhaps not neoliberal, subject. Yet, these images have also given way in US popular culture to the emasculation of almost any form of Asian American masculinity (Chua and Fujino 1999, Ling et al. 2017). "Hot springs" and "cherry blossoms" therefore construct a very typically feminized, othered, and Orientalized Japan in binary opposition to the masculinized road trip that the rest of the episode follows.

The couple are suddenly cut off at traffic lights by another car speeding in front of them. Schmidt beeps his horn at the other car, which proceeds to reverse back to nearer to their car, and a dreadlocked topless man emerges from the car, repeatedly saying his name – "Toby! Toby!" – and calling Schmidt a "bitch". Instead of standing his ground, Schmidt repeatedly apologizes, looking distressed, from behind a closed window. Back at the characters' loft apartment, he declares "the froofy Japanese bachelor party is off" – the Orientalized Japan here used as the other against Las Vegas – "we're going to Vegas on a road trip! Like men!". Despite Cece imploring that "just because a scary man yelled his name in your face doesn't mean you can't like sake[2] baths", Schmidt's ideas for his bachelor party remain stereotypically manly, requesting the car rental company's "toughest convertible", and rejecting Nick's attempt at a hug, as "hugs are not tough". In very typical hangout sitcom fashion, Schmidt's anxiously masculine douchebag roots haunt him.

The trip unfolds with a series of setbacks and obstacles that are caused by attempts from Schmidt to behave in a typically manly fashion, which in turns causes a downward emotional trajectory for Schmidt, managed by Nick. In the first setback, they struggle with transport hire. After Schmidt proclaims that yellow convertibles are for "horny beach trash", Nick steps in and obtains two "motorcycles" for him and Schmidt while the rest of the party ride along behind in Schmidt's cousin's family mini-van (the same cousin as in Chapter 4, played by comedy jock Rob Riggle) which has been masculinized by his "BG SCHMT" number plate. It is revealed that the motorcycles, however, are something closer to three-wheeled scooters. The shot pans down from the sky, playing the rock song "Thunderstruck" by AC/DC, revealing a panoramic long shot that is a pastiche of the typically masculinized road movie, a mise-en-scène that alerts us to a glaring mismatch

Figure 4.4 Replacing Harley Davidsons with trikes hints at the subversion of the road trip genre's subtextual homoeroticism that "Road Trip" will later become.

Bromance, homosociality, heterosexuality, and relationships 109

with the two emasculated men riding three-wheeled scooters with firmly tied helmets. Like the *How I Met Your Mother* episode, much of the rest of this episode can be read as a homosocial road movie – specifically, a homosocial road movie that turns subtextual homoeroticism into textual non-erotic love.

The second setback comes minutes later and leads to a more involved form of emotional management from Nick. Mid-driving, Schmidt pulls out a cigar, and attempts to light and smoke it. Unable to co-ordinate driving and smoking at the time, Schmidt loses control and barrels into the dusty landscape at the side of the road, eventually falling off his scooter as it comes to a standstill. The following exchange ensues:

Nick: Hey, it could have happened to anybody, Schmidt.
Schmidt: No, it couldn't have. It could only happen to me.
Nick: You crashed. You chunked. You beefed. You came off your bike. That's cool as hell. You got injured.
Schmidt: Yeah, you know, my neck does feel a little ... I don't know ... off.
Nick: Well, yeah, your neck's off. It's hurt. You got hurt on a hog, man. And what are you gonna do with that pain? What does a man do about that pain?
Schmidt: He takes a bubble bath.
Nick: No. He drinks the pain away. Here's what we're gonna do. You see that biker bar? We're gonna walk inside. You're gonna take your helmet off. You're gonna slam it down. You're gonna tell somebody to watch it. You're gonna put Seeger on the jukebox. And you're gonna drink some whiskey.
Schmidt: Some clear-cut accomplishables. That sounds pretty manly.
Nick: All right, my man. Give me some skin. [Nick clearly fakes his hand being hurt.] Ah-ha, Schmidt!
Schmidt: Come on, that didn't hurt.
Nick: It's too hard. It hurt. It honestly hurt. You're strong.
Schmidt: Look, man, I do ... you know.
Nick: Feel good?
Schmidt: I am, I'm feeling better.
Nick: You back? Who's the butchest guy on this roadside?
Schmidt: Me.

As with Ted and Marshall, there are two things going on here: first, the retention of certain masculinized or patriarchal structures, and second, the internal transformation of those structures. The road trip remains, at least for now, a masculinized space, where a man "drinks the pain away", is "butch", and is "strong". It is also one associated, at least partly, with closeness in the doing, specifically smoking cigars and drinking whiskey. Yet it is also a road trip where expressive support and love is not only acceptable but encouraged. No scenes in *Easy Rider* (1969) feature Peter Fonda or Dennis Hopper supporting the other through a personal crisis in masculinity.

When they get there, the "biker bar" is a dive bar held together by corrugated sheets of iron and populated by aggressive-looking redneck stereotypes. Schmidt moves toward the jukebox, and, attempting to show masculine nonchalance, taps a few buttons without looking. The song it lands on is "Roar" by Katy Perry, a pop anthem about female empowerment – its first line is "I used to bite my tongue and hold my breath", with a chorus refrain of "'cause I am a champion and you're gonna hear me roar". Schmidt cuts it short by pulling out the plug, and Nick suggests he apologize by buying a round of drinks for the entire populace of the bar. He approaches the bar and asks for a glass of whiskey on ice, angering local patrons furious about city folk asking for ice in the drought-stricken Nevada desert. The dispute escalates, and eventually the locals challenge Nick and Schmidt to a fight, but not before Nick says, "but first we gotta go to the little boys' room together". As they enter the bathroom, Nick immediately makes a beeline for the window, attempting to open it and escape. When Schmidt points out how non-manly it is to run away, for the first time in this episode, Nick calls out Schmidt's performative masculinity on this trip, saying "enough with the butch stuff, Schmidt". He responds by saying "it's not because I got yelled at, it's because I got yelled at in front of Cece", aspiring toward the househusband's heterosexual romantic masculinity, associated with middle-class professionalism. He just, as the douchebag often does, misdiagnoses the reason why he falls short of being the househusband. Nick relents, and the two exit the toilet to face up to the fight.

As the fight begins outside, Schmidt and Nick are hopelessly outnumbered by a group of at least five of them versus their two. Schmidt, bizarrely, attempts to demonstrate his manliness by puffing his chest and saying his name repeatedly and loudly, an echo of the incident at the beginning of the episode. Three of the other groomsmen hear Schmidt's pre-game ritual and join them, and the fight begins. Edited in slow motion and set to the non-diegetic Katy Perry's "Roar", the protagonists are humorously and roundly beaten in a slapstick fight routine, involving tripping up, apologies, being bested by women and children, and a plethora of incompetent fighting. The slow motion fight continues a Hollywood parody, demonstrating the artifice of masculinity by modifying the elements of a typical fight scene. Our heroes lose, while the normal rock music is replaced by an anthem of female empowerment.

After the fight Nick and Schmidt nurse their and each other's wounds on the back of the open trunk/boot of the other Schmidt's car. Offering Schmidt a plaster, Nick asks "doggies or trucks?" referring to the two different plaster patterns available. Schmidt says he does not deserve trucks, and Nick says "I'll be the judge of that. You deserve trucks". They then have this conversation:

Schmidt: I got this calendar bod, but it doesn't hold up in battle.
Nick: Look, it's 2016. She's not looking for a strong husband. That … no, tha-that's not what I was gonna … That's not where I was going with this.

Schmidt: I'm getting married, Nick. How am I going to defend Cece? She deserves the best husband in the world, and what if I don't have what it takes?

Nick: Of course you have what it takes to be a modern husband. Do you have what it takes to be a husband of the old world? God, no. They would use you as a pelt. Today, you fought, kinda. You're gonna make a great husband to Cece.

Schmidt: How do you know?

Nick: Because I know.

Schmidt: Because why?

Nick: Because.

Schmidt: Look what happened here today. Because why?

Nick: Beca ... ever since I've known you, you've been there. Okay, you're always there. Even when I don't want you there, you're there. That's what a husband does. You fight for me. That's what a husband does. You care about what I eat. That's what a husband does. You've cooked for me, even when I don't ask. That's what a husband does. When I pass out, you comb my hair so there's no knots in it. That's what a husband does. So, guess what. You're gonna be a great husband to Cece because you're a great husband to me. So that's how I know. You're, you're like my husband. You're like my wife, but ... Yeah, so that's how I know.

Schmidt: Thanks for saying that, man.

Nick: Yeah, man. (Runs away to cough and gag loudly) I need this to be done, okay?

Schmidt: Well, you can't take it back. I heard you say it, Nick.

It is worth first reiterating that this exchange takes place in a heteronormative context; Schmidt is concerned about being a good enough husband for Cece. In addition to this, the metaphors Nick uses to comfort and encourage Schmidt reference this context, too. There is also an extent to which it is undercut by Nick's disgust with himself in supporting his friend on like 25. However, when the two reconvene with the other groomsmen, they decide to return to Los Angeles, to which Winston asks, "but what about your bachelor party, Schmidt?", to which he replies "Who could want anything more from a bachelor party than their best friend telling him that they love him?".

Indeed, the entire exchange is markedly different from the one we saw from Chandler and Joey at the beginning of this chapter that was broadcast two decades earlier. When Chandler and Joey reference marriage, it is a knowing intertextual gag that continues to make absurd the notion that two men might engage in the same patter as a married couple. When Nick and Schmidt do it, it is not a joke, and is not repaired wordlessly. Instead, the two of them adopt entirely expressive roles, with textual homoeroticism: "you're gonna be a great husband to Cece because you're a great husband to me". Their bromance is at least as much romance as bro.

Homoerotic presents and straight futures

Much of the previous chapter examined how masculinities in the hangout sitcom are oriented toward straight time, and remain, in their romantic relationships, resolutely heteronormative. I argued in this chapter that male homosociality in the hangout sitcom is a space of a more significant transformation, textualizing homoeroticism while undermining masculinized instrumental friendships – and particularly that these changes can be charted over time as the subgenre develops. There remains, however, a limit to this, which is that such friendships occupy only the present moment, and the shows usually end by splitting the men apart into their own private homes. *How I Met Your Mother* tells us via flashforwards and the finale episodes that Ted lives as a widower in a New York flat with his two children, while Marshall lives in New Jersey with Lily and their children. The final three-years-later season of *New Girl* leaves Nick married to Jess in Oregon, while Schmidt, Cece, and children, live in suburbs of Los Angeles. In *The Big Bang Theory*, Sheldon and Amy are married with children, living opposite Leonard and Penny, also married, also with children. And while Joey's future is uncertain, thanks to the unfinished spin-off *Joey* (2004–2006), this was not narrative choice; meanwhile, Chandler moves with Monica and family to the suburbs.

As such, where Michael DeAngelis (2014a, 215) argues that some filmic bromances, those whose futures remain uncertain offer queer readings that "signal a dissatisfaction with the demands of heteronormativity while simultaneously inducing a sense of longing for a version of the future in which homosocial intimacy might be harbored or sustained without judgment", it is difficult to make the same argument about the bromance in a genre where futures are as certain and as heteronormative as can be. Some of DeAngelis's suggestions are applicable here, in that, for example, Ted and Marshall appear to long for a future where they can remain "bros" despite the interloping of femininity; similarly, in *The Big Bang Theory* Sheldon eventually demonstrates both happiness and sadness at the prospect of both marrying Amy and no longer living with his friend. Homosocial friendship longs for its own futures in the hangout sitcom, but is usually beaten to the finishing line by straight time.

I say usually: Raj in *The Big Bang Theory* is notable for a few reasons, first, because he does not really fit into any of the subject positions explored in Chapter 4, but also because he is the only notable male character with a completed narrative arc that does not end in a straight relationship. He is also, of course, notable for the fact that he is the only immigrant main character in any show here – the links between masculinity, sexuality, homosociality, and race are explored next.

Notes

1 The limits of some, though not all, of this research – particularly around the contested and problematic notion of "inclusive masculinities" – have been well-documented (see O'Neill 2015).
2 The Japanese rice wine.

Filmography

Baywatch. 1989–1999. [TV] Berk, Michael, Douglas Schwartz, and Gregory J. Bonann, Creator, NBC, First-run syndication: USA.
The Big Bang Theory. 2007–2019. [TV] Lorre, Chuck, and Bill Prady, Creator, CBS: USA.
Easy Rider. 1969. [Movie] Hopper, Dennis, Creator, Columbia Pictures: USA.
Friends. 1994–2004. [TV] Crane, David, and Marta Kauffman, Creator, NBC: USA.
How I Met Your Mother. 2005–2014. [TV] Bays, Carter, and Craig Thomas, Creator, CBS: USA.
Joey. 2004–2006. Silveri, Scott, and Shana Goldberg-Meehan, Creator, NBC: USA.
Marley & Me. 2008. [Movie] Frankel, David, Creator, 20th Century Fox: USA.
New Girl. 2011–2018. [TV] Meriwether, Elizabeth, Creator, Fox: USA.
Scrubs. 2001–2010. [TV] Lawrence, Bill, Creator, NBC, ABC: USA.

References

Alberti, John. 2013. "'I Love You, Man': Bromances, the construction of masculinity, and the continuing evolution of the romantic comedy." *Quarterly Review of Film and Video* 30 (2):159–172. doi: 10.1080/10509208.2011.575658.
Anderson, Ben. 2016. "Neoliberal affects." *Progress in Human Geography* 40 (6):734–753. doi: 10.1177/0309132515613167.
Becker, Ron. 2014. "Becoming bromosexual: Straight men, gay men, and male bonding on US TV." In *Reading the Bromance: Homosocial Relationships in Film and Television*, edited by Michael DeAngelis, 233–254. Detroit, MI: Wayne State University Press.
Brabon, Benjamin A. 2013. "'Chuck Flick': A genealogy of the postfeminist male singleton." In *Postfeminism and Contemporary Hollywood Cinema*, edited by Joel Gwynne, and Nadine Muller, 116–130. Basingstoke: Palgrave Macmillan.
Brecher, Bob. 2012. "The family and neoliberalism: Time to revive a critique." *Ethics and Social Welfare* 6 (2):157–167. doi: 10.1080/17496535.2012.682503.
Chua, Peter, and Dune C. Fujino. 1999. "Negotiating new Asian American masculinities: Attitudes and gender expectations." *The Journal of Men's Studies* 7 (3):391–413. doi: 10.3149/jms.0703.391.
Clough, Patricia Ticineto, ed. 2007. *The Affective Turn: Theorizing the Social*. Durham, NC: Duke University Press.
Cohan, Steven, and Ina Rae Hark. 1997. "Introduction." In *The Road Movie Book*, edited by Steven Cohan, and Ina Rae Hark, 1–15. London: Routledge.
de Boise, Sam, and Jeff Hearn. 2017. "Are men getting more emotional? Critical sociological perspectives on men, masculinities and emotion." *The Sociological Review* 65 (4):779–796. doi: 10.1177/0038026116686500.
DeAngelis, Michael. 2014a. "Queeness and futurity in *Superbad*." In *Reading the Bromance: Homosocial Relationships in Film and Television*, edited by Michael DeAngelis, 213–229. Detroit, MI: Wayne State University Press.
DeAngelis, Michael, ed. 2014b. *Reading the Bromance: Homosocial Relationships in Film and Television*. Detroit, MI: Wayne State University Press.
Goedecke, Klara. 2018. "'Other guys don't hang out like this': Gendered friendship politics among Swedish middle-class men." Doctoral thesis, Centrum för Genusvetenskap, Uppsala universitet.

Grogan, Josh. 2005. *Marley & Me: Life and Love with the World's Worst Dog*. London: HarperCollins.
Hamad, Hannah. 2018. "The one with the feminist critique: Revisiting millenial postfeminism with *Friends*." *Television & New Media* 19 (8):692–707. doi: 10.1177/1527476418779624.
Harris, Malcolm. 2017. *Kids These Days: Human Capital and the Making of Millenials*. London: Little, Brown and Company.
Illouz, Eva. 2007. *Cold Intimacies: The Making of Emotional Capitalism*. Cambridge: Polity.
Lang, Robert. 1997. "*My Own Private Idaho* and the new queer road movies." In *The Road Movie Book*, edited by Steven Cohan, and Ina Rae Hark, 330–348. London: Routledge.
Ling, Xiaodong, Chris Haywood, and Máirtín Mac an Ghaill. 2017. *East Asian Masculinities and Sexualities*. London: Palgrace Macmillan.
Lotz, Amanda D. 2014. *Cable Guys: Television and Masculinities in the 21st Century*. New York: NYU Press.
McQueen, Fiona. 2017. "Male emotionality: 'Boys don't cry' versus 'it's good to talk'." *NORMA* 12 (3). doi: 10.1080/18902138.2017.1336877.
Migliaccio, Todd. 2010. "Men's friendships: Performances of masculinity." *The Journal of Men's Studies* 17 (3):226–241. doi: 10.3149/jms.1703.226.
O'Neill, Rachel. 2015. "Whither critical masculinity studies? Notes on inclusive masculinity theory, postfeminism, and sexual politics." *Men and Masculinities* 18 (1):100–120. doi: 10.1177/1097184X14553056.
Reeser, Todd W., and Lucas Gottzén. 2018. "Masculinity and affect: New possibilities, new agendas." *NORMA* 13 (3):145–157. doi: 10.1080/18902138.2018.1528722.
Roberts, Shari. 1997. "Western meets Eastwood." In *The Road Movie Book*, edited by Steven Cohan, and Ina Rae Hark, 45–69. London: Routledge.
Robinson, Stefan, Eric Anderson, and Adam White. 2017. "The bromance: Undergraduate male friendships and the expansion of contemporary homosocial boundaries." *Sex Roles* 78 (1):94–106. doi: 10.1007/s11199-017-0768-5.
Rosen, Steven L. 2000. "Japan as other: Orientalism and cultural conflict." *Intercultural Communication*. http://www.immi.se/intercultural/nr4/rosen.htm. Accessed 12 February.
Roseneil, Sasha, and Shelley Budgeon. 2004. "Cultures of intimacy and care beyond 'the family': Personal life and social change in the early 21st century." *Current Sociology* 52 (2):135–159. doi: 10.1177/0011392104041798.
Said, Edward. 2003 [1978]. *Orientalism*. London: Penguin.
Scoats, Ryan, and Stefan Robinson. 2020. "From stoicism to bromance: Millenial men's friendships." In *The Palgrave Handbook of Masculinity and Sport*, edited by Rory Magrath, Jamie Cleland, and Eric Anderson, 379–392. Oxford: Palgrave Macmillan.
Swain, Scott. 1989. "Covert intimacy: Closeness in the same-sex friendships of men." In *Gender in Intimate Relations: A Microstructural Approach*, edited by Barbara J. Risman, and Pepper Schwartz, 75–87. Belmont, CA: Wadsworth.
Wood, Robin. 2003. *Hollywood from Vietnam to Reagan ... and Beyond*. Chichester: Columbia University Press.
Yandoli, Krystie Lee. 2016. "Matt LeBlanc gushed about his friendship with Matthew Perry and now I'm dead." BuzzFeed. https://www.buzzfeed.com/krystieyandoli/i-love-that-guy. Accessed 20 November 2022.

5 Breaking the circle

Challenging whiteness in the hangout sitcom's surrogate families

I mean, especially in the black community, there'd always be absolute criticism pulled at Friends because like, there's no black characters. It's so white! Especially in the year it were made at the time when the Wu-Tang Clan, who came from New York, were absolutely massive, which, like, that's turned a lot of people off sitcoms.

Kurt, aged 25, northern England, 2017

They were utter dogshit questions, and utter dogshit to then ask, can you both be on the show? You can, yeah, absolutely! You don't just need one black guy, you can have a bunch of them on a show.

Jake Johnson at the "Vulture Festival" of media, 2020 (Vulture, 2020)

When I carried out my PhD research, Kurt was the participant least familiar with *Friends* – he was also the only black participant. Invoking the hip hop group Wu-Tang Clan, he points out that the moment when *Friends* (1994–2004) exploded into the zeitgeist was hardly one in which New York City's black culture and black communities were invisible, even for a working-class black boy in the north of England. In fact, the first *Friends* episodes coincided with the so-called "golden years" of East Coast hip hop, 1994 marking the release of Nas's seminal album "Illmatic", while in 1995 The Notorious B.I.G. collaborated with Michael Jackson on the song "This Time Around". Whether or not it was a conscious decision, casting all six friends as white, while waiting until season nine to introduce a black character with any serious arc, was neither a necessary nor even a particularly credible writing choice. Debuting in a moment when the city's black culture was achieving global recognition, the whiteness of *Friends*, is therefore not just a description of the color of the actors' skins, but a description too of the show's wider institutional and production context.

Fast forward 17 years from the US broadcast of *Friends*' pilot episode to 2011 and *New Girl*'s (2011–2018) pilot episode casts two non-white actors in its core cast of five: Damon Wayans Jr., whose father Damon Wayans starred in his own black sitcom *Damon* (1998), as Coach, a competitive and masculine main character who coaches basketball; and Hannah Simone as Cece Parekh, a half-Indian model and best friend of main character Jess. Then, when the two-season hangout sitcom *Happy Endings* (2011–2013) was picked up by broadcast network ABC at the same time as *New Girl* was by Fox, and Wayans opted to stick with the former show, in his place they cast another black character, hiring Lamorne Morris to play Winston, a childhood friend of Nick's. In short, diversity in some sense seemed more important to *New Girl* in 2011 than *Friends* 17 years earlier. To quote a black sitcom, what's happening here?

Naming whiteness

Race is taken in this book to be a material-discursive, and therefore historically determined, construction, though it takes rather different if intertwined shapes to gender or sexuality. In the US, Theodore Allen (1994) charts how the "white race", consisting in a whole range of settler-colonial populations who had previous been considered racially different, emerged in the 17th century onwards as a method of labor- and class-based social control over Africans and the various indigenous groups. Such methods of control arose, of course, with and through slavery – today, it is perpetuated through violent methods such as police brutality and incarceration (see Hunter and Westhuizen 2022, Alexander 2010). Yet, in response to global and ideological shifts, other mechanisms of racialized social control have proliferated through the 20th and 21st centuries within the Global North.

Such a development allowed for the "unmarking" of the white race, a non-racialized status that gives it a semblance of universality, against a range of racialized others. Scholars engaged in critical whiteness studies have been interested in dispelling this appearance of universality through the naming and analyzing of whiteness as a construct rather than a taken-for-granted norm. This thereby produces a critique of the ways in which whiteness and white supremacy are sustained as structural norms (Applebaum 2010, Garner 2007). The contradiction presented by a non-racialized racial group, simultaneously visible and invisible, was explored in the 1990s by Richard Dyer (2017 [1997], 45), whose study of a range of movies and TV from across the 20th century demonstrated that

> whites must be seen as white, yet whiteness as race resides in invisible properties and whiteness as power is maintained by being unseen. To be seen as white is to have one's corporeality registered, yet true whiteness resides in the non-corporeal.

Whiteness, Dyer suggests, is that which provides body and agency, but is simultaneously unacknowledged – this is not clearer in one genre more than the 70-year-old TV sitcom.

How white is the sitcom?

The nuclear family around which US post-war reconstruction revolved, and which served as the sociopolitical context from which the sitcom emerged (Spigel 1992), was a heavily racialized – i.e., white – construction (Haralovich 2009). This shaped the early televisual families that populated the suburbs, such as the Cleavers of *Leave it to Beaver* (1957–1963) or the Andersons of *Father Knows Best* (1954–1960). Periodizing the depiction of race in the sitcom, Robin Coleman et al (2016) call this early period of the 1950s and 1960s the "non-recognition era", which largely ignored black actors for roles, apart from as the occasional help. There was during this period some limited Latinx representation, such as with Ricky Ricardo in *I Love Lucy* (1951–1957), followed by an entire Latinx family in the 1960s who were represented as magical and threatening outsiders to the neighborhood in *The Addams Family* (1964–1966).

The representation of race in the sitcom continued to change and evolve. Herman Gray (2005, 78) describes how, through the late 1960s and early 1970s, networks began

> offering programs featuring all-black casts and themes, accompanied by a smaller number of short-lived shows with a sprinkling of black-cast members, [which] continued a pattern of black visibility and invisibility on television that began the early 1970s, following the urban rebellions of the 1960s.

As the anti-racism of the Civil Rights movement were folded into mainstream political discourse, television executives uncovered in black America a thus far untapped market. A brief "assimilationist era" followed until around 1971, with several shows that featured majority black casts, but with black characters who largely conformed to white societal norms. *Julia* (1968–1971), for example, had some commercial and critical success. It had a mostly black cast, following a black nurse through her career for three seasons, and its lead actor, Diahann Carroll, even won a Golden Globe for her efforts. However, *Julia* never made it into national popular consciousness, perhaps partly because it was critiqued for featuring black characters who were defined largely in relation to white norms (Bodroghkozy 2012, 196–199).

Through the 1970s, several sitcoms that were part of Norman Lear and his relevancy-com's domination of the schedules followed black people and families while addressing some, limited, black sociopolitical issues in the US – notably *Sanford and Son* (1972–1977) and *The Jeffersons* (1975–1985). These sitcoms, which we might call black sitcoms both in terms of representation and culture, rarely achieved multi-racial demographic success. Instead, black programming and white programming remained mostly separate in a re-assertion of a type of "separate but equal" doctrine (Gray 2005).

However, in the 1980s *The Cosby Show* (1984–1992) broke into the white mainstream, becoming the most popular sitcom and TV show of the decade in the US. Sut Jhally and Justin Lewis suggest that for white audiences in particular, however, the show exemplified the "post-racial" logic in which racism was cast as a historical moment rather than an existing structural problem (Jhally and Lewis 1992). Even while the show occasionally offered arguably subversive or positive messages to black audiences, the success of the black middle-class Huxtable family for white culture was often seen as evidence that racism was no longer a significant structural barrier.

Indeed, what followed *The Cosby Show* was what Coleman et al (2016, 285) define as the "neo-minstrelsy" era, an explosion of black sitcoms in the late 1980s and early 1990s inspired by *The Cosby Show*'s success, which, rather than a nuanced exploration of black sociopolitical issues, was mostly defined by "a return to black sitcom tropes popularized on the original minstrel theatre stage". The presence of stereotypical black stock characters in this era attempted to construct a society so far beyond racism that racist stereotypes were seen to be a legitimate comedic choice (see Cummings 1988). However, where white family sitcoms had more faithfully represented the real concerns of white families, even if those situations were exaggerated for comic effect, many of the sitcoms of this era relied on racialized stereotypes for their characters. Coleman et al (2016, 286) describe this era's "all-time low in 1998, as UPN premiered the short-lived 'slave-com' (as it came to be called colloquially) *The Secret Diary of Desmond Pfeiffer*", a sitcom euphemistically about Abraham Lincoln's black 'manservant'.

If we were to continue the project of Coleman et al in periodizing the representation of black programming beyond the turn of the millennium, we might clunkily name the majority of the 2000s (perhaps until 2008 and the election of Barack Obama as US President) a "neo-non-recognition" era, dominated by *Friends* and other white hangout sitcoms that mostly ignored black culture and concerns. Black programming here declined significantly; as the hangout sitcom took hold in a neoliberal era of middle-class professionals, white sitcoms prevailed. Yet, over this conjuncture, on-screen racial representation changed, such that by the time *New Girl*, the last major hangout sitcom, aired, its cast was notably diverse, not just dealing with non-white characters, but with sociopolitical issues of race in the US.

Post-race and post-white

I argue that the hangout sitcom's shifting politics of representation is made possible by a shift in neoliberalism's racial politics. In general, the neoliberal impulse to mandatory individualization (Eagleton-Pierce 2016, McGuigan 2013) manifests as a politics of colorblindness – that the best course of action in the face of structural racial injustice is to ignore or not acknowledge race or its attendant material effects, and instead to focus on the capacities and agency of individual people. Michelle Alexander (2010) shows how this colorblind racial politics of what we might call the Obama era offers little to no threat to unequal racial politics. Rather, it assumes that the inclusion of non-white people in institutions of power (be that in entertainment, politics, finance or anywhere else) that have been defined historically by whiteness is evidence that race is no longer an issue in the USA. Whiteness here remains unchallenged and unmarked. However, colorblind politics shifts in its postracial logic over the era of the hangout sitcom, a shift that is structured into the subgenre's changing politics of racial representation.

In chapter three I briefly outlined what Sut Jhally and Justin Lewis (1992) describe as the "post-racial" consensus of the 1980s, readable from *The Cosby Show* (1984–1992) in particular, where racism is cast as a historical moment and not a structuring logic, and where the legal and cultural hegemonization of the Civil Rights movement combined with the canonization of its figureheads are perceived to represent the end of racism as a major national problem. This privileges a blackness that has assimilated to respectable consumer subjectivity, which has its roots in Western histories, both geographically specific and Eurocentric (Lemke 2001). In the post-racial USA, race can be overlooked for those who participate in acceptable normative activities, hence the popularity of the unthreatening middle-class Huxtables of *The Cosby Show*. In short, neoliberalism, in its desire to expand markets, makes consumers of all individuals, across identity and cultural boundaries. Will Kymlicka (2013, 109) identifies that "the defining feature of neoliberal multiculturalism is the belief that ethnic identities and attachments can be assets to market actors". This post-race consensus, dominant from the 1980s, endures through until today, but takes a somewhat modified form.

Mike Hill (2004) suggests that since the 2000s, US racial politics has shifted toward a "post-white" consensus where, rather than race per se, white dominance is cast as a historical moment. Hill argues that US culture and politics operates on an assumption that white people are becoming a minority group within the US, resulting a "post-white national imaginary" in which whiteness is no longer an invisible norm (Hill 2004). The place of neoliberal individualization here is more complex, immanent in what Hill calls "racial self-recognition" (2004, 12), where the reality of racial identification is imbricated within an increasing postmodern dissolution of overarching structures at the expense of individual determination. Racism is cast as a subjectivized reality rather than a structural one, requiring complex, localized, and even individual solutions. Meanwhile, the accepted fact of the end of whiteness tends to result in a politics of racial recognition that sometimes verges on fetishization of otherness.

This intra-conjunctural shift from a post-racial consensus toward a postwhite consensus contextualizes for the hangout sitcom's shift in racialized representation from *Friends* through to *New Girl*, characterized by a move from active, aggressive policing of whiteness in the former, through to a contradictory form of fetishization and attraction of otherness in the latter. Such a shift, I suggest, informs the treatment of a range of racialized masculinities, including white ones, in the hangout sitcom.

Black and white masculinities

Race and whiteness have always been imbricated within gendered structures, as critical whiteness studies has long theorized (see Dyer 2017 [1997], 145–183), and as much as the hangout sitcom is about gender, intimacy, and communal belonging, it also tells us a lot about how whiteness is imbricated within those terms. Indeed, much of the hangout sitcom's politics of race revolves around the sustaining and legitimization of white, heterosexual, masculinities.

In much the way that masculinities in *Friends* are defined by a sense of insecurity about their place in society in terms of gender, white masculinities also present as feeling threatened by non-whiteness, and in particular blackness. The range of very briefly appearing stereotypical black masculinities speak to this sense of threat, and in particular the ways that black masculinities are rebuffed and ignored. Meanwhile, non-white women in *Friends* threaten the white men not just racially, but sexually, too. This logic largely continues into *How I Met Your Mother*, too.

I further argue that the inclusion of non-white masculinities among the casts of *The Big Bang Theory* and *New Girl* indicates moves toward a fetishization of othered masculinity that is not matched by a more direct interrogation of white masculinities. Here, I deploy Mike Hill's suggestion that post-whiteness has a complex relationship with masculinities where, "according to an unlikely composite of racial benevolence and U.S. neofascism, white men's relation to alterity is writ *doubly* as an attraction *and* an aversion to the future forms of racial multiplicity they cannot quite embody" (Hill 2004, 15). The material result of such discursive work is the preservation and continued legitimization of whiteness.

In the last part of the chapter, I argue that the changing treatment of Jewish masculinities in the hangout sitcom is defined by a shift from "conceptual Jewishness" (Brook 2010) in *Friends*, to a more explicit but purely aesthetic Jewishness in *The Big Bang Theory* and *New Girl*, further reflecting the shift from the post-racial to post-white consensus, all while continuing to police the boundaries of whiteness.

The white circle

The hangout sitcom, then, like the wider genre in which it is situated, is a white subgenre. Purely in terms of numbers, Table 5.1 shows that, counting the Jewish characters as white, 83% of all main characters across the four shows are white. The percentages in the table have been rounded, while the asterisk (*) is used to indicate a Jewish actor playing a non-Jewish character, or, vice versa, a non-Jewish actor playing a Jewish character, the complexities of which are explored later in the chapter. The dagger (†) also denotes that Joey's whiteness is complicated by his Italian immigrant background.

Breaking the circle: Challenging whiteness in the hangout sitcom   121

Table 5.1 Racial demographics in the US hangout sitcom.

	White Gentile	Jewish, or implied	Black	Indian American
Friends	Chandler, Joey†	Ross, Monica*, Rachel*, Phoebe*	-	-
How I Met Your Mother	Barney, Marshall*, Lily, Robin	Ted	-	-
The Big Bang Theory	Sheldon, Penny, Amy, Bernadette*	Howard, Leonard*	-	Raj
New Girl	Jess, Nick*	Schmidt	Winston, Coach	Cece
Total number	12 (50%)	8 (33%)	2 (8%)	2 (8%)

Whiteness in the hangout sitcom is not just about representation and pure numbers, though, but cultural norms or sensibilities. Phil Chidester (2008) argues that the *Friends* characters police membership to their friendship group with a particularly aggressive policy toward non-white characters. Chidester (2008, 150) states:

> first, the sitcom reinforces whiteness's exclusive freedom to convert its public spaces to private ones; and second, it argues for whiteness's continued right (and concurrent responsibility) to maintain its core sense of purity against racial outsiders by limiting and regulating contacts with the racialized Other.

The overwhelming whiteness of the show is actively maintained both by how characters treat non-white characters, and through the construction of the public sphere as white. Indeed, the fact that the Jewish and Italian cast members of *Friends*, backgrounds that have not always been considered white, are part of this circle demonstrates the ever-shifting content of whiteness as a construction.

Chidester suggests that the circle is visually and physically manifest in the way that the white cast occupy and assume their superior claim to public space. He says, "the circle serves as a visual boundary between included and excluded, as a perimeter to be doggedly defended against anyone who might challenge the in-group's physical solidarity and cultural unity" (Chidester 2008, 163). Chidester cites two examples, both love interests of Ross's, in Charlie Wheeler played by Aisha Tyler who is black, and Julie (surname unknown) played by the Chinese American Lauren Tom. Neither are allowed in any meaningful way to become a part of the show's closed white circle of friends.

Chidester (2008, 164) observes: "Charlie does manage to insert herself into the coffee shop scene during a short run on the programme, but on both occasions she is joined by only a few members of the central cast", while "Julie does manage to breach the perimeter – but the viciousness with which she is treated as an interloper, particularly in comparison to other (white) women Ross dates in these episodes, speaks to a threat well beyond her presence".

Shelley Cobb (2018, 715) suggests there is a gendered facet to this,

> that Charlie and Julie, in addition to the plot work of delaying the union of Ross and Rachel and reinforcing the group's intimacy when they leave, also do ideological work, doubly functioning to confirm the fated-ness of Ross and Rachel as a couple, as well as the whiteness of the postfeminist tropes of fate and retreatism that Diane Negra (2009) has identified.

Here, she is referring to Negra's (2009, 5) suggestion that the subject of postfeminist culture "is represented as having lost herself but then (re)achieving stability through romance, de-aging, a makeover, by giving up paid work, or by 'coming home'". Cobb argues that Julie and Charlie, both of whom have doctoral degrees, appear better matches for Dr. Geller – when listing the pros and cons of Rachel and Julie, Ross's patronizing notes include on Rachel's cons list, "just a waitress" (*Friends*, "The One with the List"). As such, it is their non-whiteness that disqualifies them from being a legitimate love interest. Non-white femininities in *Friends* threaten Rachel's sense of postfeminist, perhaps neo-traditionalist, desserts – Ross as husband and father to her children – which plays out mostly as jealous behavior from Rachel toward the two women.

While black men do exist in the *Friends* universe, there are *no* non-white male love interests in *Friends* despite its setting. Instead, when black men do appear, they occupy a variety of stereotypes, and rarely appear beyond individual episodes. First, following in the post-racial footsteps of Cliff Huxtable, several career-successful black men appear through the show, often interacting with Chandler in a work capacity, and whose roles seem mostly to act incredulously at his social faux-pas. Mr. Tyler, a man who interviews Chandler for a new job (*Friends*, "The One with the Cooking Class"), is appalled at his inability not to laugh at the scatological homonym of the word "duty", while Monica's old friend Steve who offers Chandler an unpaid internship at his advertising firm is miffed after being told that Chandler and Monica are "supposed to have sex tonight – actually, she's probably at home naked right now" (*Friends*, "The One Where Rachel Goes Back to Work").

Second, emerging around the same time as the so-called era of "neo-minstrelsy", there are also several somewhat feminized and campy black men, typified by a director at an audition of Joey's, who flamboyantly demonstrates his dancing technique and several times flourishes his "jazz hands" (*Friends*, "The One with All the Jealousy"), or the singing black neighbor with suspenders whose operatic insistence that "morning is here" irritates Rachel on

Breaking the circle: Challenging whiteness in the hangout sitcom 123

Figure 5.1 The singing black man evokes the racially charged images of minstrelsy (Cobb 2018, 714).

a Saturday morning (*Friends*, "The One with All the Haste"). Third, there is also the working-class black guy, defined by his usually manual or at least mundane labor – we meet a librarian, a security guard, a delivery guy, and a waiter. The career-based, campy, and working black men all play on generic stereotypes about black masculinities.

There are some black men who do not embody these stereotypes, but they are not treated well by the main cast. In season 3, Joey teaches an acting class, and he and a black student of his named Cal, played by Khalil Kain, go for the same role in a play (*Friends*, "The One with the Race Car Bed"). After Cal gives Joey a taste of his audition, Joey's response to which is an amazed and sincere "wow ... that was ... that was good!", Joey decides to try to sabotage Cal's attempt. Cutting immediately to Central Perk, Chandler loudly exclaims to Joey, "you told him to play the boxer gay!?". Though Joey is reprimanded by his friends, his unpleasant behavior is eventually rewarded when he returns to his acting class, and confesses what he has done, only to receive applause from his students who assume he has just delivered a heartfelt monologue. Black masculinities in *Friends*, in short, are somewhat one-dimensional, never allowed near the main cast.

Conditional entry

Premiering 11 years after *Friends*, *How I Met Your Mother* has several non-white recurring characters who are allowed a certain conditional entry into the main friendship circle, and there are three non-white men here worth noting. The first is a fringe character named Ranjit Singh, played by Marshall Manesh, a Bangladeshi American taxi and limousine driver who appears sporadically. Ranjit is not subject to any character development or arc; instead, his comedy foreign accent and large moustache appear to be the entire joke, as he introduces himself in every appearance with a cheery and heavily accented "hello!". On the occasions when he engages with the other characters more substantively, he occupies something of a mysterious spiritual adviser role that plays into Orientalist tropes around spirituality (Imawura 2011), while his evident older age works with his race to exclude him from the circle.

Beyond Ranjit, the racial politics of *How I Met Your Mother* does mostly abandon the aggressive policing of whiteness we see in *Friends*. However, in its place, *How I Met Your Mother* adopts a colorblind policy; non-white people exist in the show, and appear not irregularly, but their race is either virtually unmentioned, or non-white characters are discursively constructed as "white". Whiteness here remains culturally and visually present. Played by Kal Penn (famous for playing a stoner in the *Harold & Kumar* movies) in season seven, Kevin Venkataraghavan is an example of this. He is an Indian American love interest of Robin's with a substantial amount of screen time, and the first non-white male love interest in a hangout sitcom. However, the references to Kevin's brownness are scant. His surname is a genuine Hindi surname, though is played as a joke next to his very generic English first name. We see his mother for all of three seconds and one line in a brief joke when he realizes Robin shares characteristics with his mom, and Kal Penn's own fame to an extent informs the audience of the character's racial background. Beyond this, Kevin could be played by anyone. His relative shedding of his racialized identity grants him limited access to the group, but it is extremely conditional. Like Julie and Charlie, Kevin is comically well-qualified, which perhaps assists in his breaching of the white circle, having studied at Princeton and Harvard, attending the latter university twice, which also plays into a variety of stereotypes about Asian American over-achieving (Lee and Zhou 2015).

Midway through his arc, the main cast gather at Lily and Marshall's home to paint a bedroom for their unborn child, where Kevin joins them (*How I Met Your Mother*, "Mystery vs. History"). Here, he takes up a similar role to Chandler's black colleagues, shining a light on the unhealthy and entitled behavior of the other cast members, as Barney and Robin contrive to find out the gender of the baby against Marshall and Lily's wishes. Kevin accuses the group of being "the most codependent, incestuous, controlling group of people I've ever met". The show cuts to a series of demonstrative flashbacks, interspliced with a series of incredulous looks from Kevin. Chastised by Robin, though, he apologizes and offers to paint the entire room by himself while the others talk, leaving himself socially ostracized for the remainder of the episode. In the final scene, when the group learn their inevitable lesson and engage in a group hug, the lonesome Kevin looks on. While the main characters literally hug and learn, Kevin remains outside the circle. Kevin

Breaking the circle: Challenging whiteness in the hangout sitcom 125

Figure 5.2 The *How I Met Your Mother* gang hug while Kevin struggles to get involved, Chidester's circle metaphor realized physically.

learns here that his otherness only presents an obstacle to membership if he challenges or questions the group's behavior.

The perhaps more interesting non-white man in *How I Met Your Mother* is Barney's gay black adoptive brother, James Stinson, played by comedian Wayne Brady. James is a messy, metatextual postmodern gag: a sex-obsessed gay black man played by a heterosexual actor, adoptive brother to a sex-obsessed heterosexual white man played by a gay actor. His introductory episode in season two (*How I Met Your Mother*, "Single Stamina") plays with this throughout. With the other characters having already met James, Lily informs Robin (and by proxy the audience) "he's exactly like Barney"– he loves his suits, uses the same catchphrases, and loves to have sex – to which Ted says, "well, Barney and his brother aren't exactly alike. James is gay. I just wanted you to have a heads up, so you don't act all surprised when he gets here". When the black James enters, Robin sarcastically comments, "thanks for the heads up". Ted then demonstrates the sort of post-racial politics that the hangout sitcom to this point has embodied, as he, jokingly, says to Robin, "is he black? I guess I'm the kind of person that focuses on who people are on the inside rather than the color of their skin". Though this appears to be a takedown of such a politics, James's blackness is barely acknowledged.

In short, despite being black and gay, James *is* exactly like Barney, his blackness almost unacknowledged, and his gayness masculinized by his sexual conquests. Barney and James, and by proxy the audience, never really get a clear explanation from their white mom about their different color skins, meaning James grew up in a white household, while his former life as a sex addict can be interpreted via discourses that attach an active, animalistic quality to gay sex that stems from emasculation and effeminophobia (Lamb et al. 2018). Additionally, when he is introduced in that first episode, he serves as a foil to Barney's character development. The episode is at pains to tell us that James is as sexually driven as Barney, except concerned with a different gender. Yet as the narrative unfolds, more and more clues lead to the reveal that James is engaged, which serves as a lesson to Barney about adhering to notions of normative straight time and growing up (Freeman 2010). The gay black guy here performs straight white chrononormativity so that the straight white guy learns his lesson.

Breaking the circle

Both critics and the viewing public from the beginning criticized the whiteness of *Friends*, and the vociferousness with which the show's narrative defended it. Kurt's comments at the start of this chapter highlight the criticism among black communities globally, while in 1995, as *Friends* was taking off as a cultural phenomenon, the six actors were interviewed by Oprah Winfrey, who suggested "I'd like y'all to get a black friend", to somewhat awkward responses from the cast (Cobb 2018). The television industry, eventually, responded. Some black sitcoms returned to TV screens from the late 2000s, while some non-white characters and some non-white social and political issues were assimilated into white shows, including the hangout sitcom.

Desexualizing Raj

The first regular non-white character in a hangout sitcom is Raj in *The Big Bang Theory*. Raj's gender and sexuality are the butt of constant jokes – there were childhood rumors he was "more comfortable in a sari", he regularly expresses his love for romantic comedy movies (and particularly Sandra Bullock ones), and when the four characters lose a bet and are forced to dress as female superheroes, Raj shows more confidence than normal dressed as Catwoman while the other three mope (*The Big Bang Theory*, "The Wheaton Recurrence"). Similarly, while none of the four male nerds are romantically adept, Raj's psychological inability to even talk to a woman, which he can only overcome by either drinking alcohol or taking experimental anti-anxiety medication, is the most extreme form of this; Sheldon is unable to perform basic social niceties to anyone, Leonard performs typical schlemiel slapstick but is probably the most "normal" of the four, and Howard is sex-crazed if often sexually successful. There is little suggestion that Raj's emasculated manhood has its roots in any socioeconomic changes, rather than in a form of racialization in which men of Asian heritage (be that East Asian or subcontinental Indian) are feminized and emasculated in US culture (Park 2013, Eng 2001). Therefore, despite *The Big Bang Theory* being the first hangout

Breaking the circle: Challenging whiteness in the hangout sitcom 127

Figure 5.3 Raj's smiley confidence as Catwoman (right) is a stark contrast to the glum faces of Batwoman, Wonder Woman, and Super-Woman.

sitcom to feature a non-white regular character, Raj's role as the racialized other is usually to legitimize the heterosexuality of the other three main characters' oft-questioned nerd masculinities thereby sustaining the whiteness of heterosexuality.

Most obviously, Raj never stands a chance with any of the main white female characters – neither Penny nor Bernadette entertains any prospect of him being a serious love interest. When Howard and Bernadette are dating, Raj misinterprets Bernadette's kindness as romantic interest and begins to daydream about her (*The Big Bang Theory*, "The Thespian Catalyst"). Throughout the season, these daydreams develop into writing poetry about her. When Bernadette finally becomes engaged to Howard, Raj struggles to accept it. He begins to spend a lot of time with Penny instead, and the two of them grow close. After a few drinks in the season four finale, the episode ends on a cliffhanger when Raj and Penny wake up next to each other without clothes on. The first episode of season five quashes the potential for real romance when Raj reveals that the two did not have sex after all, prompting Penny to request they try to remain friends.

Raj is even shown to be less heterosexually successful than the mostly asexual Sheldon. When first introduced, Raj's parents – who fulfill all the pushy, controlling, racialized stereotypes one might expect of fictional depictions of Indian parents – set him up with a woman named Lalita who knew him from childhood. He goes on the date having consumed several alcoholic drinks so that he can talk to her, which naturally results in an awkward conversation as he opines five or six times about how great it is that she "isn't fat anymore" (*The Big Bang Theory*, "The Grasshopper Experiment").

Penny, Leonard, Howard, and Sheldon are sat at the bar in the same establishment watching the date when Sheldon realizes that Lalita resembles the illustrations from a children's book his mother used to read him about an Indian princess named Princess Punchali. When Raj formally introduces Lalita to the group, Sheldon, mostly by accident, charms her by referencing his fond memories of the book, that he can "practically smell the Lotus blossoms woven into your ebony hair", or that "it was said that the gods fashioned her eyes out of the stars, and that roses were ashamed to bloom in the presence of her ruby lips". Sheldon and Lalita leave together, much to Raj's chagrin, to go for a meal just the two of them, leaving Raj abandoned. If Sheldon is asexual, where does that leave Raj?

If gender is defined in relation to the heterosexual matrix, then we might ask questions of Raj's gender as well as his sexuality – the show explores these questions diegetically. Ann-Gee Lee (2015) points out that the Indian subcontinent already has its third gender in the hijra, a social category of people defined as beyond male and female roles. As Lee observes, within Indian popular culture hijra tend to be othered characters providing comic relief, like the role adopted here by Raj. However, season five sees some serious steps toward heterosexual chrononormativity for the other three men, with Howard and Bernadette married, Sheldon and Amy declaring boyfriend/girlfriend labels, and Leonard and Penny formally dating for the second time. With white heterosexuality now affirmed by its performance and not requiring a racialized other, Raj's storylines begin to move beyond comic relief and allow his character to develop much more – notably, by the end of season six, after breaking up with his first serious girlfriend Lucy, he develops the ability to talk to women.

Raj then dates Emily Sweeney, a dermatologist with whom he reconnects after having gone on a disastrous date with her in season seven, through most of seasons eight and nine. However, even when he achieves the sustenance of a successful adult heterosexual relationship, Raj continues to be emasculated throughout. The end of the relationship is a case in point, indicative of the shape of it in the previous season and a half. The seeds of the end are sowed when Emily expresses a liking for a lamp that resembles a fake severed head, violent imagery that contrasts with Raj's domesticated response: "I guess I'm just more of a Pottery Barn, Crate & Barrel kind of guy" (*The Big Bang Theory*, "The Commitment Determination"). Similarly, when he finally breaks up with Emily in season nine, it is he who ends up crying, not her (*The Big Bang Theory*, "The Valentino Submergence").

By season 12, however, Raj's family background is treated by the show and characters as less of a punchline. In previous seasons, Raj's parents' multiple attempts to organize an arranged marriage for Raj were not just met with derision by Raj but also treated as an absurd comic proposition by the show in general. In season 12, he asks his parents to set up an arranged marriage (*The Big Bang Theory*, "The Wedding Gift Wormhole"). His parents find a woman named Anu, and after she and Raj find that they enjoy each other's company, they call off the engagement, deciding instead that it would be better to get to know each other romantically before marriage. When Anu is offered a permanent job in London, Raj resolves to travel to London to marry her (*The Big Bang Theory*, "The Maternal Conclusion"). At the airport, in a pastiche of the romantic comedy genre Raj loves, Howard runs into shot and implores with him, "stay here with ... the people who love you". Despite the increased respect with which Raj's Indian background is treated throughout this narrative, he is doubly emasculated by the situation, both by the homosocial pastiche of a heterosexual plot, and Raj's passive position within it that continues to at least limit Howard's emasculation. At the same time, Raj's last chance of a happy, straight, chrononormative ending is sacrificed, his desexualized masculinity continuing to legitimize and regulate white heteronormativity.

Men and race in New Girl

With the debut of *New Girl* in 2012, not only was its cast the most ethnically *diverse* of any hangout sitcom, but from the beginning the show addressed issues of race directly. However, the casting of Damon Wayans Jr. as Coach followed by Lamorne Morris as Winston produced some difficult questions about "tokenism". While, for example, a blog post was written for *Time* magazine praising the happy accident that led to having two black men in the cast (Poniewozik 2013), white cast and creators were asked on numerous occasions "can you *have* two black guys in the show?", drawing unimpressed responses. The official line from executive producer Dave Finkel appealed to a typical colorblind anti-racism, asserting that the recasting had "nothing to do with race" (Finkel in Andreeva 2011), while Jake Johnson, who plays Nick, responded at a television and culture festival that they could have a "bunch of" black people on one show if they wanted. Yet there were striking similarities to the two characters at the beginning that lend credence to allegations of tokenism, Coach, a competitively minded former basketball coach, Winston, a competitively minded former basketball player. This was underlined by narrative: in episode six, Winston discovers he has a hidden talent for playing the handbells and upsets the students in Jess's school handbell club with his aggressive motivation and perfectionism (*New Girl*, "Bells") – an almost identical storyline to Coach's pilot storyline in which he struggles to non-aggressively motivate and encourage a woman employing him as a personal trainer (*New Girl*, "Pilot").

By season three, though, perhaps to differentiate the two characters, Winston is an entirely different, somewhat feminized, character. He spends much of his time gossiping with Cece and is the doting owner of an exotic shorthair tabby cat named Furguson. This change in character does not appear to emerge from a character arc or development, rather than shifting some of the basic characteristics of Winston. Whereas Jess, Nick, Schmidt, and Cece in the pilot are consistent with their characters in later episodes, alongside the hugging and learning that characterizes the hangout sitcom, the Winston who Nick described as "incredibly talented but he's a jerk about it" and "one of those guys that he'll never pass the ball if he thinks he can score" in the show's sixth episode (*New Girl*, "Bells") is not recognizable as the same character by as early as season two. After a directionless opening season, including a brief stint as a nanny (highlighting the hangout sitcom's fondness for a caring masculinity), he works as a personal assistant to a locally famous radio host on the fictional KQTO station. He eventually becomes the host of his own show, before quitting impulsively and without a plan in season three. The following episode (*New Girl*, "Basketsball"), he decides he wants to become a police officer, which is where his narrative really begins.

There is a significant amount of both academic and popular scholarship about the racial politics of the police in the USA, and particularly in relation to masculinity. Black men are far more likely than any other group to be the subjects of police violence, and the names of those killed in recent years by serving police – Trayvon Martin, Breonna Taylor, George Floyd, and more – have become clarion calls for Black Lives Matter and other anti-racist movements. In a similar vein, William Hoston (2014, 4) traces the disproportionate incarceration rates of black men in the USA back to the gendered treatment of slaves, observing that police brutality toward black men today deploys the same images of black masculinity as a threat to white masculinity as were used to justify the different forms of cruel punishment and discipline several centuries ago between enslaved men and women. How does *New Girl* then parse this complex political situation? Indeed, the black police officer who wrestles with the contradictions produced by his (and most often *his* and not her) identity and career choice, is a not uncommon fixture in popular media these days – cop sitcom *Brooklyn Nine-Nine* (2013–2021) has two senior black police officers, one a precinct captain, who both struggle with the contradictions of their positions at times and ultimately decide to work within the system.

Comparing contemporary inequalities to the Jim Crow laws of the 19th and early 20th century, Michelle Alexander (2010, 235) asks: "how can something akin to racial caste system exist when people like Condoleezza Rice, Colin Powell, and Barack Obama are capable of rising from next to nothing to the pinnacles of wealth and power?". Her answer is this: "far from undermining the current system of control, the new caste system depends, in no small part, on black exceptionalism. The colorblind public consensus the supports the new caste system insists that race no longer matters" (Alexander 2010, 235). She argues that, in accordance with neoliberal individualism, "in short, mass incarceration is predicated on the notion that an extraordinary number of African Americans (but not all) have freely chosen a life of crime and thus belong behind bars" (Alexander 2010, 235).

This is the same logic that governs Winston's choice to join the police. If black individuals can choose to overcome the barriers and succeed in white society, they can also choose to commit crimes, or even choose to join the police force. Such a colorblind logic, one that is determined at least partly in relation to a neoliberal and post-white politics, thereby constructs black masculinities that are both oriented by, but simultaneously struggle to challenge, those white norms. In an episode actually written by Lamorne Morris who plays Winston, (*New Girl*, "Par 5") he dates a black woman named KC who is an activist against police brutality. Even here, the show does not substantively address the role whiteness plays in structuring such institutions – this narrative features only two references to whiteness. The first is a flashback joke during the trial of O.J. Simpson in which a teenage Nick questions why the news needs to label the Simpson's car "white", and the second does not call out Nick's own potentially complicity in his lack of understanding why black people might be scared of the police, but just states that he would not understand it, when Winston says, "I love you, but you're white, I'm black". Whiteness is not formulated as a problem because it is constructed as an individualized identity rather than a structuring norm, which is a function of its dominance portrayed as being over a long time ago. In *New Girl*, the fate of the male character is a case in point: Winston's career is in an arm of the state, while Nick's dead-end bartending work gives way to a career as an indie author. Schmidt presents, though, an interesting case, beginning as the show's must successful male character with a career in advertising, and eventually becoming a stay-at-home dad, while performing a form of Jewishness influenced by New York Yiddish culture, as explored next.

Conditional whiteness in New York

So far I have suggested that racialization in early hangout sitcoms was governed by colorblindness – as Chidester (2008, 158) puts it, "a modernist insistence on presence as the carrier of meaning and influence", which "holds that texts free of overt or explicit references to race simply cannot communicate racial meanings". So, as long as *Friends* steers clear of acknowledging race, it simply has nothing to say about the controversial terrain of racial politics. Yet, the decision to limit the inclusion of non-white characters is political precisely because of the unmarked status it gives to whiteness, further highlighted by the subsequent treatment of the eventual non-white characters. There is, however, depending on the way you see it, either a complex subsection of white culture or a marginalized group that is sometimes conditionally accepted by white culture that structures *Friends*: I am talking about the subgenre's relation to New York's Italian and, particularly, Ashkenazi Jewish immigrant communities.

New York City's culture has been shaped by immigrant communities since Europeans first colonized North America, many of whom have historically occupied positions of what we might call "conditional whiteness" – notably, Irish, German, Italian, and Eastern European Ashkenazi Jewish groups.

The whiteness of each of these groups is non-identical and confusing, not least because the final group, unlike the others, does not derive from a single nation-state. The liminal spaces these identities and communities occupy in relation to national and ethnic identity therefore can be difficult to read or understand. In the case of many of these New York groups, food is quite frequently a signifier, not least because of how foods brought over by them have become synonymous with east coast US cuisine: New York pizza, beigels, cheesecake, pickled gherkins, burgers (see Diner 2001). Indeed, food is one of the key markers of Joey's relative otherness, and he is as close as *Friends* gets to a non-white main character. He is the only main cast member to end up without a partner at the end of the show, and though this may be partly down to his eponymous spin-off, Joey is a notorious lothario, echoing the deviant and excessive sexual appetites of othered Latinx masculinities on-screen (Martinez-Cruz 2020). Joey's otherness comes from his Italian background, an identity that is bound up almost entirely in food. When we are first introduced to Joey's relationship with his father, Joey Sr., an Italian New Yorker with an accent to match, Joey Jr. is cooking with mushrooms, a herb that appears to be basil, and tomato sauce (*Friends*, "The One with the Boobies"); the gang's local pizza joint are familiar with the "Joey special", which is two pizzas stacked on top of one another (*Friends*, "The One With Ross's Wedding, Part 1"); in his spin-off show, he bonds with his siblings over lasagna (*Joey*, "Joey and the Taste Test"). There is more to be written, for sure, on Joey's Italian masculinity, but Jewishness and Jewish masculinity, partly by virtue of their relation to New York, structures the hangout sitcom in ways that Italian masculinity does not.

Table 5.1 demonstrates myriad complications in terms of individual characters' Jewishness – there are the simple cases of explicitly Jewish characters played by Jewish actors, of which there is at least one in each sitcom. Then there are the cases of non-Jewish actors playing Jewish characters: Courtney Cox as Monica Geller, and Jennifer Aniston playing Rachel Green, a character that *Friends* creators Marta Kauffman and David Crane have said they conceived of as Jewish, though where this comes from and its exact nature remain unclear, as noted by Brook (2003, 125). There are also several cases of Ashkenazi Jewish actors playing white non-Jewish characters, such as Jason Segel as Marshall, Melissa Rauch as Bernadette, and Jake Johnson as Nick. Then there are further questions hinted at by the title of the second column, "Jewish, or implied", such as, what are we to do with a character named Leonard Hofstadter whose name reads as sonically Jewish, but whose religious background is never discussed and whose actor Johnny Galecki appears to have no Jewish ancestry? And how are we to interpret the Jewish Lisa Kudrow playing Phoebe, a character never particularly conceived of as Jewish but who finds out her biological father is played by the Jewish "Woody Allenish little man" (Brook 2003, 125) Bob Balaban? Or Zooey Deschanel, a Jewish convert via marriage, playing Jess?

Breaking the circle: Challenging whiteness in the hangout sitcom 133

Then there is, of course, the obvious fact that proto-hangout sitcom *Seinfeld* (1989–1998) is, both in terms of representation and narrative, at least as Jewish a sitcom as it is white. Its title is the Jewish surname of one of its Jewish creators, while the other Jewish creator, Larry David, based the half-Jewish character George Costanza on himself. Carla Johnson (1994) shows that George and Jerry can be respectively read, respectively, as instantiations of Yiddish stock comedy characters the schlemiel and schlimazl,[1] while Jerry and George's anxieties are both constructed via a particular construction of a skittish anxious New York Yiddishkeit, which refers to an evocation of Eastern European Ashkenazi Jewish cultures (Brook 2003, 106–109). Following the legacy of *Seinfeld*, half of the characters in *Friends* are Jewish, and over the period of the hangout sitcom, 33% of the characters are Jewish.

The hangout sitcom is, in short, both a white sitcom and a Jewish sitcom, which raises a wider question: should this Jewish history be flattened out as a form of whiteness, or acknowledged as a contradiction within the sitcom's white history? Or, as much of the answer to this will depend on, how white is Jewishness? There is no easy answer to this question, and the relationship between whiteness and Jewishness in the USA is one that is provisional, unstable, and complex.

Gendering assimilation anxieties

Prior to the Second World War, Jewishness had an at best ambiguous relation to whiteness. After the war, a variety of societal upheavals saw Jewishness shed at least some of its otherness. The initial post-war period for the global Jewish diaspora was of course marked by two major events: the dark shadow of the Shoah, and the culmination of Zionism in the founding of the state of Israel. Though the founding of Israel, and its ongoing centrality to the identities of many Jewish people around the world, may have heightened a sense of otherness among Jews' identities, Karen Brodkin (1998, 141) suggests that as it became more aware of "general horror of the Holocaust, [the USA] became positively philo-Semitic in its embrace of Jewish culture". Subsequently, within the post-war reconstruction that centered the nuclear family, Jewish families eventually came to serve as something of a "model minority culture". Their provisional incorporation into whiteness was granted on their assimilation into white values and a constant self-policing of outward Jewishness; Brodkin (1998) describes this as "a male-centred version of Jewishness that was prefiguratively white, and a specifically Jewish form of whiteness, a whiteness of our own". Yet this form of whiteness, it is widely accepted, has remained fraught with tensions that "the entrance of Jews into the white mainstream did not resolve" (Goldstein 2006, 4). Eric Goldstein suggests "impulses for distinctiveness" from mainstream whiteness appear to bubble back and forth – in recent years, perhaps partly influenced by the post-white consensus from which a resurgent antisemitic far right have benefitted (Tanner 2021). Indeed, much of this ambivalence seems to stem from American Jews themselves, and the difficulties in personally negotiating the long history of Jews as outsiders and their recent acceptance into the mainstream.

This did not come without its anxieties, many of which were on display in *The Goldbergs* (1949–1956), an NBC comedy drama (which actually began as a TV show in 1929, and was on the edge of the sitcom genre) that followed a middle-class Jewish family in the Bronx area of New York City. Riv-Ellen Prell (1999) shows how *The Goldbergs* negotiated the difficulties between maintain Jewish identity and assimilating to American identity. This was most represented by Jake Goldberg, the patriarch of the family, whose sense of religious Jewish propriety about gender roles clashed with the new construction of the housewife as the lead consumer in the new all-American consumer family; here, "Jewish women were coded as usurpers of power and excessive consumers in their suburban life" (Prell 1999, 173). Jake Goldberg's wife Molly, "while an immigrant, was both suburban and acculturated" – when she decided that "the family's gifts to Rosalie for her birthday should include a cashmere sweater and a third watch … her knowledge of what a young woman should own demonstrated how much more successfully she had Americanized than Jake" (Prell 1999, 172). This concerned the Goldberg patriarch significantly, as he found himself left behind by socioeconomic happenstance, his Jewish masculinity at odds with the cultural whiteness in which Jake found himself. In short, this is as much about white assimilation anxiety as anything else – Jewish gender stereotypes' "continuity in the form of male-female hostility suggests that in the United states gender relationships are affected by Jews experience as a minority within a dominant culture" (Prell 1999, 19).

The masculine anxieties of Jake Goldberg are very similar to those of Jerry and George in *Seinfeld*, except in place of the post-war consensus shift toward consumer capitalism and culture is the shift toward neoliberal capitalism and culture (see Buerkle 2011). For Jerry and George, this is the source of a plethora of anxieties that are overdetermined by their Jewishness. The two men are anxious about their position in the world, about what is often framed as threats to the hegemony of men and of patriarchy, and produce anxiety about heterosexual romance (Brabon 2013, 2007). The Jewishness of such romantic anxiety pits the sexual temptation of an alluring consumerist non-Jewish femininity against the characters' compulsion to preserve Jewish outsider identity. Jerry and George make a big deal of Elaine's "shiksappeal"[2] after the group attend a bar mitzvah during which the newly anointed man kisses Elaine (*Seinfeld*, "The Serenity Now"); the implication, suggests Shany Rozenblatt (2014, 46) is that "'conquering' the shiksa is proof of manhood for Jews … By marrying 'shiksas' they are leaving behind the image of the emasculate" Jewish man. Anxieties here stem from a perceived double-outsider status, a Jewish identity combined with a fear of the empowered postfeminist femininities of neoliberal, "shiksa", women.

Anxious, conceptual, Jewish masculinities

Vincent Brook (2003, 3) identifies from 1989 a growing "Jewish sitcom trend", defined as "situation comedy series featuring explicitly Jewish protagonists". By Brook's criteria, the 14-year period between 1989 and the publication of his book in 2003 saw the advent of at least 33 Jewish sitcoms, compared to just six in the preceding four decades; today, we might add several more to the list, not least the three shows featured in this book that premiered post-2003. Brook identifies in that short 14 years three overlapping "phases" of the Jewish sitcom. He suggests the first phase, initiated by the controversial *Chicken Soup* (1989), was influenced by the influx of black sitcoms in the years preceding them, and particularly by a new industry logic that "expression of ethno-racial identity became not only permissible, but even desirable, almost obligatory" (Brook 2003, 67). However, where this first phase differed from the black sitcom trend was in debates over the correct amount of Jewishness in the shows – industrial discussions over whether they were too Jewish or not Jewish enough, the result of an ambiguous whiteness. *Seinfeld* was even rejected by NBC for being "too New York, too Jewish" (Mirzoeff 2007, 74).

Brook then suggests that the second phase – in which he places *Friends* – is characterized by "conceptual Jewishness". Many of the characters in *Friends*, he points out, were "literally *conceived*, more than *represented* as Jews" (Brook 2003, 124, emphasis original), written as well as read by audiences culturally as Jewish, but without any explicit textual reference to Jewishness – Rachel in *Friends*, for example, embodies most of the stereotypes of the "Jewish American princess", and the show's writers have said that they wrote her character Jewish, but the text only tangentially references this identity. This peculiar positionality, suggests Brook, should be read in two contexts: the anxieties that emerge from the provisional whiteness of American Jews, combined with a postmodern condition in which identity is shed of material genealogy, similar to Baudrillard's conception of the simulacrum (Baudrillard 1994 [1981]). This, I argue, is what determines the tendency for the postfeminist male singleton (PMS) in the hangout sitcom to be vaguely/maybe Jewish – a complex history of male Jewish assimilation and gender anxieties reduced to an aesthetic marker of anxiety, rather than a sociocultural or material identity.

The unambiguously Jewish Ross in *Friends* perhaps marks the turning point here, his Jewishness a fraction more relevant to his masculine anxieties than the PMS in the other shows.[3] Ross, most of the time, seems threatened and intimidated by women who are stronger or smarter than he is, while looking down on those who he sees as below him. Yet, it is notable that his fated on-off love interest, Rachel, is the stereotypical Jewish American princess, a media stereotype of a spoiled, entitled Jewish daughter of a wealthy family that Brodkin (1998, 163) argues embodies "Jewish men's projections of their own nightmares about whiteness onto Jewish women". An Americanized

Jewish femininity who embodies both the desire to assimilate and differentiate, Rachel can be read as much as an extension of Ross's simultaneous Jewish and masculine anxieties as her own.

The two PMSs that follow Ross have considerably more tangled and tangential relations to Jewishness. In terms of Ted, Josh Radnor is of Jewish background, but it is not until season six that he outwardly states he is "half-Jewish" (*How I Met Your Mother*, "Natural History"), which we might assume to mean having one Jewish parent. But none of his anxieties seem remotely related to this, as opposed to his ongoing failure to find his fated partner. In *The Big Bang Theory*, though Leonard's religious background is never textually addressed, "Hofstadter" reads as a sonically Jewish or Yiddish name. Furthermore, though I have not managed to find any creative admission, it is reasonable to assume that the fictional physicists Sheldon Cooper and Leonard Hofstadter were named for Nobel Prize-winning physicists Leon Cooper and Robert Hofstadter respectively – the latter of whom *was* Jewish. None of this is to say that we can reasonably assume anything about the character's religious and ethnic identity, but that there is a signified or implied Jewishness to Leonard that runs parallel with the character's televisual lineage. The PMS's Jewishness is reduced to empty signifier only, assimilation anxiety giving way to postfeminist anxieties. However, there is an explicitly Jewish character in *The Big Bang Theory* in Howard, who occupies a very similar position to Schmidt in *New Girl*.

Jewish masculinities after whiteness

In *The Big Bang Theory* and *New Girl*, masculine Jewish anxiety transfers to the douchebag via Howard and Schmidt, whose masculine Jewish anxieties are consciously reintroduced as a racial other, separate from wider masculine socioeconomic anxieties. This, I suggest, is made possible by the logic of the post-white settlement – governing the assumption of the end of whiteness is an imperative to re-open and re-assert difference from within whiteness, which is simultaneously combined with the individualization of racial identity. As such, American Jewishness is to some extent decoupled from whiteness whilst it also becomes separated from its material and social histories, such that it becomes difficult to talk about or conceive of the intersection of assimilationist and gender-based anxieties. The result is Howard and Schmidt's ambiguously white Jewish pride, which is completely unrelated to their anxious postfeminist masculinities.

Howard's Jewishness is a cliché, embodying a range of arguably antisemitic stereotypes, "represented as the prototypical Jewish male; he is thin, gawky, weak, and domineered by women" (Rubin 2021, 334), both his overbearing Jewish mother and his wife. Daniel Rubin (2021) suggests that Howard is something of an anachronism, a return to pre-war stereotypes of effeminate Jewish masculinities that affirmed and conferred a racialized otherness on Jewish men in an era before a conditional class-based entry into

Breaking the circle: Challenging whiteness in the hangout sitcom 137

whiteness. His Jewish heritage is a source of pride; it very much plays into his ego when a sex worker his friends hire for him named Mikayla pretends to be "Esther Rozenblatt", to provide him with the "Jewish girlfriend experience" (*The Big Bang Theory*, "The Vegas Renormalization"). They seem instead to be related entirely to his masculinity, that he is a nerdy, short in stature, romantically unsuccessful man threatened by assertive postfemininities. He is not attracted to his Catholic wife Bernadette's "shiksappeal", but they bond over their similarly overbearing mothers. In short, though his Jewishness is something to be negotiated, it is a purely aesthetic, othered, and comedic identity, rather than something with a proper material impact on his life.

Schmidt, too, is proud of his background; in the show's first Christmas episode, the gang drive past a house with a menorah outside it, leading Schmidt to proudly declare, "oh, a menorah! Judaism, son!" (*New Girl*, "The 23rd"). Yet where entire episodes explore and examine Winston's relationship with blackness, there is little about Schmidt's Jewishness. Instead, his religious or racialized masculinity is again an aesthetic decision, earmarking a certain white male anxiety about women. Without rehashing old ground too much, his continual worries about being "good enough" for Cece seem to derive from her successful postfeminst femininity, combined with his own former fatness (again something of a Jewish masculine stereotype). Though the Jewishness of each is far more emphasized and explicit than with Ross or Ted, it rarely interacts with his gendered concerns.

Mike Hill (2004, 78) suggests that in the present post-white situation, "otherness has never been more sought out nor more divisively manipulated than it is in U.S. culture and politics today". Specifically, both white liberal and neo-fascist dispositions toward race fundamentally rely on a desire for

Figure 5.4 Schmidt marries Cece with his yarmulke visible.

racialized otherness. This is demonstrated by contemporary portrayals of Jewish masculinity in the hangout sitcom; a renewed, still often white, otherness, emphasized by stereotypes but reduced to aesthetics. The assimilation anxiety is gone, replaced by Jewish masculinity as a general televisual signifier for a form of white postfeminist masculinity that is completely separate from Jewish identity. As such, the boundaries of white masculinities are further policed, not only by the characters that are white non-Jews, but by the separation of white masculinity and Jewish aesthetics in Jewish men in *The Big Bang Theory* and *New Girl*.

Black sitcoms in the 21st century

In something of a delayed reply to the black sitcoms of the 1980s, a spate of recent shows has resurrected a rather traditional form of family sitcom while imbuing it with a narrative focus of questions about race in much the way that the sitcom has nearly always been about gender and sexuality. For example, *Black-ish* (2014–2022) followed a black family in the suburbs, not dissimilar to *The Cosby Show*, except that, as indicated by the show's title, much of the show examines the liminality of a black family in white suburbs; following a similar premise, *The Neighborhood* (2018–present) reverses the situation, following a prototypical white suburban family who move into a majority black neighborhood. On a similar vein, there have been several shows that often adhere largely to the hangout sitcom formula, but which also center the black experience in the US – notably, *Insecure* (2016–2021) and *Atlanta* (2016–2022). These latter shows are genre hybrids, with as many elements of dramatic television and markers of "quality television" – single camera, unstable camera work, shorter seasons, variable episode lengths – as traditional sitcoms. The latter shows have been enabled by some significant changes to the television industry, notably the advent of streaming services as well as an increased willingness for smaller channels to take risks with television shows to create brand identities. *Insecure*, for example, was produced by HBO, a channel associated with quality television, while *Atlanta* was on FX, which has a reputation as an alternative channel. Because of this institutional context, combined with a contemporary popular politics of race that focuses on representation and inclusion, these sitcoms offer more ambiguous and sometimes critical musings on a range of sociopolitical issues. Such issues create a very different sitcom landscape internationally, as explored in the UK in the next chapter.

Notes

1 The schlemiel is a clumsy, inept man, while the schlimazl is his corollary, the person who is on the receiving end of the schlemiel's incompetence. Or, to roughly quote the Yiddish saying, when the schlemiel spills the soup, it lands on the schlimazl (Johnson 1994).

2 "Shiksa" is a derogatory word of Yiddish origin often used to shame or insult gentile women.
3 In a recent documentary in the UK by British Jewish comedian David Baddiel about contemporary antisemitism, David Schwimmer stated that he has never "felt white", even while asserting he "passes" as white and receives many of the benefits that come with that, also acknowledging the lack of significant markers of Ross's Jewishness (*Jews Don't Count*, 2022). This non-white interiority is an effective way of thinking about Ashkenazi Jewishness as a conditional form of whiteness.

Filmography

The Addams Family. 1964–1966. [TV] Levy, David, Creator, ABC: USA.
Atlanta. 2016–2022. [TV] Glover, Donald, Creator, FX: USA.
The Big Bang Theory. 2007–2019. [TV] Lorre, Chuck, and Bill Prady, Creator, CBS: USA.
Black-ish. 2014–2022. [TV] Barris, Kenya, Creator, ABC: USA.
Brooklyn Nine-Nine. 2013–2021. [TV] Goor, Dan, and Michael Schur, Creator, Fox, NBC: USA.
Chicken Soup. 1989. Mason, Jackie, and Lynn Redgrave, Creator, ABC: USA.
The Cosby Show. 1984–1992. [TV] Cosby, William H., Ed Weinberger, and Michael J. Leeson, Creator, NBC: USA.
Damon. 1998. [TV] Benvenuti, Leo, Steve Rudnick, and Damon Wayans, Creator, Fox: USA.
Father Knows Best. 1954–1960. [TV] James, Ed, Creator, CBS, NBC: USA.
Friends. 1994–2004. [TV] Crane, David, and Marta Kauffman, Creator, NBC: USA.
The Goldbergs. 1949–1956. [TV] Berg, Gertrude, Creator, CBS: USA.
Happy Endings. 2011–2013. [TV] Caspe, David, Creator, ABC: USA.
How I Met Your Mother. 2005–2014. [TV] Bays, Carter, and Craig Thomas, Creator, CBS: USA.
I Love Lucy. 1951–1957. [TV] Oppenheimer, Jess, Madelyn Davis, and Bob Carroll Jr., Creator, CBS: USA.
Insecure. 2016–2021. [TV] Rae, Issa, Creator, HBO: USA.
The Jeffersons. 1975–1985. [TV] Nicholl, Don, Michael Ross, and Bernie West, Creator, CBS: USA.
Jews Don't Count. 2022. [Documentary] Baddiel, David, Creator, Channel 4: UK.
Julia. 1968–1971. [TV] Kanter, Hal, Creator, NBC: USA.
Leave it to Beaver. 1957–1963. [TV] Connelly, Joe, and Bob Mosher, Creator, CBS, ABC: USA.
The Neighborhood. 2018-present. [TV] Reynolds, Jim, Creator, CBS: USA.
New Girl. 2011–2018. [TV] Meriwether, Elizabeth, Creator, Fox: USA.
Sanford and Son. 1972–1977. [TV] Lear, Norman, and Bud Yorkin, Creator, NBC: USA.
The Secret Diary of Desmond Pfeiffer. 1998. [TV] Fanaro, Barry, and Mort Nathan, Creator, UPN: USA.
Seinfeld. 1989–1998. [TV] David, Larry, and Jerry Seinfeld, Creator, NBC: USA.

References

Alexander, Michelle. 2010. *The New Jim Crow: Mass Incarceration in the Age of Colorblindness*. New York: The New Press.
Allen, Theodore W. 1994. *The Invention of the White Race. Vol. 1: Racial Oppression and Social Control*. London: Verso.
Andreeva, Nellie. 2011. "TCA: The post-pilot casting change on fox's 'new girl' helped keep it real." Deadline. https://deadline.com/2011/08/tca-the-post-pilot-casting-change-on-foxs-new-girl-helped-keep-it-real-154137/. Accessed 17 March.
Applebaum, Barbara. 2010. *Being White, Being Good: White Complicity, White Moral Responsibility, and Social Justice Pedagogy*. Plymouth: Lexington Books.
Baudrillard, Jean. 1994 [1981]. *Simulacra and Simulation*. Translated by Sheila Faria Glaser. Ann Arbor, MI: University of Michigan Press.
Bodroghkozy, Aniko. 2012. *Equal Time: Television and the Civil Rights Movement*. Chicago, IL: University of Illinois Press.
Brabon, Benjamin A. 2013. "'Chuck Flick': A genealogy of the postfeminist male singleton." In *Postfeminism and Contemporary Hollywood Cinema*, edited by Joel Gwynne, and Nadine Muller, 116–130. Basingstoke: Palgrave Macmillan.
Brabon, Benjamin A. 2007. "The spectral phallus: Re-membering the postfeminist man." In *Postfeminist Gothic: Critical Interventions in Contemporary Culture*, edited by Benjamin A. Brabon, and Stephanie Genz, 56–67. London: Palgrave Macmillan.
Brodkin, Karen. 1998. *How Jews Became White Folks and What That Says about Race in America*. London: Rutgers University Press.
Brook, Vincent. 2003. *Something Ain't Kosher Here: The Rise of the "Jewish" Sitcom*. London: Rutgers University Press.
Brook, Vincent. 2010. "Virtual ethnicity: Incorporation, diversity, and the contemporary 'Jewish' sitcom." *Emergences* 11 (2):269–285. doi: 10.1080/10457220120098991.
Buerkle, C. Wesley. 2011. "Masters of their domain: *Seinfeld* and the discipline of mediated men's sexual economy." In *Performing American Masculinities: The 21st Century Man in Popular Culture*, edited by Elwood Watson, and Marc E. Shaw, 9–34. Bloomington, IN: Indiana University Press.
Chidester, Phil. 2008. "May the circle stay unbroken: *Friends*, the presence of absence, and the rhetorical reinforcement of whiteness." *Critical Studies in Media Communication* 25 (2):157–174. doi: 10.1080/15295030802031772.
Cobb, Shelley. 2018. "'I'd like y'all to get a black friend': The politics of race in *Friends*." *Television & New Media* 19 (8):708–723. doi: 10.1177/1527476418778420.
Coleman, Robin R. Means, Charlton D. McIlwain, and Jessica Moore Matthews. 2016. "The hidden truths in contemporary black sitcoms." In *The Sitcom Reader: America Re-viewed, Still Skewed*, edited by Mary M. Dalton, and Laura R. Linder, 279–294. Albany, NY: SUNY Press.
Cummings, Melbourne S. 1988. "The changing image of the black family on television." *The Journal of Popular Culture* 22 (2):75–85. doi: 10.1111/j.0022-3840.1988.2202_75.x.
Diner, Hasia R. 2001. *Hungering for America: Italian, Irish, & Jewish Foodways in the Age of Migration*. Cambridge, MA: Harvard University Press.
Dyer, Richard. 2017 [1997]. *White*. London: Routledge.

Eagleton-Pierce, Matthew. 2016. "On individualism in the neoliberal period." PSA 66th Annual International Conference, Brighton.
Eng, David L. 2001. "Racial castration: Managing masculinity in Asian America." In *Perverse Modernities*, edited by Jack Halberstam, and Lisa Lowe. Durham, NC: Duke University Press.
Freeman, Elizabeth. 2010. *Time Binds: Queer Temporalities, Queer Histories*. Edited by Jack Halberstam, and Lisa Lowe, *Perverse Modernities*. Durham: Duke University Press.
Garner, Steve. 2007. *Whiteness: An Introduction*. London: Routledge.
Goldstein, Eric L. 2006. *The Price of Whiteness: Jews, Race, and American Identity*. Oxford: Princeton University Press.
Gray, Herman S. 2005. *Cultural Moves: African Americans and the Politics of Representation*. London: University of California Press.
Haralovich, Mary Beth. 2009. "Sitcoms and suburbs: Positioning the 1950s homemaker." *Quarterly Review of Film and Video* 11 (1):61–83. doi: 10.1080/10509208909361287.
Hill, Mike. 2004. *After whiteness: Unmaking an American majority*. Edited by Michael Bérubé, *Cultural Front*. London: New York University Press.
Hoston, William T. 2014. *Black Masculinity in the Obama Era: Outliers of Society*. Basingstoke: Palgrave Macmillan.
Hunter, Shona, and Christi van der Westhuizen, eds. 2022. *Routledge Handbook of Critical Studies in Whiteness*. Oxford: Routledge.
Imawura, Jane Naomi. 2011. *Visual Orientalism: Asian Religions and American Popular Culture*. Oxford: Oxford University Press.
Jhally, Sut, and Justin Lewis. 1992. *Enlightened Racism: The Cosby Show, Audiences, and the Myth of the American Dream*. Boulder, CO: Westview Press.
Johnson, Carla. 1994. "The schlemiel and the schlimazl in Seinfeld." *Journal of Popular Film and Television* 22 (3):116–124. doi: 10.1080/01956051.1994.9943676.
Kymlicka, Will. 2013. "Neoliberal multiculturalism?" In *Social Resilience in the Neoliberal Era*, edited by Peter A. Hall, and Michèle Lamont, 99–126. Cambridge: Cambridge University Press.
Lamb, Sharon, Elena V. Kosterina, Tangela Roberts, Medeline Brodt, Meredith Maroney, and Lucas Dangler. 2018. "Voices of the mind: Hegemonic masculinity and others in mind during young men's sexual encounters." *Men and Masculinities* 21 (2):254–275. doi: 10.1177/1097184X17695038.
Lee, Ann-Gee. 2015. "The androgyny of Rajesh Koothrappali." In *The Sexy Science of The Big Bang Theory: Essays on Gender in the Series*, edited by Nadine Farghaly, and Eden Leone, 174–188. Jefferson, NC: McFarland.
Lee, Jennifer, and Min Zhou. 2015. *The Asian American Achievement Paradox*. New York: Russell Sage Foundation.
Lemke, Thomas. 2001. "'The birth of bio-politics': Michel Foucault's lecture at the Collège de France on neo-liberal governmentality." *Economy and Society* 30 (2):190–207. doi: 10.1080/03085140120042271.
Martinez-Cruz, Paloma. 2020. "Chicano Dracula: The passions and predilections of Bela Lugosi, Gomez Addams, and Kid Congo Powers." In *Decolonizing Latinx Masculinities*, edited by Arturo J. Aldama, and Frederick Luis Aldama, 185–197. Tucson, AZ: University of Arizona Press.
McGuigan, Jim. 2013. *Neoliberal Culture*. London: Palgrave Macmillan.
Mirzoeff, Nicholas. 2007. *Seinfeld*. London: British Film Institute.

Negra, Diane. 2009. *What a Girl Wants? Fantasizing the Reclamation of Self in Postfeminism.* London: Routledge.

Park, Michael. 2013. "Asian American masculinity eclipsed: A legal and historical perspective of emasculation through U.S. immigration practices." *The Modern American* 8 (1):5–17.

Poniewozik, James. 2013. "New girl, Brooklyn 9–9, and breaking the "one black friend" pattern." Time Magazine. https://entertainment.time.com/2013/11/07/new-girl-brooklyn-9-9-and-breaking-the-one-black-friend-pattern/. Accessed 17 March.

Prell, Riv-Ellen. 1999. *Fighting to Become Americans: Jews, Gender, and the Anxiety of Assimilation.* Boston, MA: Beacon Press.

Rozenblatt, Shany. 2014. "The representation of Jewish masculinity in contemporary American sitcoms." MA, Department of Foreign Literatures and Linguistics, Ben-Gurion University of the Negev.

Rubin, Daniel Ian. 2021. "The stereotypical portrayal of Jewish masculinity on *The Big Bang Theory*." *The Journal of Popular Culture* 54 (2):322–340.

Spigel, Lynn. 1992. *Make Room for TV: Television and the Family Ideal in Postwar America.* Chicago, IL: University of Chicago Press.

Tanner, Samuel J. 2021. "Jewishness and whiteness." In *Encyclopedia of Critical Whiteness Studies in Education*, edited by Zachary A. Casey, 328–330. Leiden: Brill Sense.

Vulture 2020. "The New Girl Guys Recall the Horrible Questions Asked About Coach and Winston.." accessed 12 September 2022. https://www.youtube.com/watch?v=AACKTtWo6no.

6 First as farce, then as tragedy

Failing and flailing neoliberal men in the UK's hangout(-style) sitcoms

"They say the family of the 21st century is made up of friends, not relatives. Then again, maybe that's just bollocks".

Daisy Steiner, *Spaced*, "Leaves"

How to re-make Friends and alienate British people

At the beginning of this book, I suggested that *Friends* was not just a US TV show, but a global zeitgeisty phenomenon. This goes not just for audience reactions, but for industrial practices and patterns, too, such that in 1995 its broadcast rights in the UK were bought out by Channel 4, and it began airing that April. Yet, as is often the case with TV shows, success spawns copycats, so throughout the 1990s in the UK, several programs were commissioned that took the US formula and tried to apply it to a British setting. First came *Game On* (1995–1998) on the BBC, with its Rembrandts-reminiscent opening theme, and main cast of three friends who grew up together in Kent, and now live in London. It had three seasons, stumbling particularly after the first season when its male lead, played by Ben Chaplin, departed for the bright lights of Hollywood. Apart from a BAFTA nomination in 1997 for Best Comedy that it did not win, *Game On* received little positive reception, and was abandoned after three seasons with loose plot ends. The next effort, *Babes in the Wood* (1998–1999), came from ITV as *Game On* was ending, primarily following three young women and their romantic encounters, eking out two seasons on the back of a swathe of negative comment. Both *Game On* and *Babes in the Wood* read as rather obvious British copycats of *Friends*, transferring upbeat character and relationship development, as well as an earnest sense of aspiration and a lack of peril about material wealth, into the same kinds of settings as predecessor British sitcoms with their gaudy 1970s sets and farce-tinted humor. But neither were particularly well-received by audiences or critics or syndicated. Neither have had any lasting cultural impact.

In 1999, however, *Spaced* (1999–2001) debuted on Channel 4, introducing the Generation-X Tim Bisley and Daisy Steiner, an aspiring comic book artist and aspiring journalist respectively, who face such difficulties finding

DOI: 10.4324/9781003363538-6

somewhere to live in a ruthless rental market that they pose as a professional couple to secure housing. *Spaced* was created by its stars, Simon Pegg (Tim) and Jessica Stevenson (Daisy),[1] both still in their 20s, and has a quirky, outsider, and at times sarcastic tone. Subsequently described by Pegg as "a reaction to the emergence of these 'youth sitcoms' that were trying to be the British version of *Friends*, and usually were written by people 20 years older than the characters, I'd say specifically *Game On* and *Babes in the Wood*" (De Semelyen and Freer 2020), it is loaded with intertextual references to a range of Hollywood cinema and US television, and revels in ambiguity and uncertainty. *Spaced*, though not a rip-roaring ratings success, was very positively received by critics, nominated for several awards including an Emmy in 2001, retains a significant cult following and is easily accessible to watch (particularly on the back of several subsequent movies courtesy of most of the same group).

These few case studies demonstrate the difficulties of international TV adaptation. In Chapter 1 I used Jane Feuer's reading of Todorov to describe the naming of genre as historical rather than theoretical – that is, describing the organic emergence of similar shows, rather than prescribing what new ones should contain. Yet I also pointed out that this becomes something of a theoretical pursuit afterwards, as other shows try to follow the formula, the success of which is not purely mathematical, but demands innovation or a unique selling point (like a voice-over, or making it about nerds). For international adaptation, such need is significantly heightened (see Beeden and de Bruin 2010, Sanson 2011). The difference therefore between *Game On* and *Spaced* is that the latter show did not just follow the formula, but adapted it to a new national cultural setting, understanding the range of cultural and institutional differences across the Atlantic.

What followed *Spaced* were several shows that adapted the elements of the hangout formula in diverse ways. *Coupling* (2000–2004) began in 2000, a show with three men and three women exploring dating and intimate relationships in London, who spend a lot of time hanging around doing nothing, and which was specifically marketed as the "British *Friends*". Yet *Coupling* is more explicit in its sex references than *Friends*, and more diverse in its use of camerawork and narrative. In 2003, the darker *Peep Show* (2003–2015) premiered, following two socially incompetent men of a similar age to the other shows whose dark inner thoughts are made available to the audience via voice-over. It would not be desirable, or even I suggest possible, to read these three UK hangout-style sitcoms without considering and understanding the shadow cast over them by *Friends* and the US hangout sitcom phenomenon.

In this chapter, I compare the men in the three mentioned UK hangout sitcoms to the four US ones explored so far in this book, placing both sets of shows within the cultural and industrial frameworks in which they were produced, and the ways in which they, as *Spaced* creator Simon Pegg put it, "reacted" to their transatlantic inspiration. All three feature men trying and struggling to adapt to a new set of neoliberal socioeconomic circumstances like in the US shows. However, I argue that men in UK hangout-style sitcoms are more prone to failing at their adaptation than their US counterparts, culminating in a range of tragic masculinities – notably in terms of career, sexuality, and love life. However, following Jack Halberstam (2011), I suggest that such failure leaves open the possibility of a queer reading of both the often-ambiguous narrative conclusions of each show as well as the range of loser characters, that can read as critical commentary. Though it would be excessive to describe the British sitcoms as "subversive" of capitalism, while presuming their US counterparts frequently lapse back into neoliberal common sense, there are a range of cultural and institutional differences that mean that the British sitcom landscape can leave itself open to a more expansive range of meanings and interpretations.

Cultural and institutional difference

It would be too easy to collapse the reasons for the differences in UK and US masculinities in sitcoms into truisms about the irony and pessimism of a British sense of humor, compared to a louder and more optimistic humor in the USA. That is not to say that there is no merit at all to such a diagnosis, but that to characterize national cultural differences in comedy between the two countries is neither necessary nor within the scope of this chapter. Rather, reasons for differences between masculinities in US and UK hangout sitcoms are more specific. These can be split into institutional differences relating to the differing histories, social position, and structures of the sitcom in each country, as well as the slightly different cultural characteristics of UK and US neoliberalisms.

British capitalism, class, and the sitcom

Neoliberalism is a global ideology both in that its impacts have been felt across the world, but also in that it takes markedly different shapes across borders. The most striking difference is perhaps broadly between the Global North and Global South, but there are also important differences between nation-states. Economically and policy-wise, British neoliberalism arose as a critique of British welfarism, a form of quasi-Keynesian, quasi-social democratic state-building that combined public spending and a planned economy with the nationalization of key industries (Tribe 2009, Albertson and Stepney 2019). In contrast, US neoliberalism's predecessor was a less explicitly state-oriented political economy, more built around adaptations to the "American Dream" (see Coskuncer-Balli 2020), and embodied in the rhetorical programs of a series of presidents in the mid-century: FDR's "New Deal", JFK's "New Frontier", or LBJ's "Great Society" (see Horn and Mirowski 2009).

British neoliberalism is arguably sold on a different rhetoric, even while imbuing its neoliberal subject with a near-identical set of demands and capabilities. Rather, British neoliberalism promises, if not the end of class structure, then at least the end of the working-class (see Jameson 1991, Hall 2017). Governments from the 1980s have regularly mobilized discourses around social mobility and aspiration – indeed, Prime Minister Margaret Thatcher, famously the daughter of a grocer who found her way to Oxford University, was able to sell herself as an ideal neoliberal subject, at one point opining, "this business of the working-class is on its way out I think. After all, aren't I working class? I work jolly hard, I can tell you". This is not to say that US neoliberalism does not aim to do similar things to class structure, but that it does not mobilize political discourses that are as focused on class. Indeed, class as a discursive topic has long infused the British sitcom, one of the first important differences between British and US sitcoms.

That the British sitcom forefronts the negotiation of class in much the way the US sitcom negotiates communal belonging and domestic ideology is not a novel argument and is also not to say that US sitcoms are not fruitful sites of class conflict. Richard Kilborn, for example, shows how some of the UK's sitcoms of the 1950s, *Steptoe and Son* (1962–1974) and *Hancock's Half Hour* (1956–1961) reflected "to some extent the frustrations of members of working-class communities whose lives were still being negatively impacted by the persistence of class-bound attitudes" (Kilborn 2016, 24). Class as an issue is addressed throughout the history of the British sitcom, from Basil Fawlty in *Fawlty Towers* (1975–1979), who is very concerned that his hotel be filled only with respectable (read: middle-class) white guests, and continuing through *Blackadder*'s (1983–1989) historical reflections on British class throughout history from the Middle Ages through to World War I.

Another important difference is related to genre: British sitcoms find their roots in somewhat different genres to the US sitcom, owing perhaps more to the genre of farce than vaudeville. Jessica Milner Davis defines farce thus: it "delights in taboo-violation, but ... avoids implied moral comment or social criticism and ... tends to debar empathy for its victims" (Davis 2013, 5–6, see also Davis 2017). Frequently containing slapstick and physical comedy, but not always, farce involves the construction of comedic scenarios and characters that exaggerate real life, despite often beginning with familiar and plausible premises. British sitcoms follow many of these conventions in ways that US sitcoms do not always, particularly in the way that episodes often build toward absurd denouements. *Fawlty Towers* is archetypal here, while *Coupling* has been described as a farce by critics (Lawson 2001) and both *Peep Show* and *Spaced* have multiple episodes that reach absurd endings, ranging from the consumption of a love interest's cooked dead pet dog (*Peep Show*, "Holiday"), or the pacification of an impending mugging by starting a mimed slow motion gun fight (*Spaced*, "Gone").

However, the British sitcom, bar a few exceptions, does not occupy the same popular position as the US sitcom (the writers of *Game On* and *Babes in the Wood* perhaps struggled against this, trying to subvert or challenge the slightly less aspirational telos of the British sitcom). While US sitcoms continue to dominate ratings, British sitcoms rarely attract millions of viewers.

There are notable exceptions, often around special episodes, such as an *Only Fools and Horses* (1981–2003) 1996 special episode that drew 24 million viewers (still the highest ever for a British comedy), and *Gavin & Stacey* (2007–2010), whose 2019 Christmas day special, 9 years after the show's original ending was the most-viewed event of the year with 18 million viewers. Even yet, these programs are anomalies in a British TV landscape historically dominated by soap operas and one-off royal family-related events. No British hangout-inspired sitcom has ever had the same popular appeal as US sitcoms, even among British viewers; *Peep Show* peaked at 1.7 million viewers in 2009 (McMahon 2009), while in 2001, when *Spaced* peaked at 1.7 million viewers, *Friends* on the same channel in the UK was pulling in 2.3 million, which was not close to its peak (Deans 2001). Proportionate to population size, these numbers pale in comparison to US hangout sitcoms. In short, they do not play the same cultural role as the US sitcom.

This has several consequences. First, British sitcoms are more diverse in and between one another than US sitcoms, with more variety even within subgeneric boundaries. This is not to claim that US comedies are identical in tone and focus; for instance, *It's Always Sunny in Philadelphia* (2005–present) is effectively a dark parody of the US hangout sitcom. It is more the case that television success is measured somewhat differently, with the sitcom genre in the UK being a space for genre innovation and internal diversity. The hangout sitcom is a good example of this, a mildly diverse subgenre that consists in small changes without significant shifts. *How I Met Your Mother* added a voice-over and made explicit the fated romance of *Friends*, while *The Big Bang Theory* added nerds and *New Girl* made a woman its central character. On the other hand, *Spaced* marks a significant shift in tone and demeanor, while *Peep Show* throws in a range of voice-over and camera techniques whilst completely dropping the notion of a happy ending.

Further, British sitcoms, especially in recent years, are far more likely to be understood as high culture in contrast with the low culture stigma often associated with US sitcoms, a perception that is widespread in both US and UK media circles, often signified by single-camera work. Indeed, the US remake of *Coupling* was specifically advertised as a grown-up, quality version of *Friends* (Sanson 2011). This is because institutional circumstances in the UK create a framework where the longevity, renewal, and overall success of a TV show is measured by very different criteria relating to quality and innovation rather than US television's laser focus on ratings (see Bielby and Bielby 1994). In particular, the ownership and funding of the broadcasters responsible for the three shows explored in this chapter differ from the US's competitive broadcast market. Channel 4, who produced and broadcasted both *Spaced* and *Peep Show*, is a publicly owned, though privately funded, channel launched in 1982 with a specific remit to create diverse programming that "demonstrates innovation, experiment and creativity in the form and content of programs" (Ofcom 2004), while the publicly owned and publicly funded model of the BBC means that shows are less beholden to the

148 *First as farce, then as tragedy*

ratings battles that usually augur the demise of US TV shows. This does not mean that British sitcoms do not reflect and negotiate contemporaneous social issues, but that, I suggest, the lack of a need to appeal to large swathes of the population offers a far more significant scope for ambiguous meanings and endings, leaving open greater possibilities for subversive reading.

Hanging out in the UK

This chapter, then, takes each sitcom in turn, as while each certainly explores forms of masculinity attempting to adapt to the sociopolitical landscape of neoliberalism within certain strictures of the hangout sitcom genre, there is a range of degrees of success and optimism among the relevant men in each. I start with *Coupling*, the most optimistic, least ambiguous, and most like the US versions, before moving to *Spaced*, which revels in precarity and ambiguity, and finally *Peep Show*, a show that I suggest is as much tragicomedy as it is sitcom or farce. As denoted by Table 6.1, there is a lot, too, to say about the sexualities of the men in the British shows, which range from unabashedly straight through to bi-curious, bisexual, and entirely ambiguous.

The three UK sitcoms chosen are, essentially, middle-class sitcoms with middle-class characters, which is for several reasons. First, like the US, most sitcoms in the UK of the era that conform to hangout conventions feature majority middle-class protagonists anyway. Second, it provides a more direct comparison to the middle-class hangout sitcoms of the US, in encoding similar masculine anxieties about the socioeconomic positions of middle-class men. On this basis, two UK sitcoms that I considered but ultimately opted not to analyze were *Two Pints of Lager and a Packet of Crisps* (2001–2011), which is a working-class hangout sitcom with slightly less anxious men (in spite of its similar three-man, three-woman cast to *Friends*), and *Not Going Out* (2006–present), which follows some hangout sitcom conventions but

Table 6.1 Male characters in *Spaced*, *Coupling*, and *Peep Show*.

Show	Character	Actor	Apparent sexuality
Spaced (1999–2001)	Tim Bisley	Simon Pegg	Heterosexual
	Brian Topp	Mark Heap	Ambiguous
	Mike Watt	Nick Frost	Ambiguous
Coupling (2000–2004)	Steve Taylor	Jack Davenport	Heterosexual
	Jeff Murdock	Richard Coyle	Heterosexual
	Patrick Maitland	Ben Miles	Heterosexual
Peep Show (2003–2015)	Mark Corrigan	David Mitchell	Heterosexual/bi-curious
	Jeremy Usbourne	Robert Webb	Bisexual

First as farce, then as tragedy 149

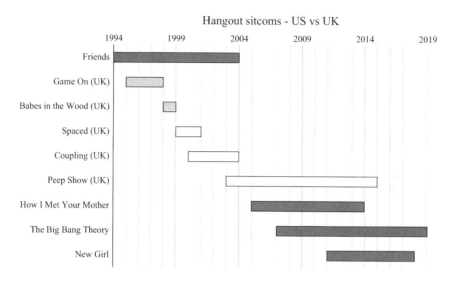

Figure 6.1 Timeline of US and UK hangout sitcoms.

has a more revolving cast and a central character who is the only one appearing in every episode, unlike the ensembles of most shows here.

Coupling and conservatism

Steven Moffat created *Coupling* in 2000, and it ran for four seasons. It was broadcast by the BBC and ended somewhat ambiguously; although a fifth season has long been mooted, it is not likely to materialize. In response to fan demand, Moffat published an online happily-ever-after epilogue (PiersB 2006) several years ago, though its status as canon is ambiguous. *Coupling*, including in its own promotional material, is frequently described as "the British *Friends*" – it had a laugh track, was multi-camera, and had a main cast consisting of three men and three women in London working their way through 21st century heterosexual intimacy, often sitting on a sofa facing a camera facing a sofa in a public place, though it was in a bar rather than a café. It is certainly the closest of any of the UK shows to the established US hangout formula, and its notable departure from the British sitcom canon is that class is almost entirely absent from it, at least as narrative topic (see Rostek and Will 2016).

Jack Davenport plays Steve Taylor, seemingly the most normal of the three men, who from the opening episode is fated to end up with Sarah Alexander's feisty Susan Walker, a relationship with more than a passing resemblance to Ross and Rachel. Richard Coyle plays the woman-obsessed Jeff Murdock,[2] a character whose lilting Welsh accent indicates at his wackiness, and whose lustful attitude to the opposite sex has a passing resemblance to Joey, though he lacks Joey's charisma or success in that department. Ben Miles plays Patrick Maitland, Susan's ex-boyfriend, office worker and self-professed Thatcherite who is often mistaken as gay. Kate Isitt and Gina Bellman respectively play Sally Harper, a neurotic beautician and love interest for Patrick, and Jane Christie, Steve's posh, possessive, and self-obsessed ex-girlfriend. All the characters are white.

Perhaps the most obvious example of *Coupling*'s successful adaptation of hangout conventions to UK culture is its straightforward lewdness. Most of the sexual content in *Friends* occurs as innuendo or implication, such as when Rachel has sex with an orthodontist at his office and remarks, "It was so nice having this little sink here", alluding to the act of spitting out semen after fellatio, as the two lay on the patients' chair afterward (*Friends*, "The One with the Evil Orthodontist"). *Coupling* has no such qualms – Sally first tries to sleep with Patrick because she learns he has a huge penis (*Coupling*, "Size Matters"), while six of the nine possible heterosexual couplings from the main cast of six have sexual relations at some point, compared to just two in *Friends* (though most of them have kissed each other, including same-sex pairings). There are several possible reasons for *Coupling* being freer and easier with sex, ranging from institutional rules about what is allowed on US primetime and British post-watershed television (where swearing, violence, and sexual references are permitted if broadcast after 9pm), to cultural differences in humor and sensibility in each country. Joanna Rostek and Dorothea Will, who argue that *Coupling* reflects wider social developments in which sex and intimacy become objects of exchange, also suggest that "*Coupling* exaggerates the competitive approach to sex in order to make it laughable" (Rostek and Will 2016, 318), an argument that is difficult to make about *Friends*, a show that links intimacy, sex, and love much more than *Coupling*'s hedonistic approach. Indeed, I suggest this plays into a wider context in which *Coupling* pastiches and gives homage to the US hangout sitcom as much as it works as a transatlantic instantiation of it. Yet, I suggest that, by chance, in the character of Jeff, *Coupling* offers an example of what Halberstam (2011, 59) calls "white male stupidity" that undermines the happy ending.

Steve's American-style optimism

Coupling, the US version, went the furthest of the three US adaptations here. NBC picked up the show in 2003 – billed as the successor to *Friends*, the final season of which was airing on the same network that year – and commissioned 13 episodes. Unlike the other shows here, the scripts were almost identical to the original, the only substantive changes being tweaks to fit US institutional rules, such as the advert breaks meaning shorter episode runtimes, for example, as well as several cultural references. It received extremely low ratings and was canceled after just six episodes had been broadcast, despite more having been filmed, which Kevin Sanson (2011) attributes to the fact that the episodes are, from set to script, identical. So, viewers might just choose to watch the original rather than what reads as a pastiche considering ease of access. At the same time, it should be acknowledged that simply making it to broadcast is a significant milestone not reached by many US remakes of British shows, including *Spaced* or *Peep Show*.

There are several explanations for this (relative) success. It is possibly due to the involvement of the original show creator Steven Moffat, who produced along with his wife Sue Vertue, who also produced the UK show (as might be indicated, the characters of Steve and Susan were based on Moffat and Vertue). However, of the three British sitcoms, *Coupling* most closely resembles Friends in terms of both plot and tone. This is partly attributable to its mechanical features, both laugh track and multi-camera filming, but there are also some similarities between the two shows' characters, their relationships, how they are written, and how they develop over time. Recall Judy Kutulas (2018) on *Friends*, a show that she suggests brought viewers back each week because it made them root for the characters. In fact, there is an almost "American" feel to the optimism within *Coupling*, to the extent that the three main middle-class male characters fit just as well into the chrononormative typology as in Chapter 3 of this book. Certainly, the centrality of Steve's romantic pursuits to the show and his anxious, skittish fear of being alone fit the postfeminist male singleton. Things grow a little more complex with the other two subject positions of househusband and douchebag, as both Patrick and Jeff most closely resemble different variations of the douchebag character type, but different instances. Patrick's playboy is similar to Barney in *How I Met Your Mother*, in both his romantic and sexual success as well as his conservative, pro-capitalist politics. Barney works in corporate finance, while Patrick reveals his attachment to the British Conservative Party (*Coupling*, "Size Matters). Meanwhile, Jeff does indeed resemble Joey but perhaps his closest kindred character is Howard in *The Big Bang Theory*, in that both talk a good game sexually but are not nearly as successful as they wish to be, and that this character is bound up in a form of ethnic or national otherness, Howard wearing his Jewishness on his sleeve, and Jeff his Welshness. Nevertheless, there is a sense in which my typology could reasonably apply to *Coupling* in ways that would be difficult to do so for both *Spaced* and *Peep Show*.

Indeed, the wider point here is that, while the men of both *Spaced* and *Peep Show* are also suffused with anxiety about romance like the men in the US shows, what marks *Coupling* out is that the three middle-class men get their reprieve or their happy ending – or, rather, they get their narrative closure, which is written into the title of the show. In particular, Steve and Susan's relationship is not only the reason that the group become friends in the first place, but they are also the eponymous "couple", the show being based on the early relationship of creator Steven Moffat and producer Sue Vertue; the final episodes of seasons one, two, and three all end on a cliff-hanger about their relationship, season one when Susan asks Steve to propose to her (*Coupling*, "The Cupboard of Patrick's Love"), season two when they seem to break up after each of them flirts with another person (*Coupling*, "The End of the Line"), and season three when Susan reveals to the two other girls that she is pregnant (*Coupling*, "Perhaps, Perhaps, Perhaps"). Even the show's overall finale ends with the birth of their son (*Coupling*, "Nine and a Half Months"). But apart from the ambiguity of the season two ending, they are together from season one, episode one, meaning that a settled couple are the romantic focus of the show.

The show reads much like three intertwining romantic comedies, though, as the three couples move closer to their final destination of coupledom – in fact its finale is titled "Nine and a Half Months", a play on the Hollywood romantic comedy *9½ Weeks*. Romantic comedy is a genre that, in its typical form, tends to maintain a conservative gender politics, narratively resolving to a status quo that retains a male romantic lead/hero who actively pursues a passive heroine through a range of obstacles, to ultimately win her hand in marriage (see Jeffers McDonald 2007). There are, certainly, more recent subversions of this, as Tamar Jeffers McDonald (2007) recounts, but in general the genre tends to remain largely heteronormative as the narratives resolve back to a conservative status quo. Many of the resolutions to individual episodes of *Coupling* in which the relationship of Steve and Susan is disrupted culminate in monologues from Steve about the politics of gender that assert the primacy of women's "bottoms" in men's thoughts, naturalizing a standard male gaze. In season one when Susan finds a pornographic DVD in Steve's television and becomes jealous, Steve's rousing speech to save his relationship at the end of the show is mostly about how he, as a man, is biologically compelled to look at women's bodies.

> I want to spend the rest of my life with the woman at the end of that table there, but that does not stop me wanting to see several thousand more naked bottoms before I die, because that's what being a bloke is. When man invented fire, he didn't say, "hey, let's cook". He said, "great, now we can see naked bottoms in the dark".
>
> (*Coupling*, "Inferno")

This resolution back to a largely patriarchal status quo continues among the other characters' storylines, for the most part. Patrick's happy ending is left, perhaps, slightly ambiguous when Sally finds an engagement ring in his cupboard (*Coupling*, "Nine and a Half Months"), but Moffat gives little ambiguity in his epilogue, suggesting she said yes to his proposal. While Jane and Oliver never manage to consummate their relationship as they are repeatedly interrupted while trying to have sex, the more interesting case in masculinity here is in the fate of the character replaced by Oliver, in Jeff.

Jeff's Welsh pessimism

Jeff is the notable exception to the happy endings in *Coupling*. Jeff is, undoubtedly, a loser, both socially and romantically defined by a series of failures. In the first season we learn of a failed romantic entanglement with Susan prior to the show's beginning, while his subsequent romantic failures include a series of flirtatious encounters with an Israeli woman who only speaks Hebrew that are lost in translation (*Coupling*, "The Girl with Two Breasts"), and an attempted fling with an attractive woman who takes the same regular commuting train as him that blows up in his face after he tells a series of lies about being an amputee to elicit sympathy (*Coupling*, "The Man with Two Legs"). Meanwhile, he also has a range of extremely pessimistic social theories that are usually hyper-conscious concerns about embarrassment, such as the "giggle loop", which asserts that if you begin laughing in an inappropriate situation, you will continue to laugh at the inappropriateness of the laughing, and so on (*Coupling*, "Sex, Death and Nudity"), or the "nudity buffer", which states that a man has a maximum of five minutes to talk to a woman after meeting her, before he has fully imagined her naked and finds himself unable to speak monosyllabically (*Coupling*, "The Girl with Two Breasts").

Jeff's actor, Richard Coyle, left the show at the end of season three, to be replaced by a love interest for Jane. Toward the end of Jeff's final season, the show had made several indications that he and Jane would eventually couple up – but Jeff never gets an unambiguous ending. Two endings have been offered, both canonically ambiguous. The first possible ending comes in Moffat's published epilogue, as follows:

> Jeff is still abroad. He lives a life of complete peace and serenity now, having taken the precaution of not learning a word of the local language and therefore protecting himself from the consequences of his own special brand of communication. If any English speakers turn up, he pretends he only speaks Hebrew. He is, at this very moment, staring out to sea, and sighing happily every thirty-eight seconds.
>
> What he doesn't know, of course, is that even now a beautiful Israeli girl he once met in a bar, is heading towards his apartment, having been directed to the only Hebrew speaker on the island. What he also doesn't know is that she is being driven by a young ex-pat English woman, who is still grieving the loss of a charming, one-legged Welshman she once met on a train. And he cannot possibly suspect that (owing to a laundry mix-up, and a stag party the previous night in the same block) he is wearing heat-dissolving trunks.
> As the doorbell rings, it is best that we draw a veil.
>
> (Moffat in PiersB 2006)

154 *First as farce, then as tragedy*

The ambiguity to Moffat's ending continues to emphasize Jeff as an outsider, and someone who rejects the chrononormative – while I compared him to Joey in *Friends*, Jeff never had his own spin-off show like *Joey*, even though that ended prematurely. The second ending to consider, though, is a dream sequence of Steve's in the show's finale episode, with the return of a version of Jeff who now presents as a trans woman named "Jeffina", played by cis woman Samantha Spiro affecting a deepened voice. Asked by Steve "what happened", Jeffina explains that after traveling, pre-transition, to the Greek island of Lesbos, a place she believed to be full of lesbians, she "started to wonder if there was any way [he] could ever see a woman naked again – at that point, Steve, I ... I may have lost my sense of proportion". To see women naked, Jeff became one to see a naked woman in the mirror. Though Jeffina is not introduced as a serious plot point, and gender reassignment surgery is written to act as a punchline here, I suggest that Jeffina's failure to understand and appreciate the limits of male heterosexuality offers a queer reading that undermines and deconstructs the male gaze. In fact, the sketch reads rather like Jack Halberstam's reading of the movie *Dude Where's My Car?*, where the two main characters, essentially stupid straight white guys, unironically perform a deep long kiss in the car as they mimic and compete with a straight couple in the car next to them. Halberstam asks whether this scene shows "competitive male heterosexuality to be the result of homoerotic mimicry",

Figure 6.2 Richard Coyle as Jeff (above), and Samantha Spiro as "Jeffina" (below).

ultimately suggesting that "their gormless plunge into manly gay sex [and] their knowing mimicry of ... barely submerged homosexuality" (Halberstam 2011, 67) of attractive white guys reveals the contingent and constructed nature of heterosexuality, if read with a queer lens. Jeff, in attempting to perform male heterosexuality, gives up the performance of manhood altogether in becoming so desperate to see naked women. *Spaced* and *Peep Show* expand further on the possibilities of failure, sometimes through apathy and sometimes stupidity.

The precarity of Spaced

Spaced was created by Simon Pegg and Jessica Hynes, and was produced by Channel 4, running for just two seasons comprising 12 episodes, all directed by longtime collaborator Edgar Wright, who also had significant creative input. Pegg and Hynes also star, the former playing Tim Bisley, a nerd and aspiring comic book artist, and the latter Daisy Steiner, an aspiring writer. Tim and Daisy meet while looking separately for somewhere in London to live, the former having been dumped by his girlfriend, and the latter moving out of a squat, and decide to search for a place together. When the place they both like and can afford is advertised for "professional couples only", they pose as a professional couple, and move in. Tim's best friend is Mike Watt, played by Nick Frost, a military fanatic who constantly wears army uniform, with a deliberately ambiguous sexuality. In their building's basement apartment lives Brian Topp, an elusive and strange "conceptual artist" played by Mark Heap, who again has an ambiguous sexuality, while the cast is rounded off by Katy Carmichael as Daisy's flighty friend Twist Morgan who has a relationship with Brian, and Julia Deakin as the chain-smoking landlady Marsha Klein, who regularly makes sexual advances on Brian. All the characters are white.

Spaced could be reasonably described as something of an innovator in the genre – it is one of the first single-camera sitcoms, eschews a laugh track before any other live-action sitcom, US or UK, I have been able to find, and trades in a range of intertextual pop culture references, pastiching famous movie scenes and making frequent comments about other texts (particularly the *Star Wars* trilogies). On the back of its positive reception, Fox commissioned and made a pilot for a US version in 2007 without the involvement of (but with credit to) the original creators. The pilot never aired, allegedly receiving very negative reactions in test screenings, but footage found its way online several years later, revealing some attempted concessions to its transferred institutional setting. Brian becomes Christian, a Latin American artist with a patchy grasp of the English language; the names Tim and Daisy, less common in the US than the UK, become Ben and Apryl; and Mike is not an army nut, but an effeminate glutton obsessed with "cream puffs". The little that can be determined of the theme song seems to indicate a tonal shift to a more heartwarming communal friends-as-family US hangout sitcom, an upbeat pop song with the refrain "I'm hanging out here", a strong contrast to the quote from the show at the beginning of this chapter. While these things are subjective, it is difficult to find much positive to say about the pilot. Edgar Wright subsequently suggested that the very premise of a US translation comprehensively misunderstands the original's intertextual relation to US pop culture: "part of the charm of *Spaced* is its people in north London acting out stuff from American films, you know, Hollywood in kind of suburbia. American TV is much more glamorous. It doesn't make any sense". In this sense, *Spaced* is deeply intertextual, a show that for large stretches would look and sound unintelligible for those not embedded within Anglo-American pop culture.

Precarious space

The premise of *Spaced* both distinguishes it from and identifies it with its US counterparts/inspiration. It is a banal point, but as Neil Ewen (2018, 725) has put it,

> the implausibility of a group of twenty-somethings, who spent much of their time lounging around drinking coffee, being able to afford sizable Manhattan apartments, and enjoying relatively privileged lifestyles was often noted by fans and critics during the original run of *Friends*.

The point of *Spaced* is that its characters have insufficient financial, cultural, and social capital to live such lifestyles. Where Ewen labels this "insulated precarity" in *Friends*, in *Spaced* Tim and Daisy appear precarious without the insulation, despite what appears to be middle-class backgrounds. I use the word "appear" deliberately – while Tim and Daisy's precarity is the premise of the show, considering their career choices it is somewhat implausible that they would have been able to afford their apartment at the time *Spaced* was released and set. This does not, however, mean that the show does not take some care to embed the characters in real material situations and remain somewhat less optimistic about their futures than the US shows.

Lauren Jade Thompson (2018) has argued that *Friends* constructs domestic space as a gendered phenomenon via the two apartments in which most of the show's action takes place – Rachel and Monica's multicolored apartment, the iconic image of *Friends*, against the bachelor pad across the hallway of Joey and Chandler, with its foosball table, TV and speakers, and dartboard. Thompson suggests that, despite narrative moments of disruption in which the topic of domestic space is not irregularly the subject, *Friends* maintains a conservative position on gendered space, in which gendered boundaries are preserved at the end of any episode which forefronts their narrative disruption. In *Spaced*, there is only one central domestic space where action takes place, which is Tim and Daisy's apartment. The first thing to say here is that

First as farce, then as tragedy 157

the internal space of the apartment in *Spaced* is nowhere near as important as the domestic internal space in *Friends*. The centrality of the flat or apartment and domestic space in the US sitcom has an extensive legacy, probably beginning with *I Love Lucy* (see Wojcik 2010), and *Friends* is no different, its lilac walls and turquoise cabinets instantly recognizable. If *Spaced* has an iconography, it is not in the apartment's internal fixings but the external view of the building, which contains not just Tim and Daisy's place, but also that of the landlord Marsha and Brian's basement apartment. Part of the house's mythology lies in the fact that it is a real building in London, and something of a pilgrimage for the show's fans and general aficionados of Pegg and director Edgar Wright's "Cornetto Trilogy", three thematically but not canonically related movies created and written by the duo between 2004 and 2013. In fact, while Pegg, Hynes, and Wright were filming the post-show documentary *Skip to the End* (2004) outside the house, they encountered a pair of *Spaced* fans taking pictures of the house, an incident they included in the final cut.

Indeed, part of the point of both the internal and external apartment in *Spaced* is precisely that it could be anywhere, that it lacks a significant identity. There is no immediately recognizable architectural style to the building that would for most viewers identify it as being in London or a particular part of the city, compared to the distinctly New York City apartment block in *Friends*. Similarly, while the interior of the *Friends* apartment has all sorts of identifying knick-knacks and oddities, from its unusual color scheme to its harlequin dining suite, there are very few individual signifying identifiers for *Spaced*. While the *Friends* apartment is rarely seen beyond three or four camera angles, the *Spaced* apartment is rarely seen via the same shot twice. This is not to say the show is pessimistic or downbeat, nor that the characters are not idiosyncratic. In fact, if anything, some of the *Spaced* characters are heightened to caricatures, such is the tone of the show. Rather, the nondescript spaces of *Spaced* serve as a deliberately non-descript background that is defined by the characters and the ways they negotiate the space rather than by significations of the space itself.

Within such a milieu, the show declines to gender the space of the apartment beyond Tim and Daisy's separate rooms. Instead, it acts as an empty public space on which neither Tim nor Daisy are particularly bothered to leave their gendered mark. Daisy does at one point try to compel Tim to help her clean the apartment (*Spaced*, "Gatherings"), but she is not the paragon of cleanliness that, for example, Monica is in her semi-sexual love of cleanliness and tidiness (see Rockler 2006). Similarly, we often see Tim lounging on the sofa playing video games, but so too does Daisy, which is presented as the status quo rather than a disruption. *Spaced* presents a sense of apathy toward the gendering of space, not an explicit or obvious critique, but an indifference toward it. In fact, where *Friends*, as well as *The Big Bang Theory*, keep two gendered apartments either side of a hallway, in *Spaced* the shared apartment is analogous to the sense of community, friendship, and camaraderie that one

158 *First as farce, then as tragedy*

Figure 6.3 The recognizably New York exterior of the *Friends* apartment (above), and the less placeable exterior of the apartment in *Spaced* (below).

might have expected of the surrogate family that models the hangout sitcom. When Tim and Daisy throw a party, Mike's voluntary role as "hired security" at the party serves to demonstrate its openness. Mike stands at the door in his camo gear, pistol in hand, a serious look on his face, getting hidden behind the door every time someone new enters, without reacting (*Spaced*, "Gatherings"). Comparatively to the policing of space in *Friends*, *Spaced* makes a point of not policing space at all. In failing to do so, it therefore offers a possible reading of public space that eschews its typical masculine attachments.

Precarious love

Spaced does not just play with precarity of space, but also with the notion of romantic fate. The will-they-won't-they heterosexual couple is never entirely resolved by the show, as Tim and Daisy's often-implied mutual attraction is played with but never acted on. In one episode, for example, among the opening scenes is a close-up shot of Tim and Daisy's faces, non-diegetic slow jazz playing, as they lie in what appears to be a bed, smoking cigarettes, Tim expressing that "I'm glad we did that", and Daisy agreeing that "there would have been a hell of a lot of tension if we'd left it any longer" (*Spaced*, "Gatherings"), the obvious implication that the pair have just had sex. The camera then pans out to reveal a tidied apartment with them lying fully clothed on the floor of the living room.

It is a not uncommon trope for love stories to begin with the breakup of the previous relationship, for them to find solace in their new one. Both *Spaced* and *New Girl* deploy this storyline with striking similarities, almost beat-for-beat identical, with *Spaced*'s opening scene being Tim's tear-laden break-up with his ex-girlfriend (*Spaced*, "Beginnings") and subsequent desperation to win her back bearing a strong resemblance to Nick's ongoing struggles in *New Girl* to move on from his ex-girlfriend Caroline. For at least the first season, both pine for ex-girlfriends who broke up with them, while living with a female main cast member love interest – Daisy for Tim, and Jess for Nick. At the end of season one of each show, the two men are re-acquainted with their ex-partners and are both excited to make things work with them (*Spaced*, "Ends"; *New Girl*, "See Ya"). Nick agrees to move in with Caroline, and they get a mortgage together, before he backs out; Tim does not go as far, and meets Sarah at the pub to "talk things through". Meanwhile, both Jess and Daisy display considerable ill-feeling about the rekindled relationships, ostensibly concerned about whether returning to their exes will make them happy, underlined by jealousy and unresolved sexual tension, both men seemingly unaware of their roommates' feelings for them. By the end of the season one finale episodes, both men end up back at the communal apartments, apparently shed of their residual romantic feelings for their exes from the beginning of season two. Both episodes end on shots of them dancing – Nick and Jess separately in their rooms, and Tim and Daisy together on a dancefloor. And, perhaps most strikingly, the conversations in which things end between the men and their exes take place off screen, which also produces the most striking difference – with Nick, we are left in no doubt that it was he who ended things, recognizing what it would take for him to be happy, and taking control. With Tim, there is perhaps a similar realization that Sarah would make him unhappy, but his over-eager justification and dulcet tone leave ambiguous the reality of who ended the relationship. After things have ended, he invites Daisy to the pub, and, with Tim looking glum, the following exchange ensues.

Tim: Before you say anything it was my decision.
Daisy: Really?
Tim: Yeah, she, she wanted me back, but, err, I said no.
Daisy: Wow.
Tim: I just had a … had a moment of clarity, you know, I just, I woke up, you know. It's like, you know when you have an orgasm on your own? You know, you're sort of, err, lying on the sofa watching some porn movie you bought on a drunken lonely night in Soho, and, and, you're lying there and everything is really great, you know, you're getting totally turned on by these absurdly graphic images. Everything seems so right,

you know, and suddenly [blows raspberry], bingo. You know, you wake up, and you're lying there sweating and desperately looking for the tissue which you just know is still in your pocket, and the remote control which is somewhere on the floor, and it's like, walking in on yourself. You know, it's just like, what you doin'? That's how I felt tonight, sitting here feeling my heart miss a beat every time the door opened, you know, "the fuck are you doing?".

Daisy: Well, that's love, innit? Load of old wank. [Laughs.]

Tim: Life just isn't like the movies, is it, you know? We're constantly led to believe in resolution, in the re-establishment of the ideal status quo, and it's just ... it's just not true. Happy endings are a myth, designed to make us feel better about the fact life is just a thankless struggle (a live band starts playing the blues song "Is You Is or Is You Ain't My Baby"). D'you wanna dance?

Daisy: D'you know what? I think I do.

(*Spaced*, "Ends")

Tim's immediate grasp at agency in the relationship's end suggests that he may not be entirely honest about the situation, while the lengthy, directionless monologue avoids truisms or clear meaning. Meanwhile, ambiguity of telos is articulated and funneled through pop culture – life is not like the things you see on-screen, he says, on-screen, while he lifts a definition of narrative almost directly from television studies when he names "the re-establishment of the ideal status quo", and the song choice not only hints at the will-they-won't-they storyline, but also leaves us wondering whether it is directed at Daisy or Sarah. The dramatic irony is that this scene is the resolution back to the status quo, it just is not the *ideal* one in Tim's head, but is permanently stuck in a liminal moment with the ending in continual jeopardy. *Spaced* never guarantees its ending. Despite almost identical beats in storyline, one that offers narrative resolution, the other being ambiguous. Both love stories play with the notion of fate, but where Nick and Jess's fate is set, Tim and Daisy's remains open, not a guaranteed romance, but a friendship. Their narrative is not defined by a telos we all know is coming, but as a constant state of becoming without an ending. This lack of an endpoint questions the inevitability of heterosexuality or chrononormativity.

Peep Show as a tragicomedy

Peep Show was created by Andrew O'Connor, Sam Bain, and Jesse Armstrong, aired on Channel 4 from 2003, and ran for nine seasons, though each contains just 6 episodes each, totaling just 54, equivalent to just two and a half seasons of a US sitcom. It follows two housemates in London: Mark Corrigan, an anxious and nerdy office worker played by David Mitchell, and Jeremy 'Jez' Usbourne, an unemployed and deluded musician living off an inherited nest-egg, played by Robert Webb. In the final season it is revealed that Jeremy is bisexual, as he joins a straight couple to become a "thrupple". Mitchell and Webb were a comedy duo before *Peep Show* was created, having emerged from the Cambridge Footlights together, and subsequently having written their own TV and radio sketch shows. Darker in tone and topic than any sitcom studied in this book, most of *Peep Show*'s comedy emerges from the extremely dysfunctional relationship between the two, who have an unhealthy and co-dependent relationship. They are joined by a recurring cast of characters. 'Super Hans' is a drug-addicted comedy relief character played by Matt King, while Mark's intimidating boss, played by Paterson Joseph, is Alan Johnson, who causes Mark to question his heterosexuality, and is the only regular black character in these three British shows. Mark's recurring love interest is his co-worker Sophie Chapman, played by Olivia Colman, who Mark accidentally marries, then divorces, then impregnates, then thoroughly resents by the end of the show; for Jeremy it is 'Big Suze', an extremely posh and implied aristocratic actress played by Sophie Winkleman (who became a real-life member of the extended British royal family when she married Lord Frederick Windsor, King Charles III's second cousin).

Peep Show follows some unusual conventions, in that the camera regularly records the first-person views of Mark and Jeremy, who also both have their own voice-overs. Though this lends itself to comparisons with *How I Met Your Mother*, that show uses voice-over mostly as exposition, whereas in *Peep Show* it provides access to the dark, unchecked ids of the two lead characters. The resultant counterpoint in *Peep Show* between inner thoughts and on-screen events is a comedic device that reveals a deep unhappiness with Mark and Jeremy's positions in the world, offering a series of often explicit critiques of contemporary capitalism, as Phil Wickham (2013, 2017) demonstrates. Indeed, it is a show whose status quo is pessimism and sadness, restored at the end of each episode after a brief hint at a positive step forward. I suggest it is informative to understand *Peep Show* through the prism of the theatrical form of tragicomedy, which David Hirst (1984) suggests may rather unsettlingly combine elements of the tragic and the comic that, in recent times, is often geared toward satire and social commentary by skewering the absurdity of social norms by merely presenting them as common sense. As Hirst (1984, 125) says of playwright Peter Barnes, contemporary tragicomedy "sees the world as mad and it is his intention to drive home to his audience a full awareness of this folly". Such an approach can elicit almost painful audience responses as the characters descend into farcical situations, inevitably ending by re-establishing the same absurd status quo that was established at the beginning of the narrative. As such, it deploys a tragicomedy vernacular to regularly parody the hangout sitcom. It is this absurd and pessimistic status quo that has meant a variety of US remakes of *Peep Show* have struggled to adapt to new national circumstances.

A pilot for a US version of *Peep Show* was commissioned and filmed in 2005, but it was never picked up by a network. As with *Spaced*, the pilot emerged online several years later, and makes for interesting viewing, not least that Mark is played by Johnny Galecki, who two years later was cast as Leonard in *The Big Bang Theory*. Though it keeps the voice-overs, the US version removes the signature first-person camera shots – tonally, there is nothing done to remedy the disjuncture between the original show's pessimism and US television conventions, with the characters as pitiful, the voice-overs as bleak, and situations as hopeless as in the original, resulting in a pilot with very little laughter. Other remakes have been attempted, including a 2008 commission by Spike TV, written by Armstrong and Bain, that never went to series (IMDb 2008), and the announcement in 2019 that the network FX had commissioned a pilot for a gender-swapped US version, with the involvement of Bain, but so far nothing has come from it (Loughrey 2019).

Tragic heterosexuality

Peep Show often comments on the sexual profligacy of hangout sitcom characters, as in Jeremy's voice-over when he meets American love interest Nancy (Rachel Blanchard): "we'll be friends, like the friends on *Friends*, who got bored of being friends and started screwing each other" (*Peep Show*, "Gym"). Mark and Jeremy both have a significant number of relationships or sexual partners, except that none of them last, nor trigger growth or character development. Mark and Ted Mosby in *How I Met Your Mother* both use the same phrase in their search for a wife, constantly speculating on the existence out there of "the one". For Mark, that search for the one is largely driven by a sense of class-based duty and a recurring fear of becoming a male spinster, a marked difference with Ted's head-in-the-clouds romanticism. Mark worries about the class background and presentation of his partners, putting this concern above his or her happiness. After spending the first few seasons pining after Sophie, by season three the two are dating, but Mark never seems happy in the relationship. When Sophie introduces Mark to a group of her friends at a club, and the group all take ecstasy, Mark only pretends to take his, and when dancing with another of Sophie's friends, his voice-over states, "this guy is literally a moron" (*Peep Show*, "Jurying").

Most of Mark's love life is based on an acute sense of class duty and anxiety. As if to emphasize Mark's class hyper-consciousness, in season four we meet Sophie's family, who live in a grand old house in the countryside (*Peep Show*, "Sophie's Parents"), upper-class in both financial and cultural capital. Sophie's father, Ian (who, in a turn of fate that Mark very much resents, is the namesake of a child he and Sophie conceive post-divorce) wears tweed jackets and flat caps, and partakes in the pastime of hunting pheasants; Sophie's mother Penny is a dissatisfied housewife with a needy adult son who still lives at home, who seduces and sleeps with Jeremy when they visit. Mark shows himself to be as uncomfortable in their world as he is in the one he lives in every day, failing to twist the head off a hunted pheasant to kill it efficiently

First as farce, then as tragedy 163

Figure 6.4 David Mitchell as Mark (below) shakes hands with Paul Clayton as Ian Chapman (above), Sophie's dad. This also demonstrates the first-person camera often deployed by *Peep Show*.

when he joins Ian on a hunt, and instead covering himself in spurting pheasant blood.

Though Ted has his own anxieties about women, they are far less concerned with class position, and much more about his own unsuitability for love, having almost given up on women before he meets his wife Tracey. The argument in *How I Met Your Mother*, though, is that your destined perfect partner probably does exist, exemplified by the range of near-misses Ted has with Tracey before finding her, from dating her roommate, to commandeering her yellow umbrella that she left at a party they both attended before meeting. Indeed, the yellow umbrella became a symbol of the show's commitment to fated love. The argument in *Peep Show* is the opposite, suggesting that believing in "the one" constructs a tragic masculinity built on a sense of duty, but doomed to failure. Indeed, the premise of "the one" is certainly congruent with neoliberal notions of a middle-class individualism and romanticism (Redman 2001) that *Peep Show* thereby skewers.

Jeremy, on the other hand, is not bothered about finding "the one", nor about romantic stability, nor chrononormativity in employment or love. He is habitually unemployed and seems to spend most of his time masturbating and playing video games. He certainly enjoys having sex with women, and is remarkably successful with it, but his sexuality throughout the show is often ambiguous. In season one, Jeremy spends an episode trying to remember "the bad thing" he and Super Hans did one night while very high, which turns out to be Jeremy performing fellatio on Hans (*Peep Show*, "Mark Makes a Friend"), while his job working as a "handyman" for a fictional washed up musician called Russell, stage name "The Orgazoid", for which one of his responsibilities is to, as he puts it, "give him a hand" (*Peep Show*, "Handyman").[3] There are a number of occasions, though, on which *Peep Show* examines the relationship between sex and power via both characters' voice-overs, which contain frequent attempts to repress gay sexual urges – and not only this, gay sexual urges that are fundamentally attached to the moments when they have power over one another. When Jeremy drugs Mark with an overdose of cold medication to keep him away from a psychedelic drug party, his voice-over states, "I *could* rape him … I'm not going to rape him" (*Peep Show*, "Shrooming"); when Mark wrangles a job interview for Jeremy at JLB, Mark muses in his mind over his excitement at being able to give his friend orders at work, wondering, "I'll be able to order him around, not horrible, just, Jeremy, could you file this for me? Jeremy, could you take that for me? Jeremy could you suck this for me? Jesus, where did that come from?". These mental failures to think heterosexually deconstruct the performativity and contingent nature of heterosexuality by suggesting it lies in the repression of other sexual urges. By attaching sex to power, then, *Peep Show* to some extent unveils and to some extent deconstructs heterosexuality, which is not achieved without caveats even within the most positive of homosocial relationships in the US hangout sitcom – Nick in *New Girl* runs away and retches multiple times to get over simply expressing affection for Schmidt (*New Girl*, "Road Trip").

Tragic work

The fictional company JLB, and the esoteric nature of Mark's work there, are a similar joke to Chandler's bullshit job (Graeber 2018), though Mark's work is slightly better defined – we know he is a credit manager. Yet, where Chandler finishes season ten of *Friends* having achieved a comfortable executive position, at the end of *Peep Show* Mark is unemployed. At the beginning of season six he does get a promotion at JLB, but the company dissolves very soon afterwards (*Peep Show*, "Jeremy at JLB") and Mark's career never recovers. Over the next few seasons, he works various jobs: as a history tour guide for Jack the Ripper walks through London for just one episode (*Peep Show*, "Jeremy in Love"), briefly as a waiter in a Mexican restaurant from which he is fired (*Peep Show*, "A Beautiful Mind"), and then loses another job as a bathroom salesman after he tries to trick a customer into making a purchase and his nephew defecates in a display toilet (*Peep Show*, "Big Mad Andy"). He finally gets another job as a loan manager, but is fired in the series finale, leaving his future uncertain (*Peep Show*, "Are We Going to Be

First as farce, then as tragedy 165

Alright?"). These career-based failings somewhat instantiate late capitalist/neoliberal versions of James C. Scott's (2008 [1985]) notion of "weapons of the weak", which are "hidden transcripts", sometimes deliberate, sometimes not, that ask questions about and resist the capabilities and performance of successful capitalist subjectivity. Mark's career path is, in short, an ode to neoliberal precarity, and once again questions neoliberal chrononormativity. Like in his love life, Mark at JLB plays the game and follows the rules, but things still do not end up positively.

In fact, Chandler achieves career advancement despite being apathetic about work throughout, compared to how Mark apportions a thoroughly inflated sense of importance to his work. Neil Ewen (2018) draws parallels between Chandler's friends' attitude toward his work and toward his sexuality, arguing that the two are interlinked, and that the emasculation of his sexuality is imbricated within the same set of discursive patterns as a form of capitalism that rewards ill-defined, arguably emasculating, labor. Mark, too, is subject to questions about sexuality based on his work, but they do not come from his friends, but his own voice-over, and his boss.

JLB takes a physical form in *Peep Show* in the figure of Mark's boss, Alan Johnson, usually called by his surname only, a ruthless jargonistic loan manager who is the subject of a crisis of sexual identity for Mark. We meet Johnson from Mark's point of view as the two of them engage in a mock interview exercise in front of other coworkers (*Peep Show*, "Mark Makes a Friend"). Apart from voice-over of Mark telling himself he can't "screw this up", the first lines of dialogue in this episode are Johnson dismissively and patronizingly asking Mark, "so Mr Corrigan we've examined your loan application, and I just have one question for you. Are you a pathetic, worthless punk? Because I'm going to turn you down as if you were a hippy parasite". Mark's response to the barrage of abuse he receives during the exercise is enthusiastic admiration in the voice-over: "oh, yes, yeah, I like it", "brilliant, that is just so spot on", followed by "Alan Johnson, I'm in love". Mark continues to be impressed by Johnson's masculine ruthless streak – throughout the same episode, he is accused by Sophie at another point in the episode of making another co-worker cry, which Mark defends, and then at the behest of Johnson admits that Sophie has a "fat arse", then ogles at Johnson's brand-new BMW and his claim that he is "insured out of my arse, mate. Nothing can touch me, I'm covered". As the rest of the episode ensues, Mark wonders if he is gay, bisexual, or bi-curious, musing in his head about whether he would kiss Johnson, and settling down to watch a DVD of gay pornography to test the waters. So, *Peep Show* comedically presents the links between the immaterial labor associated with neoliberalism and emasculation to the extent that Mark's job, which in the US hangout sitcom would put him somewhere around the hegemonic masculinity of the aspirational househusband, leaves him wondering whether he is performing masculinity at all. Here, again, via ambiguous sexuality, a queer reading is barely needed to show how the UK's diversity of hangout sitcoms' tragic masculinities' failures highlight the contradictions that inhere performing gender within neoliberalism.

Dystopian pasts, utopian futures

There are lots of people who find *Peep Show* funny but find its almost visceral depressiveness a difficult watch, which is a reasonable reaction to it. It can be a difficult watch, with its sad, pokey apartment and most of the time reprehensibly selfish and solipsistic main characters. It is the opposite viewing experience to *Friends* or *How I Met Your Mother*, shows whose finales are written to elicit affecting emotional responses following the journeys of their characters. It is precisely because of this infusion of tragedy that masculinities in British sitcoms offer the possibility of some respite from contradictory neoliberal maxims. In the US, heterosexual coupling is fated; in the UK, the romantic fate of the implied couples is either disastrous, as in Mark and Sophie's eventual unhidden contempt for one another in *Peep Show*, or ambiguous, as in *Spaced* and *Coupling*. It reads as an almost dystopian realism, a tragic exaggeration of its contemporaneous UK.

However, writing in the left-wing British magazine *Tribune* in 2022, James Greig (2022) describes *Peep Show* as a "utopian fantasy", suggesting that Jeremy's slacker lifestyle is possible to read as a desirable, comfortable, and real possibility. Living on "the dole", British slang for receiving welfare from the state, throughout the 1980s had become part of a romanticized artistic lifestyle, a slacker who could be comfortable living entirely off the state and pursuing a life of leisure, pleasure, and luxury, a sort of gritty working-class flaneur, which is Jeremy's self-image throughout most of *Peep Show*'s run. He compares himself to a range of musicians latterly associated with such a scene, such as The Prodigy and The Chemical Brothers. We, as viewers, are very much aware that this is a lie that Jeremy tells himself to justify his existence. Such a cultural phenomenon, though, as Greig points out, is today a fantasy. Living comfortably on benefits for the extended period of time Jeremy does is no longer possible in the UK, which dates early episodes of the show – its first five seasons could only occur in the period in which they were produced. Instead of reading as a dystopian satire on early 21st-century Britain, in the current climate Jeremy reads as a utopian vision of what might be politically possible with a more compassionate state. Indeed, this is perhaps what accounts for the sense of incongruity in later seasons of the show, which continued through into 2015 and a different era. In short, the long 1990s are over, and neoliberalism is in its death throes, though it is certainly not dead yet, and the resultant ideological landscape is uncertain. Within this milieu, the hangout sitcom, as well as genre itself are on their last legs, but that is not to say it leaves no legacy, as the next chapter explores.

Notes

1 Now married and known as Jessica Hynes, which I will use for the remainder of the book.
2 Coyle, having become concerned about typecasting, was replaced in the final season four by Richard Mylan, playing nerdy comic book owner Oliver Morris. His character, only lasting a season, is not substantially discussed here.
3 In season nine, Jeremy, in a moment of irony considering his life, becomes a life coach, and ends up sleeping with his only two clients, a woman and a man, who are a couple, and eventually the three of them commence a three-way romantic relationship (*Peep Show*, "Gregory's Beard"). This treatment of homosexuality in *Peep Show* reflects the political path of the US hangout sitcom, giving Jeremy a clear bisexual identity and respecting that, rather than leaving it ambiguous. Yet, this "thrupple", too, ends in failure when the three cannot handle the jealousy they feel, denying Jeremy the possibility of even a form of respectable chrono-homonormativity.

Filmography

Babes in the Wood. 1998–1999. [TV] Deane, Geoff, Creator, ITV: UK.
Blackadder. 1983–1989. [TV] Curtis, Richard, and Rowan Atkinson, Creator, BBC: UK.
Coupling. 2000–2004. [TV] Moffat, Steven, Creator, BBC: UK.
Fawlty Towers. 1975–1979. [TV] Cleese, John, and Connie Booth, Creator, BBC: UK.
Game On. 1995–1998. [TV] Davies, Andrew, and Bernadette Davis, Creator, BBC: UK.
Gavin and Stacey. 2007–2010. [TV] Corden, James, and Ruth Jones, Creator, BBC: UK.
Hancock's Half Hour. 1956–1961. [TV] Galton, Ray, and Alan Simpson, Creator, BBC: UK.
It's Always Sunny in Philadelphia. 2005-present. [TV] McElhenny, Rob, Creator, FX: USA.
Not Going Out. 2006–present. [TV] Mack, Lee, Creator, BBC: UK.
Only Fools and Horses. 1981–2003. [TV] Sullivan, John, Creator, BBC: UK.
Peep Show. 2003–2015. [TV] O'Connor, Andrew, Jesse Armstrong, and Sam Bain, Creator, Channel 4: UK.
Skip to the End. 2004. [Movie] Mudford, Dan, Creator, Channel 4: UK.
Spaced. 1999–2001. [TV] Pegg, Simon, and Jessica Stevenson, Creator, Channel 4: UK.
Steptoe and Son. 1962–1974. [TV] Galton, Ray, and Alan Simpson, Creator, BBC: UK.
Two Pints of Lager and a Packet of Crisps. 2001–2011. [TV] Nickson, Susan, Creator, BBC: UK.

References

Albertson, Kevin, and Paul Stepney. 2019. "1979 and all that: A 40-year reassessment of Margaret Thatcher's legacy on her own terms." *Cambridge Journal of Economics* 44 (2):319–342. doi: 10.1093/cje/bez037.

Beeden, Alexandra, and Joost de Bruin. 2010. "The Office: Articulations of national identity in television format adaptation." *Television & New Media* 11 (1):3–19. doi: 10.1177/1527476409338197.

Bielby, William T., and Denise Bielby. 1994. "'All hits are flukes': Institutionalized decision making and the rhetoric of network prime-time program development." *American Journal of Sociology* 99 (5):1287–1313. doi: 10.1086/230412.

Coskuncer-Balli, Gokcen. 2020. "Citizen-consumers wanted: Revitalizing the American dream in the face of economic recessions, 1981–2012." *Journal of Consumer Research* 47 (1):327–349. doi: 10.1093/jcr/ucz059.

Davis, Jessica Milner. 2017. *Farce*. Edited by Arthur Asa Berger, *Classics in Communication and Mass Culture*. Oxford: Routledge.

Hirst, David L. 1984.Davis, Jessica Milner. 2013. "From the romance lands: Farce as life-blood of the theatre." In *At Whom Are We Laughing?: Humor in Romance Language Literatures*, edited by Zenia Sacks DaSilva, and Gregory M. Pell, 3–18. Newcastle upon Tyne: Cambridge Scholars Publishing.

De Semelyen, Nick, and Ian Freer. 2020. "*Spaced*: The Complete History." *Empire Magazine*, 24 October, Retrieved 12 July 2022, from https://www.empireonline.com/movies/features/spaced-oral-history/.

Deans, Jason. 2001. "C4's M&S film fails to attract." *The Guardian*, 26 February. https://www.theguardian.com/media/2001/feb/26/overnights.

Ewen, Neil. 2018. "'If I don't input those numbers… it doesn't make much of a difference': Insulated precarity and gendered labor in *Friends*." *Television & New Media* 19 (8):724–740. doi: 10.1177/1527476418778425.

Graeber, David. 2018. *Bullshit Jobs: A Theory*. London: Allen Lane.

Greig, James. 2022. "Peep Show is now a utopian fantasy." Tribune. https://tribunemag.co.uk/2022/10/how-peep-show-became-utopian-fantasy. Accessed 21 October 2022.

Halberstam, Jack. 2011. *The Queer Art of Failure*. London: Duke University Press.

Hall, Stuart. 2017. *Selected Political Writings: The Great Moving Right Show and Other Essays*. Durham, NC: Duke University Press.

Hirst, David L. 1984. *Tragicomedy*. Edited by John D. Jump, *The Critical Idiom*. London: Methuen.

Horn, Rob Van, and Philip Mirowski. 2009. "The rise of the Chicago school of economics and the birth of neoliberalism." In *The Road From Mont Pèlerin: The Making of the Neoliberal Thought Collective*, edited by Philip Mirowski, and Dieter Plehwe, 139–179. Cambridge, MA: Harvard University Press.

Jameson, Fredric. 1991. *Postmodernism or, the Cultural Logic of Late Capitalism*. London: Verso.

Jeffers McDonald, Tamar. 2007. *Romantic Comedy: Boy Meets Girl Meets Genre*. London: Wallflower.

Kilborn, Richard. 2016. "A golden age of British sitcom? *Hancock's Half Hour* and *Steptoe and Son*." In *British TV Comedies: Cultural Concepts, Contexts and Controversies*, edited by Jürgen Kamm, and Birgit Neumann, 23–35. Basingstoke: Palgrave Macmillan.

Kutulas, Judy. 2018. "Anatomy of a hit: *Friends* and its sitcom legacies." *The Journal of Popular Culture* 51 (5):1172–1189. doi: 10.1111/jpcu.12715.

Lawson, Mark. 2001. "A farce repeating itself." The Guardian. https://www.theguardian.com/g2/story/0,3604,545851,00.html. Accessed 9 November 2022.

Loughrey, Clarisse. 2019. "Peep show remake: US network FX working on gender-swapped version of sitcom." The Independent. https://www.independent.co.uk/arts-entertainment/tv/news/peep-show-remake-us-version-fx-david-mitchell-robert-webb-american-a8931446.html. Accessed 1 August.

McMahon, Kate. 2009. "Brown and Peep Show bump C4's ratings." Broadcast Now. https://www.broadcastnow.co.uk/brown-and-peep-show-bump-c4s-ratings/5005900.article. Accessed 20 November 2022.

Ofcom. 2004. "Channel 4 Licence." https://www.ofcom.org.uk/__data/assets/pdf_file/0017/7073/c4licence.pdf. Accessed 27 June 2022.

"Peep Show (TV Movie 2008)." 2008. IMDb. https://www.imdb.com/title/tt1358239/. Accessed 1 August.

PiersB. 2006. "Coupling: How it all ends." *Fat Pigeons*. https://fatpigeons.com/2006/05/18/coupling-how-it-all-ends/. Accessed 1 Novemer.

Redman, Peter. 2001. "The discipline of love: Negotiation and regulation in boys' performance of a romance-based heterosexual masculinity." *Men and Masculinities* 4 (2):186–200. doi: 10.1177/1097184X01004002006.

Rockler, Naomi R. 2006. "'Be your own windkeeper': *Friends*, femnism, and rhetorical strategies of depoliticization." *Women's Studies in Communication* 29 (2):244–264. doi: 10.1080/07491409.2006.10162500.

Rostek, Joanna, and Dorothea Will. 2016. "From ever-lusting individuals to ever-lasting couples: *Coupling* and emotional capitalism." In *British TV Comedies: Cultural Concepts, Contexts and Controversies*, edited by Jürgen Kamm, and Birgit Neumann, 311–325. London: Palgrave Macmillan.

Sanson, Kevin. 2011. "We don't want your must-see TV: Transatlantic television and the failed '*Coupling*' format." *Popular Communication* 9 (1):39–54. doi: 10.1080/15405702.2011.538256.

Scott, James C. 2008 [1985]. *Weapons of the Weak: Everyday Forms of Peasant Resistance*. London: Yale University Press.

Thompson, Lauren Jade. 2018. "'It's like a guy never lived here!': Reading gendered domestic spaces of *Friends*." *Television & New Media* 19 (8):758–774. doi: 10.1177/1527476418778414.

Tribe, Keith. 2009. "Liberalism and neoliberalism in Britain, 1930–1980." In *The Road from Mont Pélerin: The Making of the Neoliberal Thought Collective*, edited by Philip Mirowski, and Dieter Plehwe, 68–97. Cambridge, MA: Harvard University Press.

Wickham, Phil. 2013. "British situation comedy and 'the culture of new capitalism'." PhD, College of Humanities, University of Exeter.

Wickham, Phil. 2017. "Twenty-first century British sitcom and 'the hidden injuries of class'." In *Social Class and Television Drama in Contemporary Britain*, edited by David Forrest, and Beth Johnson, 201–213. London: Palgrave Macmillan.

Wojcik, Pamela Robertson. 2010. *The Apartment Plot: Urban Living in American Film and Popular Culture, 1945 to 1975*. Durham, NC: Durham University Press.

7 Masculinities after the hangout sitcom

> Unfortunately for the creators of hangout sitcoms, it's no longer believable that a group of friends would sit around and talk without simultaneously looking at their smartphones, only half-engaged in their current surroundings and conversations. Is my cynicism for my peers showing? Probably, but I've too often seen the best minds of my generation spend half of brunch Instagramming their food while it gets cold.
>
> Lauren Le Vine (2018) for *Refinery29*

In terms of being clear and obvious instances of the hangout sitcom, there is, as far as I can see, only one that remains on the air, which is the recent *How I Met Your Mother* follow-up *How I Met Your Father* (2022–present), set in the same universe, and in fact in the same flat, but with a new cast (and cameos from some of the old cast and supporting characters), on streaming platform Disney+. It has received mixed reception. Then there is the parodic *It's Always Sunny in Philadelphia* (2005–present) on FX, a pay television channel known for alternative output, which has been going since 2005, and is as perhaps more a parody of the hangout sitcom than a straightforward instance of it. Meanwhile, the second half of the 2010s also saw the success of a cluster of genre-mixing shows with majority black writers and casts that are as much dramas exploring issues of racialization in the USA as they are hangout sitcoms. Examples include Donald Glover's *Atlanta* (2016–2022), also on FX, or Issa Rae's *Insecure* (2016–2021), on HBO, both shows with creators and writers who are simultaneously co-stars. Instead, the more dominant sitcoms on broadcast television of the past few years have been good a mix of a recuperated and societally up-to-date family sitcoms, as well as a group of workplace sitcoms with similarly up-to-date representation. In short, the hangout sitcom's hegemony appears, for now, to be over. Why?

An essential part of Stuart Hall's thesis about conjunctures is that they are by nature impermanent. The conjunctural shift toward a privatized economy and individualized culture that Hall (2017 [1979]) observed at the beginning of the neoliberal conjuncture only heralded the end of history, as Francis Fukuyama infamously put it, for a brief 20-year interlude. Inasmuch as any conjuncture or ideology has internal contradictions, Hall suggests that its

DOI: 10.4324/9781003363538-7

end is simply the exposure and coincidence of its contradictions. With the global financial crash of 2008, global neoliberal economics was put under significant strain, but it would be overstating it to suggest neoliberalism is no longer hegemonic. Rather, if anything, neoliberalism has tightened its hegemony. For Hall and others such as Philip Mirowski (2013), the reason that neoliberal common sense emerged as the solution to its own moment of economic crisis was the lack of intersecting cultural, political, and social crises as well as the absence of an alternative narrative, so all-encompassing has neoliberal logic become. Similarly, the political crisis engendered by the rupturing moments in 2016 of the election of President Donald Trump and the UK's opting for Brexit did not hark a clear end to neoliberalism.

This has led a range of authors to apply to the post-2008, even post-2016, version of neoliberalism a range of descriptive labels indicating, rather than a post-neoliberalism, something closer to a faltering neo-neoliberalism – for instance, "mutant neoliberalism" (Callison and Manfredi 2019), a re-entrenchment of the role of the neoliberal state in "authoritarian neoliberalism" (Tansel 2017), as well as more evocative phrases, such as Wendy Brown's "neoliberalism's Frankenstein" (Brown 2018) and in several journalistic pieces "zombie neoliberalism" (Harvie and Milburn 2011). As the (at time of writing) ongoing COVID-19 pandemic slows, further questions continue to be asked about to what extent the virus has provoked the confluence of a range of economic, political, social, and cultural crises globally – from the seeming insufficiency of privatized and de-centralized healthcare systems in dealing with the crisis, to an international cost of living crisis, to a set of circumstantially state-driven policies, responses do appear to be expanding the range of the politically possible. Yet, it is still hard to envisage a post-COVID 19 reconstruction that re-deploys anything other than neoliberal state-building, despite the conjuncture's alarmingly creaky and collapsing popular consensus.

Shifts in technology and methods of viewership have also threatened (or at least threatened to threaten) the sitcom's pre-eminent position in US culture. As was discussed in the introduction, streaming platforms continue to climb up the ratings, and according to Nielsen, in July 2022 accounted for a plurality of the US population's viewing hours ahead of both cable and broadcast TV (Krouse 2022). Part of the appeal of the sitcom has been its sense of community, each episode the same time every week for anyone who wanted to watch. Streaming is the opposite, viewers tuning in whenever they like, with episodes often dropped in batches having been written and designed for binge-watching (Jenner 2014). This ever more dispersed and individualized viewing experience poses a potential threat to a communitarian genre such as the sitcom – and yet, as a subgenre it remains as popular as ever, having found a variety of forms and diversifications to adapt to these habits.

Out of these historical developments has arisen a range of diverse and interesting new cultural forms that range vastly, from a concerningly visible mobilization of the far right via the darker corners of the Internet

(Van Valkenburgh 2018, Finlayson 2021), to a range of online engagements with feminism (Keller 2019), to "woke capitalism" in corporate advertising (Kanai and Gill 2020). The so-called culture wars in the Global North have become a superstructural battleground exposing the contradictions within an economic base of neoliberalism that continues to lurch from crisis to crisis without a clear alternative.

The contemporary sitcoms of the 2020s, which continue to move through conjunctures as they shift and dissipate, reflect the messiness of this range of competing cultural forms. In general, sitcom subgenre innovations are often marked by initial skepticism of sociopolitical change, through to its eventual absorption. In the 1960s for instance, the women's and civil rights movements were initially treated as threats by sitcoms like *The Addams Family* (1964–1966) and *Bewitched* (1964–1972), before *All in the Family* (1971–1979) attempted to address such issues seriously. Or, through the hangout sitcom's dominant period, it begins by treating newer forms of more loving homosociality with heterosexual overcompensation, before moving toward more affectionate relationships. The (relative) demise of the hangout sitcom, then, and the wider sitcom genre's postmodern dispersal, offers some clues at the somewhat confusing hybrid cultural forms and gender regimes that a post-neoliberal conjuncture might have to offer. More widely, the hangout sitcom's treatment of anxious, neoliberal, masculinities, become the precursor to a range of men in sitcom subgenres who are less anxious about neoliberal masculinity, and more settled in its presumptions and norms.

Domestic masculinities and the workplace sitcom

While the hangout sitcom was arguably the dominant genre through most of the 1990s and 2000s, in the latter period a cluster of mockumentary or mockumentary-style workplace sitcoms achieved significant popularity.[1]

Following the prototype of *Scrubs*, a genre-straddling sitcom influenced by *Friends* as much as by *WKRP in Cincinnati*, a US version of British mockumentary sitcom *The Office* (2001–2003) ran from 2005 until 2013, developed by Greg Daniels, who subsequently went on to co-create *Parks and Recreation* (2009–2015) with Michael Schur. Schur also co-created *Brooklyn Nine-Nine* (2013–2021) with Dan Goor, as well as the subgenre-crossing afterlife/workplace sitcom *The Good Place* (2016–2020), while *Parks and Recreation*'s cast was led by Amy Poehler, known for her writing, and her comedy partnership with Tina Fey, who created and starred in *30 Rock* (2006–2013). Its gender- and increasingly race-balanced workplaces challenge notions of white public patriarchy by constructing caring or, at least on the face of it, profeminist masculinities, in ways that the hangout sitcom's men's anxious negotiations of neoliberalism made possible.

The Office (titled *The Office: An American Workplace* in the UK to distinguish it from its source material, and from hereon denoted by *The Office (US)*), more so than the other workplace sitcoms mentioned, was a similar level phenomenon as the British show of which it was a remake. In 2003, *The Office (UK)*, created by comedy writing duo Ricky Gervais and Stephen Merchant, became the first British TV show to win multiple Golden Globe Awards for Best Television Series (Musical or Comedy), prompting the commission of a pilot for the US remake. The endeavor, headed up by former writer at *Saturday Night Live* and *The Simpsons* Greg Daniels, translated a British mockumentary sitcom following the employees of fictional paper supply company Wernham Hogg to a US facsimile paper supply company, Dunder Mifflin. It was not widely expected to succeed, especially after the outcome of US remakes of *Coupling* and *Spaced*. Season one, its shiny cast led by an established comedy movie actor in Steve Carell, was six episodes long, and, character-to-character, gag-by-gag, plot-by-plot, was mostly identical to the British version, and was not a great success story, its ratings declining episode by episode.

Season two, however, made some changes that led to huge success, sweeping several Golden Globes award ceremonies, drawing reams of praise from critics and sweeping up viewing figures. For example, it reverted to the US convention of longer seasons, with 22 episodes and original writing. There was a significant tonal shift, too. While both shows are thematically organized around finding wonder amidst the mundanity of everyday late modern life, *The Office (UK)* trades on "cringe" humor in ways *The Office (US)* does not, creating characters with whom it is not always clear to what extent audiences are meant to sympathize. Here, following the previous chapter, we see the different cultural and institutional demands of transatlantic adaptation successfully navigated, Alexandra Beeden and Joost de Bruin (2010) suggesting that *The Office (US)* adapted to the national cultural and institutional specificities of the USA.

Beeden and de Bruin compare the office manager of each show – David Brent played by Ricky Gervais in the UK, and Michael Scott played by Steve Carell in the US – who are both embarrassingly desperate to be seen as funny by everyone else, but for different reasons. Whereas David

> operates within the British understanding that comedy is a form of "power" in that culture ... Michael's attempts at comedy are designed not to garner respect and power from his employees but rather to entertain them, to create a "community" within the workplace".
> (Beeden and de Bruin 2010, 12)

The latter observation, suggest Beeden and de Bruin, is related to the US sitcom's focus on community and family. However, even for the more sympathetic Michael, desperation frequently lapses into dislikeable behavior, such as racially insensitive impressions (*The Office (US)*, "Diversity Day") or hijacking an employee's wedding because of his own emotional insecurities (*The Office (US)*, "Phyllis' Wedding"). Much of the show then focuses on Michael's character arc, as he departs the show in season seven of the US show, moving to Colorado with wife Holly Flax (Amy Ryan). Michael leaves a job that has, until this point, been the thing he loves most, and the thing to which he most aspires. He shows love throughout for both Dunder Mifflin the company and his staff, and yet his happy departure comes at the drop of a hat when Holly says she cannot move to Michael because of her ailing parents in Colorado, a decision that Michael does not think about. The legacy of *Friends* and the hangout sitcom is legible as one in which the sitcom's role shifts toward telling stories about journeys rather than destinations, and particularly about masculinity. The telos remains the same: Ward Cleaver's caring, managerial, fathering masculinity, as Michael moves across the country to care for an elderly couple and his and Holly's children. Yet, as the workplace sitcom moves through the neoliberal conjuncture, the demands of this new form of masculinity imbue a brand new self-conscious political shift.

In *Parks and Recreation*, a workplace sitcom set in the parks department in the fictional Pawnee, Indiana, both central character Leslie Knope, played by Amy Poehler, and her boyfriend (and later husband) Ben Wyatt, played by Adam Scott, become elected government officials at various levels. Further, in the series finale, via a series of flashforwards, it is revealed that at some point in the show's fictional future, both Leslie and Ben are approached to run for the position of Governor of Indiana, and Ben concedes the opportunity to Leslie. It is later implied, though left ambiguous, that one or both of them are elected President of the United States. Ben's role here is not just that of the caring managerial father, but as a stay-at-home father supporting his wife's career.

A more striking example is in *Brooklyn Nine-Nine* (which interestingly had a crossover with *New Girl*, several characters from each show appearing on the other), which follows a police precinct in New York City. Once more indicating the kinds of postmodern genre pastiche with which the sitcom is now well acquainted, *Brooklyn Nine-Nine* is as much of a police procedural as a sitcom.[2] Detective Jake Peralta is played by Andy Samberg, the implied lead character (Samberg was the first name attached to the project, and was an executive producer from the beginning, while Jake's story is the focus of the first season at least) who we are told is the precinct's "best detective. He likes putting away bad guys and he loves solving puzzles. The only puzzle he hasn't solved is how to grow up" (*Brooklyn Nine-Nine*, "Pilot"). His narrative arc unfolds predictably – he grows up. This involves nearly all the beats associated with chrononormative straight time: learning to behave appropriately at work in early seasons, repairing his relationship with his absent father, a series of progressively more serious girlfriends, getting married to long-term love interest Amy Santiago (Melissa Fumero) in season five, and having a child together the following season. The expected storyline, though, would most likely have included Jake, who is Jewish like his actor Andy Samberg, rising through the ranks in the police precinct – but he does not. Amy, a Latinx woman, achieves the position of Sergeant in season six, becoming a Chief of Department at the NYPD in the series finale, while black police officer Terry Jeffords (Terry Crews) is promoted from Sergeant to Lieutenant and then Captain. Jake, however, remains a Detective and eventually quits the police force to take care of his son.

Brooklyn Nine-Nine echoes the masculinities in *New Girl* in particular, recalling Schmidt's stay-at-home dad and Winston's black cop storyline, as well as Michael's domestication in *The Office (US)*. In fact, it appears to challenge notions of white public patriarchy, transforming the public work sphere not only in terms of gender but in terms of race, too. As Jake's character is domesticized over time, he eventually abandons the public sphere altogether, as notions of care and an other-regarding ethic take over – and not just in any workplace, but in the US police, an institution with long-standing problems regarding racism and misogyny. In fact, Jake's arc can be read, with the hangout sitcom's masculinities as predecessor, as a settled and resolved form of neoliberal masculinity, following Peter Redman's (2001) idea of romantic masculinities that articulate neoliberal notions of individualism and middle-class habitus. In this way, the anxiety of neoliberal masculinities is shed, and the workplace sitcom's characters are instead pro-feminist cheerleaders, but also in Jake and his best friend Charles Boyle (Joe Lo Truglio), unquestioning supporters of racial and sexual equality. These settled presumptions are a feature of a range of new family sitcoms.

Masculinity and homonormativity in the new family sitcom

More recently, some of the most popular sitcoms of the last decade have returned to the family, but with a twist. Amidst ongoing national debate in the US about gay marriage both preceding and following Obergefell vs. Hodges (currently back on the agenda with a conservative majority on the Supreme Court emboldened following the overturning of Roe vs. Wade), the family sitcom has begun to include and address same-sex relationships and families. To an extent, these appearances "queer" the family sitcom, but they also fall into a range of homonormative tropes that transplant all the same events of straight time onto white gay men.

The family in *Modern Family* is not the white, middle-class nuclear family of the sitcoms of the 1950s and 1960s. Rather, the show follows an extended family, consisting of three households, one blended, one same-sex and adoptive, and one reasonably standard nuclear. Phil Dunphy (Ty Burrell), patriarch of the show's heterosexual nuclear family, combines two tropes of sitcom fatherhood, that of the managerial professional father – Ward Cleaver or Cliff Huxtable – and the henpecked husband emasculated by a dominant wife empowered by moves toward gender equality – Darrin Stephens from *Bewitched*, or Dan Conner in *Roseanne*. While Phil does not have quite the same gendered authority as the latter, he also does not have the same sense of loss and tragedy over his relinquished gender power as the former. Instead, he synthesizes the two in his happiness at wife Claire's (Julie Bowen) life outside of her domestic role as a wife. *Modern Family*, it should be said, was criticized for its gender politics in early seasons as Claire was primarily a homemaker. Yet, she was never a homemaker in the same way as the frustrated Lucy Ricardo with her wild schemes, but comfortable in the role that the show suggests she chose, having previously worked managing a team at a hotel chain prior to the show's beginning. Phil puts his wife on a pedestal, showering her with compliments and gifts, and when she begins working at her father's business of selling closets and storage, Phil is her biggest cheerleader. This presents a settled consensus of many of the now-hegemonic axioms of neoliberalism that the hangout sitcom negotiated. A husband's potential socioeconomic demotion thanks to the empowered postfeminist femininity of his wife is not an issue of contention and anxiety, but a source of pride. Indeed, by the end of *Friends*, Chandler is not anxious about Monica's similarly empowered postfeminist femininity, but excited about her and their future together.

This goes further for *Modern Family*, too, in Phil's attitude toward Mitchell (Jesse Tyler Ferguson), Claire's brother, and Cameron (Eric Stonestreet), Mitchell's boyfriend and later husband. In the chapter on bromance, I showed how the hangout sitcom, certainly in its earlier forms, resorted to forms of homophobia to undercut the genuine possibilities of serious friendship between male characters. Phil, on the other hand, never has any qualms about LGBTQ+ identities, and rarely, if ever, feels the need to overcome accusations of emasculation via homophobia. In quite an endearing scene, when Luke has bought a bra to prepare for potential sexual scenarios, and Phil misinterprets his owning the bra as Luke being a trans woman, he says, "if that's what you need on the outside to feel like the Luke you are on the inside" (*Modern Family*, "Spring Break"). Meanwhile, he is on the constant receiving end of emasculation by his father-in-law Jay Pritchett (Ed O'Neill), who struggles with the gay identity of his own son and nearly does not attend the wedding. This image is heightened by the fact that Ed O'Neill, who plays Jay, was previously known for 11 seasons as an extremely similar character Al Bundy in the 1990s family sitcom *Married ... with Children* (1987-1997) (to the extent that *Modern Family* sometimes seems like a sequel). Bundy was a semi-tragic and misanthropic, if affable, women's shoes salesman left behind by a feminized consumerist culture, exemplified by the way he is treated by a materialistic wife and daughter. Indeed, the reminders that Jay is simply from a different era seem to encourage viewers to both disapprove of and sympathize with his homophobia (in similar ways as Al Bundy's misanthropy is treated with affection), he is positioned as a residual, ebbing, form of masculinity in comparison to Phil.

Yet, in *Modern Family*, the forms of gay masculinity that the show represents largely exist within a homonormative framework. The idea of homonormativity suggests that a mainstream politics of queerness transfers many of the aspects of hetero- and chrononormativity onto gay politics, such as marriage, the nuclear family, and normative, acceptable workplaces. It has been observed, too, that the optics of homonormativity tend to uphold a certain norm of whiteness (Ferguson 2005), and of masculinity, too, in which white gay men come to represent queer politics. Lisa Duggan (2002) suggests that homonormativity aptly describes neoliberalism's LGBTQ+ politics, for the ways it links individualism, domesticity and consumption. Steven Edward Doran (2013) argues that Mitchell and Cameron represent such a dynamic, a white couple who get married in a season finale episode written in response to Obergefell vs. Hodges, one of whom works as a lawyer, and the other of whom works as a music teacher. Such homonormativity demonstrates the limits of Phil's profeminist masculinity. *Modern Family*, though, was a typical sitcom broadcast hit, broadcast on ABC in a primetime slot, and garnering the millions of viewers that come with that. More recently, another family sitcom has emerged as one of the most popular shows of recent decades, through means determined by contemporary cultural and technological practices.

Schitt's Creek and the future of the sitcom?

Canadian sitcom *Schitt's Creek* (2015–2020) debuted in 2015 on the state-run Canadian Broadcasting Network (CBC). It follows the wealthy Rose family, who in episode one lose everything due to financial irregularities, and wind up living in a rural Ontario town called Schitt's Creek, pun very much intended, which was their only remaining asset, the whole town having been bought as a joke for son David's birthday – or, as co-creator Dan Levy put the premise, "what would happen if one of these wealthy families would lose everything? Would the Kardashians still be the Kardashians without their money?" (Levy in Martin 2015). The Roses at the beginning of the show are four selfish, entitled, odious snobs, who treat the denizens of Schitt's Creek as dim-witted backwards simpletons. Rose daughter Alexis, played by Annie Murphy, spends the first few seasons callously playing with love interest Ted's heart, while son David, played by co-creator Dan Levy, does not shy away from being highly critical of the town's collective fashion sense – neither have really ever worked. Meanwhile, mum Moira, played by Catherine O'Hara, cannot hide her disgust for the town's mayor Roland Schitt, played by Chris Elliott. Playing the relative straight man, father Jonny, played by Dan's real-life father and co-creator Eugene Levy, is the least snobby of the group, but still shows little interest in the people and community of their adopted town.

The first season was broadcast to generally positive but not overwhelming reaction. It was picked up in the US by pay-per-view channel Pop TV the same year as it was broadcast on CBC, but still received little traction. With the commencement of its third season, however, Netflix purchased its broadcast rights in 2017, in a range of countries, and at this point (in a similar as happened to the quality TV phenomenon *Breaking Bad* (2008–2013) several years earlier), *Schitt's Creek* really took off. Critical reception was almost unanimously positive from seasons three through six, as the Rose family slowly shuffled toward their redemptive arc by taking the eponymous town to their hearts and in the process learning basic empathy and to appreciate the value of human connection. Catherine O'Hara's Moira became hugely popular, labeled a gay icon for her bizarre posh American accent and her fabulous and campy outfits – alongside the show's final season, Netflix released a documentary about *Schitt's Creek* that featured footage of a themed night club event called "The Night of a Thousand Moiras", where the challenge was to dress in one of her costumes. And, interestingly, the show received heaps of praise for Dan Levy's portrayal of David, an openly pansexual character who has relationships with both men and women in the show. *Schitt's Creek*, in short, arguably hit and mined a zeitgeist in the way a US sitcom had not done for a while.

The reason this backstory is important is because, I think, *Schitt's Creek* negotiates a post-neoliberal settlement, for three reasons. The first is its route to popularity via the amplification of fans' voices, a trend also exemplified by fan-driven revivals of season six of *Brooklyn Nine-Nine* following its cancellation after season five, as well as season six and impending movie adaptation of the sitcom *Community* (2009–2015), all largely driven by fan pressure. The second is its genre innovation. Genre innovation often occurs at moments of conjunctural imbalance, exemplified by the emergence of the hangout sitcom in the 1990s, but also, for example, the relevancy-coms of the 1970s or the magicoms of the 1960s. The premise of *Schitt's Creek*, as well as its adult children in David and Alexis, and the nature and positioning of characters who function differently to their predecessors, all suggest that the show belongs to a newer era. Though, whether, and indeed how, this might coalesce into, or at least contribute to, a wider subgenre is yet to be seen.

The third piece of evidence, considering the sitcom's strong relation to social context, is its discursive focus, in that *Schitt's Creek* negotiates a range of different issues to the hangout sitcom even while the hangout sitcom's legacy is legible. For instance, where the hangout sitcom's urban setting was indicative of a moment when neoliberalism found in cities its ideal geography, recent years have seen some ideological and public attention shift away from urban communities to the areas that deindustrialization left behind. In a linked development, we are much more likely to see critiques of the super-rich within public discourse, after leftwing movements in the USA and the UK have challenged elements of the neoliberal consensus – economic austerity, for example, has gone from political common sense to swear word in a decade, while President Joe Biden has recently canceled a vast amount of student debt. Correspondingly in *Schitt's Creek*, being rich is not necessarily a good thing.

Katharine Schaab (2020, 150), suggests that "the cross-class community building and power-sharing featured in *Schitt's Creek* offers viewers a narrative questioning the status quo by queering the prevailing, divisive social class system and imagining alternative, yet plausible, economic and social futures". Reading the show as a performance of different ways of exerting power, Schaab suggests the Roses' narrative redemption is characterized by a move from a power-over mentality, in which they consider themselves superior to, or of higher standing than, the rest of the citizens of Schitt's Creek, to a community-based form of power. The Roses by the end are much more willing to work with the people of Schitt's Creek than they were at the beginning of the show, and this certainly does appear to offer a more communal solution than the individualist work ethic of *Friends*, in which the insularity of the group offers community and belonging only within the closed middle-class white circle, and at the expense of those outside the circle. The Roses, by contrast, engage with the entire community. This perhaps offers a glimpse of a possible future beyond neoliberal hegemony, in offering a clearer challenge to neoliberalism's individualist paradigm. Rather than absorbing discourses that threaten it, instead *Schitt's Creek* threatens to challenge them from the inside.

Indeed, we might also consider how such community-based forms of power challenge, and offer alternatives to, masculinities. Feminists have long pointed out how patriarchal power tends to be oriented toward domination (Walby 1990, Millett 1970) and described how masculinities are constructed to remain complicit in such structures (Connell 2005). Meanwhile, neoliberal power is often structured along similar lines (Garlick 2020). In *Schitt's Creek*, it is no coincidence, then, that collective power comes together with its most visible male lead is the femme pansexual David – as he puts it, "I like the wine and not the label" (*Schitt's Creek*, "Honeymoon") – played by the gay actor Daniel Levy. David's venture in the town of Schitt's Creek is to start his own business, a shop selling local artisanal products and produce, and finishes by marrying his business partner Patrick (Noah Reid). This shop, named Rose Apothecary, is an extension of David's character, a man preoccupied with fashion, cosmetics, and pretty things, and reads as a feminized form of consumption. David learns his lessons on building success through community with typically feminized consumption as the means. The show deploys forms of masculinity quite different to the hangout sitcom that construct community-based power.

This, of course, has its limits. The Canadian show certainly inculcates the American Dream – though the Roses start with nothing in *Schitt's Creek*, the finale involves all but one of them leaving the town for better things, Johnny building a nationwide chain of motels, Moira to star in a reboot of the TV show for which she has been famous, and Alexis to work as a publicist in TV in New York. And though David remains behind, he does so as a successful business owner. Simultaneously, the hangout sitcom's legacy is legible in *Schitt's Creek*'s post-class politics. The Roses' class background is demarcated in much the same way as it is in *Cheers* and subsequent hangout sitcoms, as a matter of taste, aesthetics, and identity rather than material background. The fact that the Roses are members of the upper-class is less important than the idea that they simply come from a different cultural background than the citizens of Schitt's Creek, in that the things that alienate them from the town's residents are cultural tastes and class habits, such that the materiality of class position and inequalities is rendered irrelevant.

Yet, apart from Johnny Rose, who shows no interest in women beyond his wife Moira, *Schitt's Creek* is not all that interested in straight white masculinities What are the circumstances in which a sitcom, that TV show which at every era seems to capture and distill the American cultural imaginary, can lack a straight white masculinity? Just as the hangout sitcom emerges as post-white, one might ask whether what emerges from the end of the hangout sitcom is, too, a post-male consensus in which men's power is perceived to be at an end, and question where this might head in the future.

Will hyperreality expose masculinities?

Two events occurred in the latter stages of writing this book that demonstrate the continued cultural import of the hangout sitcom. In late 2022, Matthew Perry, known more commonly as Chandler Bing, published his autobiography, *Friends, Lovers and the Big Terrible Thing* (Perry 2022). Perry's private life had been well-documented throughout his time on *Friends*, having suffered from issues with addiction, a fractious social life, and an aborted Hollywood career, and both he and viewers have noted the visible fluctuations in his weight between seasons. The autobiography was unsurprisingly salacious, fleshing out details of various sexual and romantic encounters, the huge amounts of drugs and alcohol he has consumed, and the moment in 2020 when he had to pull out of a movie for health reasons because his heart stopped beating for five minutes. Combined with this, several years prior, Netflix had released the fifth and final season of their animated sitcom *BoJack Horseman* (2014-2020), which follows a fictional anthropomorphized bipedal horse who was a former star of a fictional sitcom *Horsin' Around*, in which he adopts three children as a lone father. Throughout *BoJack Horseman*, BoJack (voiced by Will Arnett) is middle-aged, washed-up, drug-addicted, sexist, and generally anachronistic, struggling to find a purpose or a way to cope with a range of past mistakes and wrongdoings. He reads as an amalgamation of a range of stereotypes about washed-up male Hollywood stars who had rocky personal lives, such as Tim Allen and Bob Saget. Matthew Perry is as good an analogue to BoJack as any of these, but all of them had significant sitcom fame, Allen with *Home Improvement* (1991-1999), and Bob Saget, of course, as the older voice-over of Ted Mosby in *How I Met Your Mother*. *BoJack Horseman* is a sitcom about a character who reads as a fusion of white men, who used to star in a sitcom, and who now struggles to find his place, specifically as a man, in the modern Hollywood.

Meanwhile, in September 2022, a scandal rocked a small subsection of the Internet. Starting with a small cluster of posts on various social media websites, details slowly emerged that Ned Fulmer, a comedian and one of four members of the comedy group and media organization the "Try Guys", had been conducting an extramarital affair with an employee (Garcia 2022). The group, a spin-off from social media website BuzzFeed's video content, formally announced Fulmer's departure within a few weeks, the other three Try Guys having signed legal documents removing him as a partner in the company (Garcia 2022). The whirlwind speed at which the allegations in less than 24 hours became a job loss was marked, as extramarital affairs rarely spell major career trouble, even in entertainment. Fulmer's chastening experience was instead because of who the Try Guys are or were, and more specifically who the character of Ned Fulmer became. The general synopsis of the Try Guys is that they try out new experiences, from the mundane, such as baking without instructions, to the more surprising, such as feeling the simulated pain of childbirth via technology, sometimes but not always guided by some sort of expert. The appeal of the Try Guys is not just in the novelty of their tasks (their most popular video is titled "The Try Guys Get Their Bones Cracked") but in the "guys" themselves, each of them with their own unique selling point. Fulmer's selling point was that he was "the wife guy" (see McIntyre & Negra 2022). In one of their first big videos, "The Try Guys Test The Legal Alcohol Limit", Fulmer spends most of the episode expressing how much he misses his wife Ariel, while his Instagram account bio still, as of 2023, describes him as "Ariel Fulmer's husband". His on-screen character, in short, was that he was a doting husband, which is why his cheating scandal hurt his career, as it undermined the character he played. But there is not much separating Ned Fulmer from Marshall Eriksen, or from Schmidt in later seasons of *New Girl*. He was a semi-real instantiation the househusband, gone chrononormatively awry.

All of this is to say that at moments when the hangout sitcom's masculinities extend into the hyperreal – from Matthew Perry, Chandler Bing and BoJack Horseman's lives leaking into one another, through to the real-life househusband Ned Fulmer's infidelities – something about those masculinities comes unstuck. Jean Baudrillard (1994 [1981]) defines the hyperreal as the breakdown between that which does and does not belong to the real, or material world, such that it becomes difficult to distinguish between what is signified and what is real. For him, hyperreality is a symptom of late capitalism (or, neoliberalism), an abandonment of a culture or superstructure no longer determined purely economistically, which instead turns cultural signification inwards, among itself, leading to porousness between the real and the fictive. Such a precarious system of signification, he suggests, is prone to a "slow implosion", as a precarious and interdependent set of signs and constructions gives way to the lack of a material reality underpinning it. Gender and masculinity are symptomatic here, as the iterative performances of neoliberal gender risk the reveal of their lack of an original, and undermine masculinity's claim, in general, to having a natural or essential form. At these moments, the neoliberalized masculinities in the hangout sitcom unveil their situation within ongoing patriarchal structures.

Legacies of the hangout sitcom's masculinities

As is customary to note, readers of this book will have noticed several areas where I could have gone further. I very briefly talked about female masculinities and their relation to postfeminist femininities, and perhaps missed a trick in leaving them aside. A range of feminist authors have pointed out how women's performances of masculinity not only help to sever the link between maleness and masculinity as a performance, but also serve to offer didactic lessons to male characters about masculinities (Halberstam 1998, Noble 2004).

Similarly, there is a lot of room for the study of both boyhood and fatherhood in the hangout sitcom, not only in related family sitcoms, but also in its use of flashbacks and how boyhood remains immanent within the male characters thus far studied. Caitlin Jordan (2020) suggests that many contemporary US sitcoms can be read as instantiations of the bildungsroman genre, with the characters in a state of delayed childhood and in a continual state of "becoming" adults, which we never fully see onscreen. Within such a reading, we might reasonably wonder how, for example, the figure of the father hangs over and haunts the masculinities of the hangout sitcom. One might consider how such depictions of boyhood contribute to generational moral panics, and ongoing concerns about the emasculation of each new generation (see Kordas 2011), especially considering the feminized qualities of the neoliberal subject.

I have mentioned *It's Always Sunny in Philadelphia* (2005–present) a few times, which reads as a dark parody of the hangout sitcom. It skewers, for example, the ways in which the hangout sitcom friendship group polices its boundaries so aggressively to reject the possibility of otherness entering, much like Phil Chidester (2008) described. The "gang", as they get called, of white main characters, all of them irredeemably selfish and unpleasant, through their actions wreck the lives of a series of fringe characters, such as Matthew "Rickety Cricket" Mara (David Hornsby), who is first introduced as a mild-mannered priest, and eventually becomes a grotesque-looking homeless man who will perform all manner of tasks for a small amount of money. Meanwhile, the character Dennis (Glenn Howerton) is a psychopathic misogynist whose treatment of women reads as a sinister version of Barney Stinson, offering a critique of the misogyny of the douchebag character.

As well as parodies, what of black hangout sitcoms such as *Atlanta* and *Insecure* that I briefly touched on? Or the recent splurge of animated sitcoms with their damaged, tragic masculine figures, such as the mentioned *BoJack Horseman* or *Rick and Morty* (2013-present)? Further, I pointed out in chapter one that many fans of *Friends*, as well as other hangout sitcoms, watch the show despite reading its politics – of gender, race, and sexuality – in a very negative light. How is this cognitive dissonance squared by viewers? Reception studies might help us to respond to such questions.

The fact that there is so much left to examine is symptomatic of the rich gender politics in *Friends* and its inheritors. I have argued that the anxious straight white men of the hangout sitcom negotiate the contradictions and pitfalls of a neoliberal, postfeminist conjuncture, in which they perceive threats to socioeconomic power and to heterosexual reward. Within this milieu, we find backlash scripts in the douchebag or the postfeminist male singleton, as well as an emerging racial politics focused more on representation than materiality, encoded congruently with homosocial relationships that offer queer readings via the forms of political smuggling in which the sitcom often engages. It is, as I stated at the beginning of this book, difficult to underestimate quite how big the *Friends* phenomenon is, and how big it continues to be, as the neoliberal conjuncture stutters, wheezing, into its fifth decade. In recent years, a who's who of Generation Z masculine icons have worn *Friends* like a badge of fashion, from Justin Bieber's appearance on *Friends: The Reunion* in the "spudnik" potato Halloween costume worn by Ross (*Friends*, "The One With The Halloween Party"), to Harry Styles publicly modeling a replica of a T-shirt worn by Rachel with the slogan "save the drama for your mama" (Hammond 2020). The show's cultural status is yet to let up.

Notes

1 Richard Wallace (2018) argues that the mockumentary is not as much of a political or parodic genre as its title suggests, and instead seeks to elicit comedy through familiarity with the documentary genre it skewers. The idea of "comedy through familiarity" makes it a comfortable match for the sitcom.
2 There is much to be written on *Brooklyn Nine-Nine*'s shift from a cops-as-good-guys narrative that predominates police procedurals, over to more critical viewpoints articulated following the wave of anti-police sentiment in 2020 after a range of high profile cases of young black people killed by serving officers. See, for example, Lauren Bernabo (2022).

Filmography

30 Rock. 2006–2013. [TV] Fey, Tina, Creator, NBC: USA.
The Addams Family. 1964–1966. [TV] Levy, David, Creator, ABC: USA.
All in the Family. 1971–1979. [TV] Lear, Norman, Creator, CBS: USA.
Atlanta. 2016–2022. [TV] Glover, Donald, Creator, FX: USA.
Bewitched. 1964–1972. [TV] Saks, Sol, Creator, ABC: USA.
BoJack Horseman. 2014–2020. [TV] Bob-Waksberg, Raphael, Creator, Netflix: USA.
Breaking Bad. 2008–2013. [TV] Gilligan, Vince, Creator, AMC: USA.
Brooklyn Nine-Nine. 2013–2021. [TV] Goor, Dan, and Michael Schur, Creator, Fox, NBC: USA.
Community. 2009–2015. [TV] Harmon, Dan, Creator, NBC, Yahoo! Screen: USA.
The Good Place. 2016–2020. [TV] Schur, Michael, Creator, NBC: USA.
How I Met Your Father. 2022-present. [TV] Aptaker, Isaac, and Elizabeth Berger, Creator, Hulu: USA.

Insecure. 2016–2021. [TV] Rae, Issa, Creator, HBO: USA.
It's Always Sunny in Philadelphia. 2005-present. [TV] McElhenny, Rob, Creator, FX: USA.
Married... with Children. 1987-1997. [TV] Moye, Michael G., and Ron Leavitt, Creator, Fox: USA.
The Office. 2001–2003. [TV] Gervais, Ricky, and Stephen Merchant, Creator, BBC: UK.
The Office: An American Workplace. 2005–2013. [TV] Daniels, Greg, Creator, NBC: USA.
Parks and Recreation. 2009–2015. [TV] Daniels, Greg, and Michael Schur, Creator, NBC: USA.
Rick and Morty. 2013–present. [TV] Roiland, Justin, and Dan Harmon, Creator, Adult Swim: USA.
Schitt's Creek. 2015–2020. [TV] Levy, Eugene, and Dan Levy, Creator, CBC: Canada.

References

Baudrillard, Jean. 1994 [1981]. *Simulacra and Simulation.* Translated by Sheila Faria Glaser. Ann Arbor, MI: University of Michigan Press.
Beeden, Alexandra, and Joost de Bruin. 2010. "The office: Articulations of national identity in television format adaptation." *Television & New Media* 11 (1):3–19. doi: 10.1177/1527476409338197.
Bernabo, Lauren. 2022. "Copaganda and post-Floyd TVPD: Broadcast television's response to policing in 2020." *Journal of Communication* 72 (4):488–496. doi: 10.1093/joc/jqac019.
Brown, Wendy. 2018. "Neoliberalism's Frankenstein: Authoritarian freedom in twenty-first century 'democracies'." *Critical Times* 1 (1):60–79. doi: 10.1215/26410478-1.1.60.
Callison, William, and Zachary Manfredi. 2019. *Mutant Neoliberalism: Market Rule and Political Rupture.* New York: Fordham University Press.
Chidester, Phil. 2008. "May the circle stay unbroken: *Friends*, the presence of absence, and the rhetorical reinforcement of whiteness." *Critical Studies in Media Communication* 25 (2):157–174. doi: 10.1080/15295030802031772.
Connell, R.W. 2005. *Masculinities.* 2nd ed. Cambridge: Blackwell.
Doran, Steven Edward. 2013. "Housebroken: Homodomesticity and the normalization of queerness in *Modern Family*." In *Queer Love in Film and Television: Critical Essays*, edited by Christopher Pullen, and Pamela Demory, 95–104. New York: Palgrave Macmillan.
Duggan, Lisa. 2002. "The new homonormativity: The sexual politics of neoliberalism." In *Materializing Democracy: Toward a Revitalized Cultural Politics*, edited by Russ Castronovo, and Dana D. Nelson, 175–194. Durham, NC: Duke University Press.
Ferguson, Roderick A. 2005. "Race-ing homonormativity: Citizenship, sociology, and gay identity." In *Black Queer Studies: A Critical Anthology*, edited by E. Patrick Johnson, and Mae G. Henderson, 52–67. Durham, NC: Duke University Press.
Finlayson, Alan. 2021. "Neoliberalism, the alt-right and the intellectual dark web." *Theory, Culture & Society* 38 (6):167–190. doi: 10.1177/02632764211036731.

Garcia, Gretty. 2022. "Breaking down the try guys drama so you don't have to Google around yourself." Cosmopolitan. https://www.cosmopolitan.com/entertainment/celebs/a41430463/try-guys-cheating-scandal/. Accessed 20 November 2022.

Garlick, Steve. 2020. "The nature of markets: On the affinity between masculinity and (neo)liberalism." *Journal of Cultural Economy* 13 (5):548–560. doi: 10.1080/17530350.2020.1741017.

Halberstam, Jack. 1998. *Female Masculinity*. London: Duke University Press.

Hall, Stuart. 2017. *Selected Political Writings: The Great Moving Right Show and Other Essays*. Durham, NC: Duke University Press.

Hammond, Natalie. 2020. "Harry styles just wore a T-shirt seen on Rachel in friends - And you can buy it for £8.99." Grazia. https://graziadaily.co.uk/fashion/news/harry-styles-friends-t-shirt/. Accessed 20 November 2022.

Harvie, David, and Keir Milburn. 2011. "The zombie of neoliberalism can be beaten - through mass direct action." *The Guardian*, 4 August. https://www.theguardian.com/commentisfree/2011/aug/04/neoliberalism-zombie-action-phone-hacking. Accessed 11 August 2022.

Jenner, Mareike. 2014. "Is this TVIV? On Netflix, TVIII and binge-watching." *New Media & Society* 18 (2):257–273. doi: 10.1177/1461444814541523.

Jordan, Caitlin. 2020. "The gang's all here: Re-reading contemporary American situation comedies as delated, ambivalent bildungsroman." MA English, Faculty of the Graduate School of Arts and Sciences, Georgetown University.

Kanai, Akane, and Rosalind Gill. 2020. "Woke? Affect, neoliberalism, marginalised identities and consumer culture." *New Formations* 102:10–27. doi: 10.3898/NewF:102.01.2020.

Keller, Jessalynn. 2019. "'Oh, she's a tumblr feminist': Exploring the platform vernacular of girls' social media feminisms." *Social Media + Society* 5 (3):1–11. doi: 10.1177/2056305119867442.

Kordas, Ann. 2011. "Wally Cleaver goes to war: The boy citizen-soldier on the Cold War screen." *Boyhood Studies* 5 (2):163–173. doi: 10.3149/thy.0501.163.

Krouse, Sarah. 2022. "Streaming tops cable-TV viewing for the first time." *The Wall Street Journal*. https://www.wsj.com/articles/americans-spent-more-time-streaming-than-watching-cable-tv-in-july-a-first-11660821/184?mod=hp_lead_pos4. Accessed 11 October 2022.

Martin, Michael. 2015. "Dan Levy discusses Schitt's Creek, his eyebrows & being a sex object." Out. https://www.out.com/television/2015/3/09/dan-levy-discusses-schitts-creek-his-eyebrows-being-sex-object. Accessed 20 November 2022.

McIntyre, Anthony P., and Diane, Negra. 2022. "Of wife guys and family defenders: Towards a typology of 21st century celebrity husbands." *Journal of Gender Studies* 32 (3):270-282. doi: 10.1080/09589236.2022.2106957.

Millett, Kate. 1970. *Sexual Politics*. Chicago, IL: University of Illinois Press.

Mirowski, Philip. 2013. *Never Let a Serious Crisis Go to Waste: How Neoliberalism Survived the Financial Meltdown*. London: Verso.

Noble, Jean Bobby. 2004. *Masculinities without Men?* Vancouver: University of British Columbia Press.

Perry, Matthew. 2022. *Friends, Lovers and the Big Terrible Thing*. London: Headline.

Redman, Peter. 2001. "The discipline of love: Negotiation and regulation in boys' performance of a romance-based heterosexual masculinity." *Men and Masculinities* 4 (2):186–200. doi: 10.1177/1097184X01004002006.

Schaab, Katharine. 2020. "Upending the status quo: Power-sharing and community building in *Schitt's Creek*." *Critical Studies in Television* 15 (2):148–161. doi: 10.1177/1749602020916449.
Tansel, Cemal Burak. 2017. *States of Discipline: Authoritarian Neoliberalism and the Contested Reproduction of Capitalist Order*. Edited by Ian Bruff, Julie Cupples, Gemma Edwards, Laura Horn, Simon Springer, and Jacqui True, *Transforming Capitalism*. London: Rowman & Littlefield.
Van Valkenburgh, Shawn P. 2018. "Digesting the red pill: Masculinity and neoliberalism in the manosphere." *Men and Masculinities* 24 (1):84–103. doi: 10.1177/1097184X18816118.
Vine, Lauren Le. 2018. "Did millennials kill the hangout sitcom?" Refinery29. https://www.refinery29.com/en-gb/2015/09/186750/hangout-sitcoms-friends. Accessed 20 July 2022.
Walby, Sylvia. 1990. *Theorizing Patriarchy*. Oxford: Blackwell.
Wallace, Richard. 2018. *Mockumentary comedy: Performing authenticity*. Edited by Roger Sabin, and Sharon Lockyer, *Palgrave Studies in Comedy*. Oxford: Palgrave Macmillan.

Index

8 Simple Rules 27
9½ Weeks 152
30 Rock 172

ABC 116, 177
active/passive binary 69, 152
The Addams Family 49, 117, 172
affect 13, 16, 89, 91, 93–94
Alexander, Jason 55
Alexander, Michelle 118, 130
All in the Family 9, 50, 71, 92, 172
Allen, Theodore 116
Allen, Tim 180
alt-right *see* far right
ambiguity: in British sitcoms 138, 144–145, 148, 153–154, 159–160; of character background 25; of character future 62, 153–154; of chrononormativity 64; between Jewishness and whiteness 133, 135; between public and private spheres 102–103; of readings of the sitcom 80, 83, 91, 138; of sexuality 148, 155, 164
American Beauty 79
American Dream 41, 42, 51, 145, 179
Amos 'n' Andy 41, 45, 52
Anderson, Eric 4
Aniston, Jennifer 22, 23, 100, 132
antisemitism 134
anxiety 5, 32, 65–66, 136, 175–176: and assimilation 133–136; and postfeminism 18, 136, 176; and race 133, 138; and sexuality 81–82, 90, 94–98, 151; in the sitcom 40, 55–57; of status 48, 136, 148, 151, 162
architecture 66, 157
Armstrong, Jesse 160, 162
Arnaz, Desi 47
Arnett, Will 180

asexuality 27, 76, 128
Atlanta 138, 170, 182
Attallah, Paul 7, 42
autism 27, 76, 104

Babes in the Wood 143, 146
baby boomer 44, 50, 71, 73
bachelor (archetype) 9, 63, 66, 72, 156
Baddiel, David 139n3
Bain, Sam 160, 162
Ball, Lucille 47
Barbie 3
Barnes, Peter 161
Baudrillard, Jean 54, 135, 181
Bays, Carter 7, 23
Baywatch 94, 96
BBC 104, 143, 147, 149
Becker, Ron 94
Beeden, Alexandra 173
Belsey, Catherine 69
Bernabo, Lauren 174
The Beverly Hillbillies 50, 53
Bewitched 49, 172, 175
Bialik, Mayim 26, 27
Biden, Joe 178
Bieber, Justin 183
binge-watching 1, 10, 171
bisexuality 148, 161, 165, 167n3
Black Lives Matter 130
Blackadder 146
blackface 3
Black-ish 138
blackness 20, 51–52, 115–120, 125, 137
Blanchard, Rachel 162
bodies 16–17, 62, 73–74, 77, 89, 152
BoJack Horseman 180–182
Bond, James 83–84
boyhood 182
Brabon, Ben 18, 64, 65
Breaking Bad 177

Index

Brexit 171
Bridesmaids (movie) 70
Bridges, Tristan 14
Brodkin, Karen 133, 135
bromance 31, 89–114, 176
Brook, Vincent 135
Brooklyn Nine-Nine 32, 130, 172, 174–175, 178
Brown, Carol 14
Brown, Wendy 17, 19, 171
Buddy movies 99
Budgeon, Shelley 19
Buerkle, C. Wesley 55
Burrell, Ty 175
Butler, Judith 75
Buzzfeed 62, 181

camp 72, 75–76, 96, 122, 178, 179
capitalism: consumer 43; "cool" 16, 51; emotional 16, 57; and the family 40; history of 14; late 12, 54, 65, 181; monetarist 51; neoliberal 13, 134; and subjectivity 62, 165; "woke" 17, 172
Carell, Steve 173
Carmichael, Katy 155
Catwoman 126, 127
CBC 177
CBS 7, 24, 26
Centre for Contemporary Cultural Studies 6
channel 4 143, 147, 155, 160
Chaplin, Ben 143
character: development 54, 124, 126, 128–129, 143, 162, 173–174; in *Friends* 11; in the hangout sitcom 20–29; in the sitcom 9, 12; types/roles 31, **62–85**, 151
Cheers 9, 10, 41, **52–54**, 56, 69
Chicago, Illinois 41, 71, 98, 101, 106
chick flick 70, 96
Chicken Soup 135
Chidester, Phil 121–122, 124, 131, 182
chrononormativity 31, **62–85**: and hyperreality 181; rejection of 154, 160, 163, 165; and sexuality 167n3; and whiteness 126, 129; in the workplace sitcom 174, 176
cis-genderedness 3
cities 12, 41, 57, 82, 178
civil rights 51, 117, 119, 172
class 20, 148: and the family 44; and masculinities 67, 79–83, 85, 110, 162–163, 166; post-class 52–54, 149, 179–180; and race 41–42, 116, 123, 134–136; in the rural-com 48–49; in the UK 145–146, 148, 156
Clayton, Paul 163
closeness in the doing 89–90, 93, 96–98, 99, 109
Clough, Patricia 91
Cobb, Shelley 122
Coleman, Robin 117, 118
college 92, 94, 98, 106
Collins, Jim 9
colonialism 93, 116
community 178
compulsory individualization 51
conjuncture 8, 13–14, 170: as analysis 30–31; historical 40–41; neoliberalism 15–17, 73, 118–119, 170–172
Connell, Raewyn 14, 40
conservatism 42, 151, 152, 156
Conservative Party (UK) 151
consumption 15, 43, 177, 179: of media 6, 9
Cosby, Bill 51
The Cosby Show 51, 54, 118–119, 122, 138, 175
Coupling 32, 144, 146, 149–155, 173
COVID-19 171
Cox, Courtney 22, 132
Coyle, Richard 148, 153, 167n2
Crane, David 21, 132
Cranston, Bryan 68
Crews, Terry 175
critical discourse analysis 30
critical whiteness studies 116, 120
culture wars 172
Cuoco, Kaley 26, 27

Dalton, Mary 57n1
Damon 115
dandy 53
Daniels, Greg 172, 173
Danson, Ted 53
Davenport, Jack 148, 149
David, Jessica Milner 146
David, Larry 11, 55, 133
Days of Our Lives 23, 96
de Bruin, Joost 173
Deakin, Julia 155
DeAngelis, Michael 90, 102, 112
Demetriou, Demetrakis 14
Dench, Judi 83
Deschanel, Zooey 4, 28, 132
discursive psychology 64

Disney 10, 46, 170
divorce 67, 81
domestic: ideology 40–50; labor 23, 43; space 18, 47, 57, 69, 92–97, 156–158
Doran, Steven Edward 177
douchebag 31, 64–66, 72–78, 83–84, 108, 151, 182–183
Douglas, Susan 49
Dow, Rebecca 18
drag 75, 81
Dream On 21
Dude Where's My Car? 154–155
Duggan, Lisa 177
Dyer, Richard 116

emasculation: of characters (hangout sitcom) 65, 80–82, 101, 109, 126–129, 165; of characters (not hangout sitcom) 25, 49, 72, 175–176; and homosociality 89–90, 92; and postfeminism 18; and race 107, 134–136; and sexuality 126–129, 165; in society 45, 182
erotic capital 73
Ewen, Neil 18, 80, 82, 156, 165

failure 145, 153–154, 163–164, 167n3
family: blended 56, 175; and consumerism 134; and individualism 64; and intimacy 76; and neoliberalism 16–17, 56–57, 80, 85, 90, 143; in the post-war period 8, 43–45, 51, 117; and race 117–118, 133–134; in the sitcom (general) 7, 10–11, 19–50, 54, 117–118, 173–177; in the sitcom (hangout) 12, 19, 62–63, 77–83, 85, 90
far right 76, 120, 133, 137, 171
farce 146, 148, 161
Farina, Dennis 71–72
fascism *see* far right
Father Knows Best 117
fatherhood: in the post-war period 43–45; in the sitcom (hangout) 71–72, 77–78, 82–83, 85, 106–107; in sitcoms (general) 45–47, 54, 174–177, 182
fatness 73, 77–78
Fawlty Towers 146
femininity: and blackness 122–123; and consumption 176, 179; and domesticity 57; fear of 19; interloping in public space 99–101, 112; and Jewishness 134–136; on men 16, 66, 80, 95, 129; and neoliberal subjectivity 5, 15–16, 31, 63–64, 90, 182; and Orientalism 107, 126; postfeminist 17, 22, 29, 84–85, 137, 176
feminism 16–17: popular 27, 172; in the sitcom 50, 57; theory 91, 179; women's movement 16, 49, 63
Feuer, Jane 6, 7, 144
Fey, Tina 172
financial crash of 2008 171
Fiske, John 8, 63
food 132
Fox (network) 28, 116, 155
Frank, Thomas 16
Freeman, Elizabeth 62
Friedman, Milton 15
Friendsfest 1
friendship: dyadic friendship in hangout sitcoms 76, 89–112, 157–160; groups in hangout sitcoms 11–12, 19, 85, 121–126; and neoliberalism 57, 86; in workplace sitcoms 50
friendship contract *see* roommate contract
Frost, Nick 148, 155
Fukuyama, Francis 170
Fulmer, Ned 180–181
Fumero, Melissa 174
FX 138, 162, 170

Galecki, Johnny 20, 26, 132, 162
Game On 143, 146
geek *see* masculinities: nerd
gender 3, 4
generation X 3, 20, 73, 143
generation Z 3, 73, 183
generational conflict 49, 71
genre: innovation 178; mixing 9, 11, 72, 138, 170, 172; parody 9, 93, 174, 182; studies 5–7, 9, 19, 144; in the UK 146
Genz, Stephanie 18
Gervais, Ricky 173
Gill, Rosalind 4, 16–18
Gilmore Girls 26
globalization 10, 14–15
Glover, Donald 170
The Goldbergs 134
golden age of television 46
Goldstein, Eric 133
The Good Place 172

Index

Goor, Dan 172
Graeber, David 80, 164
Grammar, Kelsey 53
Gray, Herman 117
Gray, Jonathan 6, 54
The Great Depression 43
The Great Migration 41–42
Greenfield, Max 20, 28, 29
Greig, James 166
Grogan, Josh 100
Gullage, Amy 73

Halberstam, Jack 83–84, 145, 150, 154–155
Hall, Stuart 6, 51, 170–171
Hamad, Hannah 2, 67, 94
Hamamoto, Darrell 42, 48, 57n1
Hannigan, Alyson 24, 25
Happy Endings 20, 29, 115
Harris, Neil Patrick 20, 24, 25, 75
HBO 138, 170
Heap, Mark 148, 155
Hearn, Jeff 14
Helberg, Simon 20, 26, 27
heteronormativity 82: disruption of 90; in the family 16, 43; and femininity 68; and homosociality 93–95, 102, 111, 112; and masculinity 50, 62, 67, 69, 85, 129; and patriarchy 66; in UK sitcoms 152
heterosexuality: of the douchebag character type 77–78; of the househusband character type 82–83; of the PMS character type 68–70; and race 127–129; in sitcoms (general) 47; in sitcoms (hangout) 12–13, 31, 62–66, 83–85, 125–126; in UK sitcoms 148, 149–152, 154, 158–160, 162–164
hijra 128
Hill, Mike 119, 120, 137
Hilmes, Michelle 52
hip hop music 115
hippies 75, 165
Hirst, David 161
Hollywood 69, 73, 144, 156, 180
Holocaust *see* Shoah
homoeroticism 90, 93, 108–109, 111–112, 154
homonormativity 175–177
homophobia 52, 89, 90, 176
homosexuality: actors 25, 27, 75–76, 179; characters 125–126, 164–165, 175–177; mimicry of 154–155; mistaken sexuality plot 80–82, 90, 94–95, 150; in UK sitcoms 167n3
homosociality 31, 89–112, 129, 172, 183
Hoston, William 130
househusband (subject position) 31, 64–66, 79–83, 110, 151, 165, 181
How I Met Your Father 170
Hulu 10
humor 8, 10, 42, 145, 173
Hynes, Jessica 144, 155, 167n1
hyperreality 180–181

I Love Lucy 7, 11, 41, 46–48, 57, 117, 157, 176
Illouz, Eva 57
immigration 11, 112, 120, 131, 134
incarceration 116, 130
individualism 15–17: in the city 57, 82; and the family 63, 82; and neoliberal ideology 51, 170; and neoliberal subjectivity 15–16, 85; and postfeminism 16–17; and race 118–119, 130–131, 136; and romance 82–83, 163, 175; and streaming platforms 10, 171
insecure 138, 170, 182
intertextuality: in the hangout sitcom 9, 57, 93–94, 111; and postmodern television 54, 63; and reparative reading 30; in UK sitcoms 144, 155–156
intimacy: within friendship groups 19, 50, 122; and homosociality 94, 112; and masculinity 89–90, 93; and neoliberalism 57, 76, 90, 150; in the sitcom 42, 63, 89–91; of television 9, 45–47; in UK sitcoms 144, 149
Israel 133, 153
Italian-American 23, 96, 120, 121, 131–132
It's Always Sunny in Philadelphia 147, 170, 182
ITV 143

Jameson, Fredric 54
Japan 107
The Jeffersons 117
Jewishness 10, 131–138: conceptual 120, 135; and otherness 120–121, 151; in sitcoms 174; stereotypes 27, 29, 76, 77; and whiteness 133–134, 139n3

Jhally, Sut 51, 118, 119
Jim Crow laws 41, 130
jock 72
Joey 23, 27, 63, 112, 132, 154
John, Elton 81
Johnson, Carla 133
Johnson, Jake 20, 28, 29, 115, 129, 132
Jones, Bridget 66
Jordan, Caitlin 182
Julia 117

Kanai, Akane 4, 17
Kauffman, Marta 12, 21, 132
Keynesianism 14, 145
Kilborn, Richard 145
Knox, Simone 1
Kudrow, Lisa 22, 23, 132
Kutulas, Judy 11, 151
Kymlicka, Will 119

labor: domestic 12, 16–17, 43; in hangout sitcoms 65, 73–75, 80–81, 165; and masculinity 19, 43, 73, 80–81, 165; neoliberal 11, 15–17, 57, 73, 80–81, 165; post-war 47; and race 116, 123; in UK sitcoms 164–165; in workplace sitcoms 52
laborer-subject 43
Landay, Lori 47
Latinx 49, 117
laugh track 8–9, 32n1, 47, 95, 151, 155
Le Vine, Lauren 170
Lear, Norman 50, 52, 71, 117
Leave it to Beaver 48, 68, 79, 92, 117, 174, 175
LeBlanc, Matt 20, 22, 89
Lee, Ann-Gee 128
Levy, Dan 177
Levy, Eugene 177
Lewis, Justin 51, 118, 119
LGBTQI+ activism 27, 75
liberalism 15, 137
The Life of Riley 48
Linder, Laura 57n1
linguistic turn 30, 91
Lo Truglio, Joe 175
London 143, 155–157, 159, 160
Lorre, Chuck 26
Los Angeles, California 28, 106, 111, 112
Lotz, Amanda 6, 89, 91
Louis-Dreyfus, Julia 55
love stories 69, 159
Luciana, Dana 62

Mad About You 23
male gaze 73, 96, 152, 154
Marc, David 42, 46, 51, 57n1
Marley & Me 100
marriage: gay 175–177; intertextual references to 95–96, 98, 101, 111; in the post-war period 44–45, 47; as telos in the hangout sitcom 12–13, 62–66, 79, 112
Married… with Children 176
Marsh, Margaret 44
Martinez-Cruz, Pamela 49
The Mary Tyler Moore Show 7, 50
masculinities: Asian American 107, 126–127; black 52, 120, 123, 130–131; caring 83, 130, 172–174; crisis in 43, 80; female 83–84; hegemonic 14, 40, 48, 62, 64, 79, 83, 165; hybrid 5, 13, 15, 18; inclusive 4, 112n1; Jewish 120, 132, 134–138; Latinx 49, 132; marginalized 14, 64; middle-class 52, 67, 79, 82; neoliberal 3, 13, 30, 83–85, 172, 174, 175; nerd 4–5, 70, 75–77, 98, 102–106, 155, 160; othered 32, 64; post-class 53; postfeminist 18; post-war 44; straight 31, 64, 179; subordinated 4, 14; subversive 5; tragic 163, 166; white 29, 64, 119, 120, 130; working-class 53
M*A*S*H 41
masturbation 55, 163
May, Elaine 43
McDonald, Tamar Jeffords 152
McGuigan, Jim 16
men's movement 84
Merchant, Stephen 173
Meriwether, Elizabeth 27
#MeToo 3
Migliaccio, Todd 89, 90
Miles, Ben 148, 150
Milioti, Cristin 25
military 41, 48, 155
millennial 3, 20, 73
Mills, David 12
Minnesota 25
minstrelsy 123
Mirowski, Philip 15, 171
misogyny: expressed by hangout sitcom characters 65, 66, 72, 75–76; the hangout sitcom being against 81, 82; in other TV 180, 182; in the police 175

Mitchell, David 148, 160
Mittell, Jason 6, 8
mockumentary 172
Modern Family 32, 56, 175–177
modernity 54, 173
Moffat, Steven 149, 151–154
moral panic 45, 182
Morris, Lamorne 20, 28, 29, 129, 131
Muzellec, Laurent 22

narrative 8, 31, 42: and character 63–64; in the hangout sitcom 12, 64, 69, 85, 91–92, 156; in love stories 69, 152; and postmodernity 54, 160; in the streaming era 10; in UK sitcoms 144–145, 160, 161
Nayyar, Kunal 20, 26, 27
NBC 10, 21, 45, 134, 135, 150
Neale, Steve 8
Negra, Diane 66, 122
The Neighborhood 138
neoliberal subjectivity 15–16: and the body 73–74, 78; and the city 57; in the hangout sitcom 63–65, 71–72, 76, 78, 85, 182; and masculinity 19, 63, 76, 83; and politics 51; and race 119; US/UK differences 145–146
neoliberalism: American 15, 145; British 145–146; capitalism 13, 15, 54; and the city 19, 57, 178; conjuncture 15–17, 144, 147, 170–172, 183; end of 166, 170–172, 177–178; and the family 17, 56, 63, 90, 91; and gender 16–18, 50, 181; hegemony 54–55, 176, 179; and human bonds 11, 57, 90, 93–94, 103–106; identity 51; individualism 15–17, 57, 119, 130, 163; and labor 80, 90, 165; and masculinities 13, 17–18, 30, 40, 83–85; and patriarchy 13, 17; and race 32, 118–119
neo-traditionalism 67–68, 71, 84, 122
nerd *see* masculinities: nerd
Neruda, Pablo 67
Netflix 2, 3, 10, 177, 178, 180
new man 44, 50
Newhart, Bob 9
nostalgia 67–68, 71
Not Going Out 148
nuclear family *see* family
Nudity 73, 153, 154

Obama, Barack 118, 119, 130
Obergefell vs. Hodges 175, 177
O'Connor, Andrew 160
The Office (UK) 172–174
The Office: An American Workplace 172–174
"The one" 24, 67, 68, 162
O'Neill, Ed 176
Only Fools and Horses 147
Orientalism 107, 124
Ortner, Shelley 14

Pacino, Al 73
paranoid reading 30; *see also* reparative reading
Parks and Recreation 32, 172, 174
parody/pastiche 9: by the hangout sitcom 57, 96, 108, 110, 129, 155, 174; of the hangout sitcom 1, 147, 150, 161, 170, 182; as a postmodern tendency 41, 42, 54–55
Parsons, Jim 20, 26, 27, 76
Pasadena, California 26
Pascoe, C.J. 14
pastiche *see* parody
patriarchal dividend 71
patriarchy 13–15, 56, 179: and femininity 85; and neoliberalism 5, 16–17, 66, 134, 181; and postfeminism 16–17; shifting versions of 18–19, 48, 53; in the sitcom 40, 64, 109, 152, 172, 175; transpatriarchies 17
Peep Show 32, 144, 146, 149, 160–166
Pegg, Simon 144, 145, 148, 155
penis/phallic imagery 68, 107, 150
Penn, Kal 124
Perry, Matthew 20, 22, 23, 89, 180–181
philo-semitism 133
Pierson, David 55
Poehler, Amy 172, 174
police 72, 116, 130–131, 174–175
pop TV 177
pornography 152, 159, 165
post-closeted culture 82
Poster, Winifred 5
postfeminism 16–17: and femininity 84–85, 134, 137, 176, 182; in the hangout sitcom 2; and Jewishness 134–137; and masculinities 17–19, 50, 136, 138; and race 122
postfeminist male singleton 31, 64–72, 151, 183

Index

post-industrialism 14, 82, 178
postmodernity 54: and morality 55; and race 119, 125–126, 135; and the sitcom 9–11, 54–56, 63, 172, 174
post-racial consensus 51–52, 118–119, 124, 130
post-war: consensus 14, 15, 51, 134; reconstruction 8, 117, 133
post-white consensus 119, 131, 134, 136–138, 180
Prady, Bill 26
Prell, Riv-Ellen 134
profeminism 3, 4, 172, 175, 177
public/private spheres: and the family 43–45; in hangout sitcoms 68, 82, 93, 99–102; and neoliberalism 57; and patriarchy 14; and race 121, 175; on television (general) 10, 12, 47–49, 52–53; in UK sitcoms 156–158
Pugh, Tison 48

queer theory/studies: and affect 91; readings 30, 91, 112, 145, 154–155, 165; subtext 93, 96; and temporality 102

race: and the family 44; in the hangout sitcom 4, 115–139; and neoliberalism 51, 54; in popular culture 3; in the post-war period 44; in the pre-war period 42; in sitcoms (general) 49, 174–175
racism 32, 51, 118–119, 175
radio 41–42
Radnor, Josh 20, 24, 25, 136
Rae, Issa 170
Rauch, Melissa 26, 27, 132
Reagan, Ronald 15, 51
The Real McCoys 49
Reception studies 182
red-lining 44
Redman, Peter 67, 82, 175
Reiner, Rob 9, 71
relationship maintenance 91, 94, 107
reparative reading 30, 78
Rick and Morty 182
road trips 93, 98, 99, 108–111
Roe *vs.* Wade 175
romance 67–69, 82–83, 110, 134, 163, 175
romantic comedy 66, 69, 126, 129, 152
roommate contract (The Big Bang Theory) 76, 103–106

Roseanne 26, 41, 175
Roseneil, Sasha 19
Rossi, Ugo 19
Rostek, Joanna 150
Rubin, Daniel 137
rurality 41, 49–50, 82, 178

Saget, Bob 25, 180
Sam 'n' Henry 41
Samberg, Andy 174
Sanford and Son 52, 117
Sanson, Kevin 151
satire 161, 166
Schaab, Katherine 178
Schitt's Creek 32, 177–180
schlemiel/schlimazl 126, 133, 138n1
Schur, Michael 172
Schwimmer, David 20, 22, 23, 139n3
Schwind, Kai 1
science fiction 102, 104
Scott, Adam 174
Scott, James C. 165
Scrubs 20, 90, 172
The Secret Diary of Desmond Pfeiffer 118
Sedgwick, Eve Kosofsky 30
Segal, Lynne 45
Segel, Jason 20, 24, 25, 82, 132
Seinfeld 10–11, 21, 55–56, 133–135
Seinfeld, Jerry 11, 55, 133
self-discipline 17, 55, 71, 72
sexism *see* misogyny
shiksa 134, 137, 139n2
Shoah 133
Simone, Hannah 28, 115
The Simpsons 54–55, 173
sitcom 7–10: animated 54–55, 182; black 117, 126, 138; British 32, 143–148; characters 9, 11; family 12–13, 46–49, 51, 57, 92–96, 138; and humor 8; "magicom" 49, 57, 178; postmodern 9–11, 54–56; radio 40–41; relevancy 50, 178; "rural-com" 49–50, 53, 57; workplace 32, 50, 90, 170, 172–175; "queer" family 32, 56, 170, 175–177
slavery 116, 130
spaced 143, 146, 149, 155–160, 173
Spike TV 162
Stenbacka, Susanna 82
Steptoe and Son 146
Stigler, George 15
straight time 63, 66, 73, 77, 112, 174

Index

streaming 9–10, 27–28, 138, 171
Styles, Harry 183
subject position 64, 112
subjectivity *see* neoliberalism, capitalism
suburbs 44: in the family sitcom 12, 48–49; and gender 44–45, 48–49; and race 117, 134, 138; and television 45–46; in UK sitcoms 156
Superbad 102
Swain, Scott 89

Television & New Media (journal) 18
Thatcher, Margaret 15, 17, 51, 146, 150
Thomas, Craig 7, 23
Thompson, Lauren Jade 18, 156
time panic 64, 66, 71, 79, 85
#TimesUp 3
Todorov, Tzvetan 6, 8, 144
Tom, Lauren 121
tragedy (also tragicomedy) 72, 148, 161, 166, 175
transgender 81, 154, 176
transvestitism 81
Twin Peaks 9
Two Pints of Lager and a Packet of Crisps 148
Tyler, Aisha 121

urban space *see* cities
US remakes of UK shows 144: *Coupling* 150–151; *The Office* 172–173; *Spaced* 155–156; *Peep Show* 162

Van Horn, Rob 15
variety shows 46

Vaudeville 46, 146
voice-over 24, 144, 147, 161–166

Wales 149, 151
Wallace, Richard 172
Wayans, Damon Jr. 20, 28, 29, 115, 129
Webb, Robert 148, 161
Wells, Paul 40, 42
Western (movie genre) 93
Wever, Merritt 78
white circle 120–126, 179
white supremacy 116
whiteness: and the family 44; in the hangout sitcom 120–138; and Jewishness 133–134, 139n3; and masculinity 62–63; in pop culture 3; and sexuality 176–177; in the sitcom (general) 116–120; in the UK 146
Wickham, Phil 161
Will, Dorothea 150
witches 49
WKRP in Cincinatti 50, 172
Wojcik, Pamela 47
women's movement *see* feminism
Wood, Robin 99
World War I 146
World War II 43, 133
Wright, Edgar 155

Yiddishness 131, 133, 136, 138n1, 139n3
Young Sheldon 76, 77

Zionism 133

Printed in the United States
by Baker & Taylor Publisher Services